T0413642

The Future of Motherhood in Western Societies

Gijs Beets · Joop Schippers · Egbert R. te Velde
Editors

The Future of Motherhood in Western Societies

Late Fertility and its Consequences

 Springer

Editors

Gijs Beets
Netherlands Interdisciplinary
Demographic Institute (NIDI)
PO Box 11650
2502 AR The Hague
Netherlands
beets@nidi.nl

Joop Schippers
Department of Economy (REBO)
Faculty of Law, Economics
 and Governance
University of Utrecht
Janskerkhof 12
3512 BL Utrecht
Netherlands
j.j.schippers@uu.nl

Egbert R. te Velde
Department of Reproductive Medicine
University of Utrecht
PO Box 85500
3508 GA Utrecht
Netherlands
e.r.tevelde@ziggo.nl

ISBN 978-90-481-8968-7   e-ISBN 978-90-481-8969-4
DOI 10.1007/978-90-481-8969-4
Springer Dordrecht Heidelberg London New York

Printed on acid-free paper

Springer is part of Springer Science+Business Media (www.springer.com)

Preface

The growing availability of reliable, acceptable and affordable forms of contraception since the 1960s contributed greatly to women's emancipation in all layers of population. This process was of inestimable value for women's liberation and independence.

However, some unforeseen problems have cropped up. Emancipation policies, developed by national governments and the European Union, are primarily directed towards women's economic independence. In these policies it is (implicitly) assumed that biological differences between women and men do not matter any more in today's society and in economic life. What a man can do, a woman should be able to do as well, is the well-intentioned thought underlying this view and indeed in many respects this is true. However, it is also the reason that little attention has been paid to motherhood. It has been assumed so far that a woman who wants to have children in addition to all her many other activities should just carry on and do so, preferably in a harmoniously decision making process with her partner. In practice, for many women, this proves to be too much to manage. Women are therefore apprehensive about having children, they put off the decision until later and have fewer children than they would really like, or even decide not to have children at all. Later on in life some of these women regret their earlier decisions. The question is whether this is the freedom of choice emancipation was supposed to offer.

From a demographic perspective we observe that the *age at first birth* has increased significantly and that the average number of children per woman has dropped rapidly since the beginning of the 1970s in most European countries to (well) below the replacement level. This will lead to an increasing proportion of elderly people who have, when becoming in need, to be cared for by a decreasing proportion of young people.

The view that differences between men and women have become irrelevant in social and economic respects is questioned over and over again. Modern biology and psychology have taught us that men and women differ in how they think, feel and act. These differences are partly due to our long evolutionary history and cannot be removed by a few well-intentioned measures within a couple of years, as many emancipation ideologists and politicians seem to think. "True" emancipation maintains an interpretation of equality that not only accepts the differences between men and women but also values them.

In his 1991 Utrecht University inaugural speech on the increasingly later age at first birth Egbert te Velde touched the dilemma of ongoing adverse health issues versus understandable socio-economic drives. Te Velde's address led to several public and scientific discussions and meetings; two readers resulted in Dutch (Beets & Verloove-Vanhorick (eds.), 1992; Beets, Bouwens, & Schippers (eds.), 1997). Being better informed about the declining success rates of having children with advancing age could facilitate the decision making process.

The book in hand is the reflection of several international meetings and consultations on these issues, driven by the observation that practically all Western countries are characterised by a rising age at first birth although levels and timing may vary significantly. In these interdisciplinary meetings the participants – medical and biological scientists, next to demographers, sociologists and economists – discussed their concerns on the ongoing further rise of the age at first birth. They aimed at a better understanding of the advantages and disadvantages of having children late, on gender relationships, (the timing of) having children and other life time preferences and commitments, as well as at discussing acceptable strategies for preventing the age at first birth to rise further.

The meetings and discussions were organised at and coordinated by the Netherlands Interdisciplinary Demographic Institute (NIDI) in The Hague, a research institute of the Royal Netherlands Academy of Arts and Sciences (KNAW) engaged in the scientific study of population (Demography). Next to the authors of the various chapters in this book, listed in a separate annex, several other researchers contributed in the scientific discussions: *Christien Brinkgreve* (Professor of Sociology, Utrecht University), *Pearl Dykstra* (Professor of Empirical Sociology, Erasmus University, Rotterdam), *Carina Hilders* (Gynaecologist, Reinier de Graaf hospital Delft), *Marli Huijer* (Professor of Philosophy, Erasmus University, Rotterdam; and Haagse Hogeschool, The Hague), *Renske Keizer* (Post-doc Researcher in Sociology, Erasmus University, Rotterdam), *Hans Merkus* (Emeritus Professor of Obstetrics and Gynaecology, Nijmegen University), *Melinda Mills* (Professor of Sociology, Groningen University), *Nico van Nimwegen* (Deputy Director NIDI), *Joyce Outshoorn* (Emeritus Professor of Women's Studies, Leiden University), *Anne van Putten* (Sociologist, Ministry of Social Affairs and Employment, The Hague), *Judith Soons* (Psychologist, Education Council, The Hague), *Anmarie Widener* (Assistant Professor of Women's and Gender Studies, Georgetown University, Washington, DC), *Frans Willekens* (Former Director NIDI), and *Boukje Zaadstra* (Epidemiologist, Researcher at the Netherlands School of Public and Occupational Health, Amsterdam).

This book is the reflection of these meetings and discussions. Some contributions were completed already in 2008, others became available more recently. We thank all persons who contributed to this book, in whatever way. Also a "thank you" to

NIDI for its efforts in organising the meetings, discussions and its final outcome. We hope the book will widen the understanding and discussion on the future of motherhood.

The Hague, The Netherlands   Gijs Beets
Utrecht, The Netherlands   Joop Schippers
Utrecht/Rotterdam, The Netherlands   Egbert R. te Velde

Contents

Contributors

Elisabeth Beck-Gernsheim Professor of Sociology, Universität Erlangen-Nürnberg, Erlangen, Germany, beck-gernsheim@soziol.phil.uni-erlangen.de

Gijs Beets Senior Demographic Researcher, Netherlands Interdisciplinary Demographic Institute (NIDI), The Hague, The Netherlands, beets@nidi.nl

Ingrid Doorten Sociologist, The Netherlands Centre of Ethics and Health (a joint venture of the Health Council of the Netherlands and the Council for Public Health and Health Care), The Hague, The Netherlands, i.doorten@rvz.net

Gøsta Esping-Andersen Professor of Sociology, Department of Political and Social Sciences, Universitat Pompeu Fabra, Barcelona, Spain, gosta.esping@upf.edu

Catherine Hakim Senior Research Fellow, Sociology Department, London School of Economics, London, UK, c.hakim@lse.ac.uk

Karen Henwood Professor of Psychology, School of Social Sciences, Cardiff University, Cardiff, UK, HenwoodK@cardiff.ac.uk

Joanne Kellett nee Procter Research Fellow, Family and Parenting Institute, London, UK, research@familyandparenting.org

Joop Schippers Professor of Labour Economics and the Economics of Equal Opportunities, Utrecht University, Utrecht, The Netherlands, j.j.schippers@uu.nl

Fiona Shirani Psychology Research Associate, School of Social Sciences, Cardiff University, Cardiff, UK, Fionashirani@cardiff.ac.uk

Dick F. Swaab Emeritus Professor of Neurobiology, University of Amsterdam, Amsterdam, The Netherlands; Emeritus Professor of Neurobiology, Netherlands Institute for Neuroscience, Amsterdam, The Netherlands, d.f.swaab@nin.knaw.nl

Egbert R. te Velde Emeritus Professor of Reproductive Medicine, Utrecht University, Utrecht, The Netherlands; Department of Public Health, Erasmus University Medical Centre, Rotterdam, The Netherlands, e.r.tevelde@ziggo.nl

Dirk J. van de Kaa Emeritus Professor of Demography, University of Amsterdam, Amsterdam, The Netherlands; Honorary Fellow, Netherlands Interdisciplinary Demographic Institute (NIDI), The Hague, The Netherlands, vandekaa@nidi.nl

Anneke van Doorne-Huiskes Emeritus Professor of Sociology, Utrecht University, Utrecht, The Netherlands, doorne.huiskes@wxs.nl

Jan A.R.A.M. van Hooff Emeritus Professor in Animal Behaviour, Utrecht University, Utrecht, The Netherlands, jaramvanhooff@planet.nl

Chapter 1
Introduction

Gijs Beets, Joop Schippers, and Egbert R. te Velde

If someone would have left the Western world some 50 years ago and would have come back at the end of the first decade of the twenty-first century what would be his first observation? Maybe the completely different built-up areas nowadays with the much more intensified traffic streams, maybe the cell phones, I-pods, black-berries and other electronic equipment that everyone seems to be carrying around all of the day. If he was a she, and especially if she was a sociologist she might be surprised by women's presence in the public room. And if he was a demog-rapher he would be caught by the high number of older people in the streets and the relative absence of young people, except for those with some sort of immigrant background. You don't have to look far, neither do you have to be a scholar to notice two of the major changes in Western societies during the past few decades: women's emancipation and the changing composition of the population. If you are a scholar or a scientist you will immediately recognize the relation between the two phenomena. Emancipation has clearly to do with birth rates and fertility. A brief overview of history or a comparison between different parts of the world seems to suggest that there is a negative trade-off between emancipation and fertil-ity rates. The more time women seem to spend on education and earning money in the labour market the less time and energy they seem to have available for motherhood.

One of the more striking, related issues is the rising *age at first birth*, observed over the past decades in most Western countries: both women and men are increas-ingly older when they become a parent for the first time. With the introduction of effective contraceptives the evolutionary link between sexuality and procreation was completely broken in Western societies. From the *health* perspective "late fertility" (defined here as having a first child when the mother is 30 years or over) is beyond the biological optimum for women. Risks on health deficiencies for both mother and first child are lowest when women are in between the age range from about 18 to 30 years. Having a first baby before the age of 18 or after age 30 is therefore

G. Beets (✉)
Senior Demographic Researcher, Netherlands Interdisciplinary Demographic Institute (NIDI), The Hague, The Netherlands
e-mail: beets@nidi.nl

G. Beets et al. (eds.), *The Future of Motherhood in Western Societies*,
DOI 10.1007/978-90-481-8969-4_1, © Springer Science+Business Media B.V. 2011

less recommendable, also in the era of assisted reproductive technology (ART) with for example in vitro fertilization (IVF). Health issues related to late fertility are, for women (and their partners), increases in the so-called waiting-time-to-conception, increased risks of remaining involuntarily childless, increased problems with conception, a higher risk of miscarriage, a higher risk of a Caesarean delivery, and a higher risk of developing breast cancer before age 75; and for babies, increased risks of a preterm delivery with adverse mental and/or health consequences, and increased risks of perinatal and infant mortality.

For many women (or men) the health perspective, however is not the primary one they have in mind when thinking or deciding about having children. First, they may not be aware of any medical risks and dangers. In many eyes having children has become a personal choice like booking a vacation to the Maladives or buying the new Harry Potter. Children are no longer a necessary insurance for a well-cared-for old age, but "an experience", something to fulfil your own emotional needs. The same attitude holds for the time path towards getting children. Unwanted conceptions can be prevented by contraceptives, unwanted pregnancies can be interrupted by abortion, and reproductive problems can be solved by doctors using their state of the art in reproductive techniques. Second, from a personal development and socio-economic perspective, late fertility is quite understandable as it offers many advantages. It gives you time to find a proper partner, it offers you the opportunity to get your career going, you might have settled down after some "wild years" during which you explore "the world", have developed into an emotional stable adult and you may even start to think you are ready for parenting a member of the new generation. Moreover, even though there are wide differences between countries belonging to different welfare state regimes in the degree of supportive measures to reconcile work and family life, there is no government in any Western country that actively supports women (and men) to have their children at an earlier stage in life than they actually do. Governments support young people's enrolment in education. They also support the prevention of teenage pregnancies. Broken families and lone mothers are considered a serious problem in many countries, and many parents underline the related parole of "look before you leap" when their sons or daughters in their 20s enter into a new relation. Altogether, the social and societal context in which young adults have to decide on having children and when to have them points emphatically towards postponement.

So, with late fertility as the main trigger and focal point this book discusses the future of motherhood in Western societies[1]: to what extend and under what

---

[1] Although not defined in detail this book refers to motherhood in *Western* societies, i.e. Europe (including Central and Eastern Europe), Northern America, Australia, New Zealand and Japan. Elsewhere first motherhood also shifts to higher ages, but not (yet) so extensively as in the most developed world. However, over time the "Western world" is expanding as of late also some new emerging countries gradually enter that world, like for example Argentina, Brazil, Chile, China, Egypt, India, Indonesia, Malaysia, Mexico, Morocco, Philippines, Singapore, South Africa, Taiwan, Thailand, Turkey. Some of these countries increasingly feature low and late fertility behaviour.

conditions are motherhood and emancipation (still) compatible? Is it possible to define an optimal time path or optimal conditions?

Earlier discussions in the Netherlands on late motherhood/parenthood and the dilemma of health issues versus personal and socio-economic motives revealed that addressing this general question, immediately brings up a series of related questions in which many scientific dimensions are involved (Beets & Verloove-Vanhorick, 1992; Beets et al., 1997). That is why we brought together an international team of scholars and scientists from various disciplines to present and discuss their view on the relation between motherhood and emancipation and the dilemmas around late parenthood. This book consists of several chapters resulting from these consultations.

The second chapter is by Egbert te Velde who elaborates on the central question of the book. He discusses the evolution of motherhood and the contraceptive revolution and its consequences for emancipation policies. After that two other natural scientists get the floor. The behavioural biologist Jan van Hooff puts into perspective current views on gender and male and female behaviour by holding a mirror up to our face showing how reproduction works with some other living species. What is the role of mothers and fathers in the animal world around us? Is there a natural order or are male and female behaviour just a cultural agreement that may change over time? From the neurobiological perspective Dick Swaab elaborates on the sexual differentiation of the brain and its consequences for male and female behaviour. He compares the effects of the neurologically determined sexual differentiation of the brain on behaviour with effects from the social environment. Then the social scientists take over. Dirk van de Kaa discusses the societal impact of modern contraception. He distinguishes between foreseen and unforeseen demographic consequences, describes the effects on sexual relations and marriage and focuses our attention on some paradoxical effects of the contraceptive revolution. Another demographer, Gijs Beets, goes into the details of facts and figures. He discusses the relation between late parenthood and issues like partnership formation, the use of effective contraceptives, childlessness, educational attainment, labour market participation, economic security, gender egalitarianism, and changing norms and values. In the meantime he disentangles complicated and often misused concepts like the Period Total Fertility Rate and the Cohort Total Fertility Rate. Joop Schippers looks at the economic perspective of individual and collective behaviour around motherhood and the timing of children. How can we explain from a private cost-benefit analysis why some women have their children earlier in life than others and how can we explain from a similar analysis that the age at which people become a parent for the first time has been rising during the last few decades? Can similar cost-benefit arguments play a part in explaining government behaviour with respect to the supply of arrangements that allow parents to combine parenthood and a labour market career in a smooth way? The latter question also guides the chapter by Anneke van Doorne-Huiskes and Ingrid Doorten. More in particular, they focus on the perspective of the welfare state and the influence different welfare states have on individual choices and behaviour. Each welfare state offers different incentives by supplying various arrangements that help people reconcile parenthood and paid activities in the labour market. The discussion on the role of the welfare state is continued by Gøsta Esping-Andersen, who puts up the question whether modern welfare states invest enough in children. He criticizes traditional family policies that have not been adapted to the new and modern ways many European citizens (like to) live their lives. A lack of proper policy measures that allow for the reconciliation of work and family life may endanger fertility. He underlines that we should not only look at the number of children, but also on the quality of children. Proper policy measures, in Esping-Andersen's view, also include fathers as a group to focus on. A more egalitarian division of paid *and* unpaid work may emerge as a bottom-line condition for future fertility. Elisabeth Beck-Gernsheim discusses into more detail the decision making process among women in a welfare state that offers reliable and relatively cheap contraceptives for most women, but also holds women responsible for "controlling" their reproductive "behaviour" and for taking their share in labour market activities. The process of emancipation has stirred up the demands women have for themselves and each other with respect to what they expect from life. The pill has given her much more freedom but turns out to have also created new dilemmas. After looking at women's decision making process it is time to focus – as already advocated by Esping-Andersen – on fathers and men. Karen Henwood, Fiona Shirani and Joanne Kellett take up this challenge by discussing the social and individual logic of men's lives. Based on their deeply felt responsibility of being a good father and a proper provider and breadwinner men are inclined to contribute to the postponement of the birth of a first child. Henwood et al. conclude that there is a lot of insecurity among men, but they also see some changes in men's behaviour ahead. Based on her preference theory Catherine Hakim foresees a twenty-first century where there will be more room for diversity among women (and men). Policy makers will – in the wake of scholars – start to recognize that not all women share the same preferences with respect to work and family. Worries about population ageing and decline will induce policy makers to develop new policy measures that will allow more women to keep the balance steady between work and activities in other domains of life, even if they have preferences that differ from the majority or some Mrs. Average.

In the final chapter the editors take the floor again to comment on some outcomes of the previous chapters, draw major conclusions, and discuss the future of motherhood and the timing of children.

References

Beets, G., Bouwens, A., & Schippers, J. (Eds.). (1997). *Uitgesteld ouderschap*. Amsterdam: Thesis Publishers, 145 pp. (in Dutch).
Beets, G., & Verloove-Vanhorick, P. (Eds.). (1992). *Een slimme meid regelt haar zwangerschap op tijd*. Amsterdam/Lisse: Swets & Zeitlinger, 147 pp. (in Dutch).

Chapter 2
Is Women's Emancipation Still Compatible with Motherhood in Western Societies?

Egbert R. te Velde

The Long Past of Motherhood

Since the origin of mammals some 70 million years ago, reproduction has been the inevitable consequence of sexuality with all its attributes such as sexual attraction, mating behaviour, passion, intercourse, orgasm, ejaculation and fertilization of the oocyte by a sperm cell as the ultimate goal. Sexual reproduction was the prerequisite for diversity and natural selection – important incentives for the progress of evolution (Short, 1994). Without sexual reproduction there would be no evolution: most species including humans, would never have come into existence.

Human evolution began some 7 million years ago when the first primitive humans emerged from a common ancestor of man and chimpanzee for whom it became advantageous to walk in an upright position. The erect posture resulted in the female pelvis being tilted and flattened such that a human baby can only be delivered by rotating and extreme bending of the head (Stewart, 1984; Rosenberg & Travathon, 2001). Hence, a human delivery lasts longer and more frequently turns out badly than in chimpanzees, our immediate ancestors. Some millions of years later humans acquired an enormous increase in brain volume and skull dimensions. As a consequence a human child can only be born prematurely before its brain has reached full size. A human baby is helpless and underdeveloped compared to the offspring of other primates. It takes a human much longer to stand on its own legs, both literally and figuratively (Potts & Short, 1999).

Within the female reproductive strategy of most mammals, primates and even more so in humans, it was profitable to develop empathic and caring abilities. During the long period to maturity, she is then better able to sense the subtle needs of her child, to anticipate and avoid outside dangers, and to find reliable allies in the struggle for life. In humans, this is related to the exceptionally large investments women have to make in the gestation, delivery, breastfeeding and rearing of their children until adulthood (Hrdy, 1999). Having adult offspring that is able to have descendants

E.R. te Velde (✉)
Emeritus Professor of Reproductive Medicine, Utrecht University, Utrecht, The Netherlands;
Department of Public Health, Erasmus University Medical Centre, Rotterdam, The Netherlands
e-mail: e.r.tevelde@ziggo.nl

G. Beets et al. (eds.), *The Future of Motherhood in Western Societies*,
DOI 10.1007/978-90-481-8969-4_2, © Springer Science+Business Media B.V. 2011

themselves is an important condition for progress in evolution. This also explains women's preference for a powerful and dominant male partner who is capable of protecting her and her children, and providing them with adequate food supplies (Buss, 1999).

Male primates may follow different reproductive strategies. One scenario is to copulate as frequently with as many partners as possible without any social commitment. Under different circumstances, however, establishing a permanent relationship with one or more females who bear his children in return for protection and food appeared to be a better alternative (Potts & Short, 1999) to assure to have offspring that will reach adulthood. This is the normal relationship maintained by most humans. Whatever strategy is chosen, the greater the male's dominance, social standing and political smartness, the more attractive he is to members of the opposite sex (De Waal, 1982). When humans appeared on the evolutionary stage, the ability of spatial orientation, assess speed and make tools also became important assets in increasing a male's suitability as a partner.

Along these lines of evolution during millions of years, motherhood always has been the fate and destiny of almost every woman during her whole reproductive life; carrying, delivering, breastfeeding, nurturing, taking care of, educating and defending her children until they were able to reproduce themselves. And even thereafter, many mothers who survived motherhood and became grandmother continued to look after their grandchildren in order to increase their likelihood of reaching adulthood (Hawkes et al., 1998).

The Contraceptive Revolution

From an evolutionary perspective something most extraordinary happened in the 1960s. Within less than 10 years – a split second in the time scale of evolution – it became possible to separate sexuality from its reproductive consequences. This so-called sexual revolution was in fact a contraceptive revolution. By the introduction of the "pill" and other safe and reliable methods of contraception, women "suddenly" became able to have full control over their own reproduction (Rensman, 2006). Before the 1960s, some primitive forms of contraception had been available (Riddle, 1997), but apart from being unreliable and clumsy, these methods usually required the cooperation of the male partner who could decide whether or not to use them. Unwanted pregnancies often occurred and masses of women felt themselves forced to have an abortion which was often complicated by life-threatening infections or serious blood loss. Moreover, millions of women got rid of their child by abandoning it after a painfully hidden gestation and delivery (Hrdy, 1999). The availability of simple and effective methods of contraception has provided the stepping stone for female emancipation for all women; not only for a small and privileged group like in former times. Naturally, women seized the chance to free themselves from the burden of reproduction and male dominance (Blossfeld, 1995; Van de Kaa, 1987). For the first time in history, women could choose between motherhood and other activities without suppressing their sexuality. They massively choose to expand their horizons, join the work force, train for jobs and careers, and enjoy the benefits of earning their own salary. They could experiment with sex and relations before committing themselves to a partner with whom they wished to have children. The word emancipation means liberation, and indeed what women have experienced since the 1960s embodies all aspects of a liberation process from the slavery of unavoidable motherhood and male suppression to the freedom of self determination. Women have become equals of men and life has become so much happier for them in comparison to the "dark ages" that lasted until the 1960s (Potts & Short, 1999; Shorter, 1991). Women will never give up their newly gained independence and freedom.

However, the availability of perfect contraception also has fundamentally changed the reproductive behaviour of humans (Van de Kaa, 1987) – especially of women – and consequently the "natural order of things": the delicate balance between men and women with their innate differences in reproductive strategies but also the balance between the generations of children, parents and grandparents on which the structure of societies was based. With the event of modern contraception these relationships fundamentally changed, lost their obvious meaning and often became problematic or superfluous. Not surprisingly in retrospect, apart from the many blessings and advantages, the contraceptive revolution also has led to unforeseen problems. These problems are so serious that the question is justified whether or not it will be possible in the future to combine the generally accepted, highly appreciated values of women's liberation with the way humans have reproduced in the past million of years. Are emancipation and reproduction still compatible in the present era of emancipation and birth control? Can this be achieved in a way that benefits both society and women?

Consequences of the Contraceptive Revolution

Since the availability of perfect contraception, motherhood became an issue of personal preferences, involving choices of voluntary childlessness and, if more than one child was desired, spacing their birth order. Most women in Europe nowadays want one or two children or no child at all. In 1965 the Total Fertility Rate (TFR) of a country – the mean number of children women deliver during a calendar year – was still three or more in most European countries. Within the following 10 years these TFRs dropped below the so-called replacement level of about two children per woman in many countries. At the same time people live longer nowadays because of better medical care and a healthier lifestyle. Falling birth rates and increasing longevity lead to population ageing. Hence, the progressively increasing expenditure for pensions and health care of the elderly has to be paid by a progressively reduced labour force (Lutz et al., 2008). This notion is expressed in the so-called old age dependency ratio, which is the proportion of persons at or above 65 divided by the proportion of the population aged 15–65 considered as the potential working age. This indicator was 25% in the EU of 2005. The age dependency ratio will increase rapidly over the following decades and will have more than doubled in the

EU of 2050. This would imply that there will be less than two persons of working age per one person above age 65 (Lutz et al., 2008).

The second problem caused by female emancipation and the availability of perfect contraception is the massive delay of childbearing (Te Velde & Pearson, 2002). From a biological perspective, the optimal period for a woman to have her first child is between 18 and 30 years, or even earlier. During the millions of years of human development, the fast majority of women had their first child during those years. But nowadays this is the appropriate age for schooling, training, having a job, going for a career and being occupied with all those other things that have a much higher priority than motherhood for most young women. Motherhood is therefore postponed to ages when having a first child seems more convenient. The mean age at first delivery increased by 4–5 years in most European countries since the 1960s and is now around 28–30 years, while most women give birth above the age of 30, so up in their 30s, when taking not only the first, but all children into account. Especially highly educated women often delay childbearing until age 35 or thereafter. But the quality of their eggs stored in both ovaries, deteriorates from about age 30 onwards and consequently, the possibility to have a healthy baby starts to decline after that age. This not only affects her chances to become pregnant; the risks of abortion and chromosomal aberrations like Down's syndrome also steeply increase (Te Velde & Pearson, 2002). Compared to women of 30 or younger, the monthly probability of a pregnancy leading to the birth of a healthy child – the measure of a woman's fertility potential; fecundability in demographic terms – is already halved by age 35 and is one fourth at age 38 (Van Noord-Zaadstra et al., 1991). At age 41 it has dropped to zero which means that the average woman is already infertile and has lost the capacity to have a child. Since all ages mentioned are mean or median values with large variations, some women are already infertile at age 36 or before while others still are able to conceive and deliver a healthy baby at age 43 or even later (Te Velde & Pearson, 2002).

Not surprisingly, delay of childbearing leads to an increase in the incidence of sub-fertility and infertility. Moreover, many couples who still manage to have a first child may not be able to have a second or third one. There are many therapeutic options nowadays of which in vitro fertilization (IVF) and its variant intracytoplasmatic sperm injection (ICSI) are the most important ones. The number of IVF treatment cycles in the Netherlands per year has risen from five in 1984, 5,000 in 1991 to about 15,000 in 2006. About 2.5% of all children born each year in the Netherlands are from IVF. In Denmark this percentage is above four and together with all additional assisted reproductive technologies (ART), it has already risen to more than six (Andersen et al., 2008). Fertility specialists estimate this percentage will further rise to ten or even more, first in the Nordic and then in all European countries. However, the success of IVF also depends on female age. After age 35 the chances of success dramatically drop and at age 40 or beyond an IVF-pregnancy leading to live birth is rare (Templeton et al., 1996; Leridon, 2004). In about 2% of women serious complications occur during IVF-treatment, sometimes life threatening (Allen et al., 2006; Luke & Brown, 2007). The spectacular rise of multiple pregnancies is the most serious threat because of the high chance of premature births associated with increased risks of infant mortality and morbidity after delivery, and of cognitive and neurological problems later in life (Allen et al., 2006; Weisglas-Kuperus et al., 2009; Helmerhorst et al., 2004). Behind the façade of success put forward by the media, the lay press and the pharmaceutical industry, the reality of IVF and related techniques is disappointing (Te Velde et al., 2007).

Older mothers-to-be have considerably more problems during gestation, have longer and more complicated deliveries, which more often have to be terminated by Caesarian sections and have more complications after delivery (Te Velde et al., 2007).

Delay of childbearing also leads to more breast cancer, the most frequently occurring female cancer in Western countries; one in ten women will have it before her 75th birthday. The relative risk of breast cancer increases with 3% every year a woman further delays the birth of her first child after age 25 (Collaborative Group on Hormonal Factors in Breast Cancer, 2001).

In conclusion, delay of childbearing leads to an increase of serious health problems, many of us are not aware of. Surprisingly, in the social, demographic and political sciences most attention is focused on the setbacks of ageing populations whereas the health problems following delay of childbearing seem to be almost neglected.

In a recent editorial the British Medical Journal comments on postponement of childbearing:

> Obstetricians and gynaecologists have seen dramatic changes alongside this demographic transition of delay and witness the resultant tragedies in their daily practice. The pain of infertility; miscarriage; smaller families than desired; or damage to pregnancy, mothers and children is very private, particularly when women blame themselves for choices made without being aware of the consequences. It is ironic that as society becomes more risk averse and pregnant women more anxious than in the past, a major cause of this ill health and unhappiness is unacknowledged (Bewley et al., 2005).

Reproduction without Sex

Although the availability of modern contraception made it possible to separate sexuality from reproduction, the majority of children are still conceived in the traditional way. However, currently it is possible to conceive a child by IVF or one of the other assisted reproductive technologies, also when there is no medical reason. For example, when a couple gets inpatient after having tried in vain for, let us say, 3 months or when a single woman wishes to have a child with the use of donor sperm or when a couple who already has a girl wants to be sure their next child is a boy. Moreover, for women who postpone childbearing until ages they are infertile, the availability of donor eggs from young women offers a realistic opportunity of still becoming a mother. In 2002 the prices for such eggs started at 3,000 US dollar and went up to 50,000 for so-called designer eggs, while the demand still exceeds the supply (Hewlett, 2002). Women who are not looking forward to a pregnancy and delivery can opt to use the services of commercial surrogate mothers. Those are women who agree to have the client's fertilized eggs implanted in their uterus, carry the child during gestation and hand the baby after the delivery over to the client. Indeed, the following phase of human reproduction – reproduction without sex – has already started on a fairly large scale in the United States, where relatively many people are ready to pay large sums of money for these treatment modalities. Infertility in America has become a highly profitable multi-billion industry (Spar, 2006).

It is expected that in due time women will be able to practice what is called "fertility insurance" by freezing their own eggs at a young age. When she is having a career of her own and becomes older and older, her eggs stored at –180°C, remain young. She may then want to use them and have a child of her own when she is 40, 50 or even 60. In this way she is able to have all good things in a woman's life at different times: first a career and then a child.

And so all the ingredients for completely separating reproduction from sexuality are in place: isolated eggs either from a donor or herself, isolated sperm from her partner or a donor, surrogate mothers, women who wish to have a career first, and doctors who wish to make a fortune. The cut-throat competition between IVF clinics for clients and the globalisation of the commerce in donor eggs and surrogate mothers will ultimately result in lower prices and reproduction without sex will become available to less affluent clients as well. These trends are occurring wherever these techniques are commercially available, also now in Europe.

Why not be happy with these developments? When the problems of reduced birth rates and increasing maternal age become unbearably hard, we may welcome the widespread use of reproduction without sex as the perfect solution. The basis for most of the techniques needed for this scenario is already available. In one particular area, that of determining the genetic make-up of an embryo from a single or small number of cells, we can expect to see spectacular progress in the coming decades, with improvements in DNA sequencing at a micro-level and the ability to relate the genetic code to desired features of the child. Because these developments will proceed in small steps, the changes will occur almost unnoticed. In the second half of this century we may well awake in a world where all problems of falling birth rates, population ageing and delay of childbirth have been solved by the blessings of assisted reproductive technologies (ART) enabling reproduction without sex. If so, emancipation apparently is not compatible with traditional motherhood any more. Are there still other, more natural solutions?

The Differences between Men and Women

Indeed, men and women are very different in their reproductive possibilities and appearances. These differences are determined by the presence of testes or ovaries and consequently in differences of exposure to different (levels of) sex hormones during the foetal period – testosterone or estrogens. But what about the more subtle differences in feelings, natural attitudes, character, behaviors, instincts, choices and preferences (Potts & Short, 1999; Buss, 1995)? The central question here is whether these psychological differences are the result of upbringing and society or of predisposition and inheritance. The answer to this question is at the heart of the nurture–nature debate where nurture stands for education, upbringing, environment, and society while nature stands for predisposition, inheritance, and genes. This debate was and sometimes still is emotional because it focuses on sensitive issues like differences between homo- and hetero-sexuals, criminals and non-criminals, blacks and whites, and also men and women. The answers to this question much depends on the spirit of times. In the 1960s and 1970s, there was an almost passionate belief in nurture and the feasibility of transforming society and human beings according to certain ideals. For example, it was believed that undesirable and unjust differences between men and women could be eliminated in a relatively short time by the implementation of appropriate measures. The feminist movement was very influential in the often fierce debates. The suggested differences between men and women were "social constructs" based on "irrelevant biological differences" propagated by men "as an excuse to suppress women and maintain male dominance" and "women are not born as women, they are made into women". These quotes from Simone de Beauvoir have inspired generations of feminists and other nurture adepts.

But much has changed in the nature versus nurture debate during the last 20–30 years. This is due to the spectacular progress made in molecular biology, genetics and evolutionary biology. The evolution theory is central in these sciences and has proved to be a robust, inspiring and so far never contradicted base for further progress in biological sciences. Among many other things, it has taught us that there is continuity between species – for example between primates and humans – not only in external features, but also in behaviour. Determining the entire human genetic code and gene content – the result of the world-wide Human Genome Project – is the biggest milestone to have occurred in recent years (Venter et al., 2001). Much research has been carried out on psychological, hormonal, genetic and behavioural differences between males and females in primates and humans, including advanced imaging studies on differences in brain structure (for a review see Baron-Cohen, 2003). The most important conclusion from this research is that there are gender differences which cannot be explained by upbringing, education and environment. Some major differences emanate from variations in hormone levels in early pregnancy and, in addition, are determined by differences in our genetic profiles as established over millions of years of evolution. With regard to the nature–nurture controversy, there is overwhelming evidence now that genetic predisposition in complex interaction with environmental factors and upbringing, do play a central role in human and animal development including male–female differences (De Waal, 1999; Baron-Cohen, 2003). This applies not only to differences in external characteristics but also to differences in behaviour, character, feelings and preferences. Both nature and nurture play an important role in determining how a man and woman eventually will be, both with regard to their similarities and their differences (Buss, 1999; Campbell, 2002). Recent scientific evidence shows we are beyond the nature versus nurture controversy because there is none, both are essential.

Emancipation Policies

Surprisingly, the nurture concept has been the prevailing concept in emancipation policies and has hardly been challenged by the growing insights from the biological sciences. According to this concept, men and women are psychologically the same at birth and the differences thereafter are the result of education and upbringing in a male-dominated society. Basically men and women are the same with regard to all their social, psychological and working abilities; women can perform almost all typical male activities and professions equally well as men (Hyde, 2005). However, women have been systematically kept out of male-dominated professions by men. All problems will be solved if women will get the same opportunities as men with regard to education, training, labour force participation and earning money, and having a career. Moreover, men can equally well carry out housework and child-care activities as women and therefore, he should undertake an equal part of these less highly appreciated activities. These were and still are the major principles of emancipation policies.

However, since governments and policy-makers in Europe have been aware of the problems related to declining birth rates and population ageing during the last 2 decades, all sorts of support measures have been introduced attempting to recon-cile the tension between female labour force participation and having a family. The influential Danish sociologist, Esping-Andersen, probably has proposed the most radical solutions. He argues for a "gender contract" in which binding agreements are to be made to create "true gender equality" (Esping-Andersen, 2002; see also Chapter 9 by Esping-Andersen elsewhere in this book). A broad-based, woman-friendly policy is necessary for which the most important conditions are: (a) fully paid and long-term maternity leave with retention of job and salary, (b) guaranteed and, when necessary, long-term leave to care for sick children, and (c) affordable and good child-care facilities. These conditions had been fulfilled in Sweden and the results of these measures seemed promising until the late 1980s, but appeared not to work in the period of recession thereafter. Apparently, having children in eco-nomically hard times is being considered as a luxury on which people are inclined to economise first like on motorcars. Esping-Andersen has wrestled with the issue of what additional changes must be made to create really true gender equality. Does this mean that women must adapt even more to the male role model? That would imply that they still further relinquish their reproductive role, which would result in even fewer children being born later, thus augmenting the problems that lie ahead. He argues there is a limit to what he calls the "masculinisation of the female life course" and comes to the conclusion that real gender equality will only be achieved if men somehow would succeed in feminizing their life course. But is the average man able and willing to do that?

In the present concept of emancipation and gender equality, the implicit assump-tion has always been that men and women are the same with regard to work, preferences, and social and economic abilities. In spite of all good intentions, the male implicitly became the standard for the female in this process of equalization: only if she is able to adapt to his lifestyle and ambitions, she will be successful in this male-dominated world. Unique female features such as the deep rooted wish to have a child to care for and her exclusive abilities to become pregnant, deliver a child, breastfeed and take care of babies, have been ignored, neglected or regarded as inconvenient and counterproductive in our efficiency-driven society. Differences in male/female preferences with regard to work and family – women being more often family-oriented than men – have not been appreciated (Hakim, 2000; see also Chapter 12 by Hakim elsewhere in this book). In fact, the existing emancipation policy unintentionally has been an instrument to equalize men and women in the sense of trying to make copies of one another: women especially had to become copies of men. If she succeeded, she usually did extremely well in his world. However, children or a family did not fit in this success story. Not surprisingly, that under such circumstances of societal pressure, women often decided to refrain from having a child or feel themselves obliged to delay childbearing to ages they have become sub-fertile or even infertile. Under the mask of true gender equality, a new form of inequality has come about, in which women get the worst part.

Unfortunately, so far no allowance has been made for the fact that some differences between men and women are the product of millions of years of evolutionary selection anchored in our genetic make-up. Now that we have taken the irreversible decision to separate sexuality from reproduction, we must not delude ourselves that the innate differences between men and women no longer exist or will disappear within a generation. Men and women are not only different in appearances and reproduction, but to some extent also in feelings, thoughts and behaviour. In emancipation policies we should account for those differences and accept them. True equality does not imply that men and women should be the same with regard to their abilities and attitudes towards work and children; the implicit assumption of most emancipation policies in Europe so far. True equality must entail the notion that both sexes are equivalent in the sense of having the same value: something quite different from being the same. True gender equality is accepting and appreciating that both sexes are different in some essential aspects (Potts & Short, 1999). Both should have equal opportunities for self-development and self-fulfilment; for many women motherhood is part of their self-fulfilment. Within this concept of equality, the differences between men and women are considered as complementary in that they supplement and enrich the life of their partner. Such a concept of gender equality is a precondition for more realistic emancipation policies because of being based on the reality of male/female differences and not on the illusion of men and women being the same.

In a society that embraces such a vision, women are offered ample opportunity to develop themselves, have a job and enjoy life just like men, but at the same time have the possibility to get children whenever they wish to have them. In such a society woman's emancipation is still compatible with motherhood.

In the words of Anne Campbell, psychologist and converted feminist (Campbell, 2002):

> If we accept that women and men are different, we can think about a society that breaks down the barriers between children and work, that allows women to see value in cooperation as well as competition and that allows women to capitalize on their linguistic and other

advantages. If evolutionary theory is correct then we cannot design twenty-first century women as if from scratch. Ideology, social policies, law and the media cannot in and of themselves make women into something they are not. What we can and should do is to give people choices that allow them the maximum freedom to be whatever they want. With that freedom, women's nature can take its own course.

References

Allen, V.M., Wilson, R.D., & Cheung, A. (2006). Genetics committee of the society of obstetricians and gynaecologists of Canada (SOGC) and reproductive endocrinology infertility committee of the society of obstetricians and gynaecologists of Canada (SOGC). Pregnancy outcomes after assisted reproductive technology. *Journal of Obstetrics Gynaecology Canada*, 28, 220–250.

Andersen, A.N., Goossens, V., Ferraretti, A.P., Bhattacharya, S., Felberbaum, R., de Mouzon, J., & Nygren, K.G. (2008). European IVF-monitoring (EIM) consortium and European society of human reproduction and embryology (ESHRE). Assisted reproductive technology in Europe, 2004: results generated from European registers by ESHRE. *Human Reproduction*, 23, 756–771.

Baron-Cohen, S. (2003). *The Essential Difference*. London: Penguin Books.

Bewley, S., Davies, M., & Braude, P. (2005). Which career first? *BMJ*, 331, 588–589.

Blossfeld, H. (1995). *The New Role of Women: Family Formation in Modern Societies*. Boulder, Colorado: Westview Press.

Buss, D.M. (1995). Psychological sex differences. Origins through sexual selection. *The American Psychologist*, 50, 164–168. discussion, 169–171.

Buss, D.M. (1999). *Evolutionary Psychology. The New Science of the Mind*. Boston, London, Toronto, Sydney, Tokyo, Singapore: Allyn and Bacon.

Campbell, A. (2002). *A Mind of Her Own. The Evolutionary Psychology of Women*. Oxford: Oxford University Press.

Collaborative Group on Hormonal Factors in Breast Cancer. (2001). Familial breast cancer: collaborative reanalysis of individual data from 52 epidemiological studies including 58,208 women with breast cancer and 101,986 women without the disease. *Lancet*, 358, 1389–1399.

De Waal, F. (1982). *Chimpanzee Politics: Power and Sex Among Apes*. Baltimore, Maryland: The John Hopkins University Press.

De Waal, F.B. (1999). The end of nature versus nurture. *Scientific American*, 281, 94–99.

Esping-Andersen, G. (2002). A new gender contract. In G. Esping-Andersen & A. Hemerijck (Eds.), *Why We Need a New Welfare State* (68–90). Oxford: Oxford University Press.

Hakim, C. (2000). *Work-Lifestyle Choices in The 21st Century: Preference Theory*. Oxford: Oxford University Press.

Hawkes, K., O'Connell, J.F., Jones, N.G., Alvarez, H., & Charnov, E.L. (1998). Grandmothering, menopause, and the evolution of human life histories. *Proceedings of the National Academy of Sciences of the United States of America*, 95, 1336–1339.

Helmerhorst, F.M., Perquin, D.A., Donker, D., & Keirse, M.J. (2004). Perinatal outcome of singletons and twins after assisted conception: a systematic review of controlled studies. *BMJ*, 328, 261.

Hewlett, S.A. (2002). *Baby Hunger. The New Battle for Motherhood*. London: Atlantic Books.

Hrdy, S.B. (1999). *Mother Nature. A History of Mothers, Infants and Natural Selection*. New York, NY: Pantheon Books.

Hyde, J.S. (2005). The gender similarities hypothesis. *The American Psychologist*, 60, 581–592.

Leridon, H. (2004). Can assisted reproduction technology compensate for the natural decline in fertility with age? A model assessment. *Human Reproduction*, 19, 1548–1553.

Luke, B., & Brown, M.B. (2007). Elevated risks of pregnancy complications and adverse outcomes with increasing maternal age. *Human Reproduction*, 22, 1264–1272.

Lutz, W., Mamolo, M., Potančoková, M., Scherbov, S., & Sobotka, T. (2008). European Demographic Data Sheet 2008. www.populationeurope.org

Potts, M., & Short, R.V. (1999). *Ever Since Adam and Eve. The Evolution of Human Sexuality.* (First edition). Cambridge: Cambridge University Press.

Rensman, E. (2006). *De pil in Nederland. Een mentaliteitsgeschiedenis.* Amsterdam: Van Gennep.

Riddle, J. (1997). *Eve's Herbes. A History of Contraception and Abortion in the West.* Cambridge (Massachusetts), London: Harvard University Press.

Rosenberg, K., & Travathon, W. (2001). The evolution of human birth. *Scientific American,* 285, 72–78.

Short, R.V. (1994). Why sex? In R.V. Short & E. Balaban (Eds.), *The Differences Between the Sexes* (3–23). Cambridge: Cambridge University Press.

Shorter, E. (1991). *Women's Bodies. A Social History of Women's Encounter with Health, Ill-Health and Medicine.* New Brunswick (USA) and London (UK): Transaction Publishers.

Spar, D.L. (2006). *The Baby Business. How Money, Science, and Politics Drive the Commerce of Conception.* Boston, Massachusetts: Harvard Business School Press.

Stewart, D. (1984). The pelvis as a passageway. Evolution and adaptations. *British Journal of Obstetrics Gynaecology,* 91, 611–617.

Te Velde, E.R., Habbema, J.D., Hilders, C.G., & Merkus, J.M. (2007). The consequences of postponing pregnancy. *Ned. Tijdschr. Geneeskd.,* 151, 1593–1596.

Te Velde, E.R., & Pearson, P.L. (2002). The variability of female reproductive ageing. *Human Reproduction Update,* 8, 141–154.

Templeton, A., Morris, J.K., & Parslow, W. (1996). Factors that affect outcome of in-vitro fertilization treatment. *Lancet,* 348, 1402–1406.

Van de Kaa, D.J. (1987). Europe's second demographic transition. *Population Bulletin,* 42, 1–59.

Van Noord-Zaadstra, B.M., Looman, C.W., Alsbach, H., Habbema, J.D., Te Velde, E.R., & Karbaat, J. (1991). Delaying childbearing: effect of age on fecundity and outcome of pregnancy. *BMJ,* 302, 1361–1365.

Venter, J.C., Adams, M.D., Myers, E.W., Li, P.W., Mural, R.J., Sutton, G.G., Smith, H.O., Yandell, M., Evans, C.A., Holt, R.A., et al. (2001). The sequence of the human genome. *Science,* 291, 1304–1351.

Weisglas-Kuperus, N., Hille, E.T., Duivenvoorden, H.J., Finken, M.J., Wit, J.M., Van Buuren, S., Van Goudoever, J.B., Verloove-Vanhorick, S.P., & Dutch POPS-19 Collaborative Study Group. (2009). Intelligence of very preterm or very low birthweight infants in young adulthood. *Archives of Disease in Childhood. Fetal and Neonatal Edition,* 94, F196–F200.

Chapter 3
Males and Females: The Big Little Difference

Jan A.R.A.M. van Hooff

Impatiently a male marmoset monkey is waiting till he can take over his baby from his female partner who is nursing it. Patiently he will then carry it around on his back till the next nursing period.

Never ever would a male hamadryas baboon consider this. He suspiciously watches the female members of the harem he herds. If one of them is so imprudent as to wander close to another male he rushes towards her to punish her with a ritualized neck bite and chases her back into his own club. She screams like hell and eventually tries to approach and embrace him.

Never would a gorilla female do this. She has joined a powerful silverback male and the females who associated with him earlier. Now she moves with them in his compact little group. Normally this male does not tolerate any other silverback near his females. As gentle as he is to these females and their infants, in as far as they are born in his presence, so ferocious he is to male invaders; his females might get frivolous thoughts. . .

Chimpanzee males have no problems with that. They are members of a population in which they form male fraternities that defend their ancestral home range against males from neighbouring groups. If it makes for a nice living in that range, females may gladly want to settle there. So no harems here. In principle the ladies are for everybody, that is to say, a bit more for the leaders than for the others.

And so we can go on for a while with examples of the enormous variety in the relationships between and within the sexes of our nearest relatives in the animal kingdom, the monkeys and the apes – a variety that is even greater elsewhere in the animal kingdom. You could say: well that's how it is; every bird is known by its note. But a biologist wants to know why one bird is known this way and the other that way. In fact this is an evolutionary question: what are the evolutionary reasons that a given structure or process has arisen and persists?

J.A.R.A.M. van Hooff (✉)
Emeritus Professor in Animal Behaviour, Utrecht University, Utrecht, The Netherlands
e-mail: jaramvanhooff@planet.nl

G. Beets et al. (eds.), *The Future of Motherhood in Western Societies*,
DOI 10.1007/978-90-481-8969-4_3, © Springer Science+Business Media B.V. 2011

Everything Turns around Reproduction

Whether you are virus, a bacterium, a fungus, a plant or an animal, ultimately there is only one thing that matters, namely whether you reproduce. However sophisticated and fabulous you are, if you don't replicate yourself in offspring you are the dead end of a till then continuous thread of life and your magnificence is of no avail. Already early on in the course of evolution it was discovered that reproduction by forming germs leading to totally new individuals was a strategy that won from replication by cloning. And sexual reproduction won from the asexual production of germs, which produces almost identical copies of a single parent individual. Although both cloning and asexual reproduction maintain themselves as strategies of reproduction under certain circumstances, they suffer from a major disadvantage in comparison with sexual reproduction in which two individuals combine and mix up their genetic programs. The latter may lead to unexpected new outcomes. For in asexual reproduction, and even more so in cloning, the chances of innovation are much less and so then is the chance of evolutionary development.

Something new can arise in two ways. There may be spontaneous changes in the genetic material that harbours the developmental program. And there may be recombinations resulting from the reshuffling of genetic material from the two parent individuals. Then, sometimes, it is "bingo": something new turns up that is a step forward and makes all the previous functional solutions obsolete. Such fortunate recombinations could occur since the developmental recipe came to be dispensed in a twofold form, namely in the two different strands of the DNA double helix that each are provided by one of the two parents.

Why the Sexes Differ

Here we see the beginning of sexual reproduction and consequently of sex, of all those processes that are necessary to bring two right partners together at the right moment. Of course bacteria do this already. Although most reproduction is simply by doubling the genetic double strand and then splitting into two new individuals, there occasionally is a sexual phase in which two individuals halve themselves; two such different halves find one another and form a new individual. But there are not two different sexes.

However, already early in evolution a specialisation of the germ cells occurred. This proved to another advance. One individual produces germ cells which in addition to the genetic material contain a load of materials necessary to provide the energy and the building blocks for the first phase of development of the germ into a self supporting larva. That is the she-cell. The other one, the he-cell is no more than the genetic material packed together with a little motor and some fuel to allow it to race around for a while in search of a she-cell. Every couple that has ever been standing at the station exit looking for a cab knows that it is more efficient to have one person waiting with all the luggage and the other going to look around than both going on a search with each one hauling half of the luggage.

The Little Difference with the Great Consequences

This small but essential difference between the egg cell and the sperm cell is associated with a specialisation in what we call a female and a male role that profoundly affects the relationships between individuals. The basic reason is that small sperm cells can be produced more cheaply and, therefore, in quantity than the egg cells with their costly load.

Lots of animals – think of marine species such as mussels, sea urchins, sea anemones, and also many fish – simply spawn their sexual products in the surrounding water. To raise the chances of meeting they do this simultaneously in response to synchronising environmental cues or signals from one another. But in what we tend to call the "higher animals" a grandiose improvement has turned up. There the egg cell remains in the female's body to meet the sperm delivered at the spot. In birds and quite a few reptiles the fertilized egg is then loaded with lots of goodies, and laid somewhere to develop, incubated or not. In a number of species, at any rate in all mammals, the fertilized egg remains in the safe wrapping of the mother where it is supplied with nutrients by the mother.

At that stage the differences between males and females become appreciable. In many species the male rapidly provides his contribution and the female is then left to make the costly investments necessary to complete the reproductive task successfully. She thus carries the burden of pregnancy and lactation, and in many cases a subsequent period of maternal care. Note that in quite a few non-mammalian species the roles may be reversed. In the sea horse the egg is deposited in an incubation pouch of the male and the female happily wanders off. The stickleback male finds himself in the same predicament. After building a nest he tries to lure visiting females into depositing their eggs there. These females are gone already by the time he has fertilized the eggs. Everything would be wasted unless he now takes care of the brood. The crux of the matter is: he or she who is left with the fertilized egg is also left with the decision to give it care. And that is different for species with external fertilization and those with internal fertilization.

This difference in the contribution of the two sexes leads to remarkable differences in the strategies the sexes employ to maximise their fitness. Charles Darwin (1809–1882) was the first to realize this (in 1859) when he developed his model of evolution by means of natural selection. He realised that natural selection must unavoidably lead to increased effectiveness and efficiency of biological functions. He unfolded a threefold argument. First he reasoned that all living things are able to produce many more offspring than the carrying capacity of their specific ecological niche allows. Their eventual reproductive success is limited by a number of factors that have an effect on the survival and reproduction of individuals, the availability of resources, in particular food, being the most important one. This was an insight Darwin got from the "Essay on the principle of population" (1798) by economist Thomas Malthus (1766–1834). From this it follows that there must always be competition for the available resources and the available places in the niche.

Secondly, he realised that individuals differ in their characteristics. At present we know that the genetic material of no two individuals is the same. In as far as this variation is reflected in differences in fenotypical characteristics and in as far as these characteristics have an effect, direct or indirect, on the reproductive success of the individual, it follows necessarily that there must be selection on the most adaptive variants, those that most effectively and efficiently contribute to survival, in as far as that leads to reproduction.

The different strategies of the sexes, at least in birds and mammals, result from the fact that their reproductive potential differs. Females can produce only a limited number of offspring during their lifetime. In primates, for instance, a female monkey has an infant on average every 2 or 3 years, a female ape even once in every 3–8 years. A female may count herself lucky if she lives long enough to produce ten offspring. Most don't reach this at all. This is true also for our own species. It even was before the pill arrived.

What would be the strategies to be followed by females that will favour selection? Of course she should behave so as to get genetically fit and healthy offspring. She can't do much about her own genetical make-up; she got it from her father and mother. But she can select that of her partner. In other words, females will be selected to have a preference for phenotypes that are correlated with "good genes". She should fall for "beautiful" males, that is strong, healthy looking and harmoniously developed males (in species where the male contributes to the rearing of the young, she should also test his inclination to give care – we will deal with that below). It is equally important that she worries about safety and access to resources for herself and her offspring. And that is indeed what females appear to be doing.

Males find themselves in a different predicament. Whereas females go for quality of a limited number of offspring, males can go for quantity. The bible mentions that King Salomon had a 1,000 wives. This must have ment quite a job for him, since a year has only 365 days. The example is a proverbial illustration that a male mammal (this doesn't apply only to humans) can have an impressive number of offspring, at least in principle. The more he has, the greater will be the chance that there will be good ones amongst them. Obviously then, natural selection will make him aim for this end. However, whether the strategy is successful will ultimately depend on whether he is able to gain access to fertile females, and to many at that.

But then there is a problem. In almost all species of mammals and birds there are about as many males as females, at least initially. If one male begets offspring from a large number of females, then there must be many males which achieve nothing. Whereas female mammals needn't worry about whether they will be fertilized, but only about by whom, males should have as their foremost worry whether they will ever fertilize a female. Otherwise they will be evolutionary zeros, the end of their line. It follows that there must be strong inter-male competition. In autumn deer stags fight ferociously for access to the hinds in the herd. The hinds don't fight. They simply wait. The stag that wins is fine. Evolutionary logic tells them: by allowing the winner to take them they will most probably get sons that will do equally well. And she couldn't care less whether that stag has been courting other females.

On the Polygamy Track or on the Careful Father Track?

How very different are things in species where the males help their females in raising the offspring. Do males do that? Yes, sometimes they have to switch from a "many mates strategy" to a "caring father strategy". That can happen in species where the way of life is so complicated that it takes a long time before a youngster can stand on its own legs. In, for instance primates and ungulates this is not the rule. By the time a zebra foal is off the mother's milk, he can eat the grass that is standing around it. For carnivores such as the wolf it is a different story. A wolf bitch would have to stray widely to fetch food for herself and the cubs to be nourished. Before the young wolves can fend for themselves, there has been a long period of learning and exercise. All this time they are dependent on prey that has to be provided to them.

Under such conditions a male finds himself in a dilemma. He could fertilize a female and leave her with the fruits of his enterprise while he searches for another female to mate with. But if the female has a small chance of successfully rearing the youngsters and if this chance is increased when the male stays to help he must consider the trade-off: which strategy will eventually yield the greatest yield for him. A simple calculation makes the principle clear. Suppose a polygynous male might succeed in mating with four different females during one mating season. Suppose each female gets five pups, of which only one grows up successfully when she has to care for them on her own. Then the reproductive success of the polygynous father will eventually be four offspring. But a male that stays with the first female to relieve her form the burden of hunting while she is lactating may see all five pups making it... Well, he has done better, and under these conditions a predisposition for paternal care will win from a predisposition for polygamy. He might also try to profit twofold: help the spouse but not miss out on an incidental mating when the chance occurs. A mix of these two strategies might sometimes even offer the greater benefits.

But then another problem arises. Hinds, merries and the females of many primate species might not care less whether the father of their young has sired many others, for a wolf bitch that is different. She cannot bear the presence of other females around her spouse. It is a major concern of her to prevent that other bitches lure him away and thus dilute his paternal investments. Wolf bitches are notoriously jealous. This is a trait they share with human females, as we will consider below.

For male animals, that is to say "our kind of animals", there is the fundamental trade-off: with which socio-sexual strategy do I ultimately score the highest "fitness", i.e. relative reproductive success. Not that the members of any species, humans included, make this computation explicitly and consciously. On the contrary, evolutionary selection has brought certain motivational drives to the fore, emotional preferences and tendencies which under the given circumstances yield the highest "pay-off".

Our Animal Relatives

Monkeys and apes are not hunters. Only the chimpanzee and some baboons hunt larger mammals occasionally, but meat is not a substantial component of their diet. Most species live of fruits, leaves, herbs, the occasional invertebrates, such as caterpillars, ants, beetles, and the occasional fledgling bird or young mammal. Males then have little "paternal potential"; they cannot contribute substantially to the growing up of their infants. Yes, they can and do protect females and young. But that is not necessarily restricted to the young of one particular female. Primate males can therefore easily go on the polygynous tour. But consequently they will meet other males there. What the one wants, the other wants too. Indeed, as is illustrated so nicely in the case of the deer stags.

What form the competition takes can vary greatly. It depends on the behaviour of the females. They determine which male strategies will be successful. The key word here is monopolisation. Can a male claim the access to a number of females and can he effectively inhibit the access of other males? That will be easier if the females, for reasons of their concern, want to live in compact cohesive groups. Females appear to do this primarily for reasons of safety; the nature and the strength of threats from predators and hostile conspecifics are major factors in female aggregation. Together the members of a group have more eyes and ears. Together they can share vigilance duties and they can join in defense.

Competing Macho Males

Whatever the reason for female association, once they operate as a group that is compact and not too large a male can, so to speak, take possession of that group and keep others at bay. This type of competition is known as exclusion or contest competition. Darwin already realised that this will lead to the selection of those physical and mental characteristics of males that will lend them superiority in this contest competition, such as strength, size and assertiveness. The evolutionary consequence of this can be "sexual dimorphism"; males are considerably larger and more aggressive than the females. Amongst our nearest relatives, the apes, the gorilla and the orangutan are obvious examples. Gorillas are the largest terrestrial primates. They live in small compact groups. Although there is some variation in their social organization the typical pattern is that of an adult silverback male with a group of females and their kids. The male fiercely wards off other adult males. The orangutan is the other example. It is the largest arborial mammal on earth. A mature adult male defends an area of tropical forest in which a number of females reside. He is fiercely intolerant against other mature males. And indeed, both species are extremely sexually dimorphic. The males are about twice as heavy as the females.

However, evolution may take a different course. If females do not find it necessary to stick together, and if they live in large and/or loose groups, then even the most powerful male cannot prevent that other males grasp the opportunities that arise here when he is elsewhere. If, in addition, females come into estrous more or less simultaneously, a monopolization strategy becomes almost impossible. This has been demonstrated clearly for hanuman langurs. These monkeys live in India. In some areas they occur in so called one-male groups, in other areas they occur in multi-male groups. Hill & Dunbar (2002) could show that populations varied with respect to reproductive seasonality. Where that ocurred groups tended to be multi-male. In other words, a dominant male did no longer try to monopolise access to all the fertile females.

When the necessity to worry about other males falls away, the selective pressures on male toughness and intolerance between males are much less as well. Animal species that find themselves in this position do indeed show less sexual dimorphism. Differences in male reproductive success are no longer determined by differences in male power. Other factors become more important in determining which male wins in the competition. This situation has become known as one of "scramble competition".

When Male Contest does not make Sense

Now the females can play their cards in a different way. Where males contest for females with one another, a female fares best by lending her favours to the winner: the greater her chance that she will have sons who will similarly prevail. In fact she may thus reinforce the selection effects of intermale competition. But in a context where the machos are no longer at an advantage, who should the female choose? Her preference should go to males who offer other benefits. For instance, to a male who has taken possession of a food source and tolerates that a female eats from the source also. Or to a male who comes to her support when she has become involved in a skirmish. Now, all at once, male courtesy counts.

Sometimes both strategies occur side by side or in some mixed form. This has been found in a field study on savanna baboons (Smuts, 1985, 1987). These animals often live in groups that are so large that it is simply impossible for a dominant male to keep other adult males at bay. When a female comes into her fertile period the dominant male forms a consort with her for the duration of that period in which he mates with her and stays close to her thus preventing that subordinate males get a chance to mate. Here his bravery is some use. But when more females are simultaneously fertile, then also subordinate males may grasp their chance. He cannot be at two places at once. The females may now choose to lend their sexual favours to males who have helped these females, also outside their fertile period. In this way it may be worthwhile for a male to buy the friendship of a female, and conversely.

Relaxed Relationships between Males

It was the starting point of our story: that big little difference. It leads to the default condition that males engage much more easily in contests for sexual partners than do females. However, when it does not pay to engage in heavy conflicts, when the benefits to be gained are more than offset by the costs in terms of time and energy wasted and of the risks incurred, and when the females are no longer tempted to go preferentially for the macho males, then what point is there in further nurturing male intolerance. Indeed, that is what we see, when we look at various species. Amongst the apes our nearest relatives, the chimpanzee and, especially, the bonobo are illuminating examples.

In the bonobo, a slender form of chimpanzee, we find fully free sexual relationships. Everybody has sexual contacts of some sort with everybody: males with females irrespective of age, adults with infants, males with males and females with females. Sex has become an expression of social bonding and is used in situations of greeting, of reconciliation and so on (De Waal, 1997). But if a female mates with many males, who then will be the father. In the bonobo it is a matter of chance. The male who mates most often (*ref. Paternity bonobos*) so that his sperm outnumbers that of other males has the greatest possibility. This phenomenon is refered to as sperm competition. It requires abundant production of sperm. This is reflected in the fact that in the bonobo and in other polygynandrous species (socio-sexual relationships of a male with many females and of a female with many males) the testicles are many times larger than in species which live in one-male-one-female (monogamous) and one-male-multi-female (polygynous) societies.

Compare this with the situation in which the silverback male gorilla lives. He is the only who mates with the females of his club and he needs to do this only when one of his females feels like it. Well, that is not too often. His females are either pregnant (which lasts about 9 months) or they are lactating (which can last up to a few years). And a female who is neither pregnant nor lactating will only be in her fertile period during a limited number of days in her menstrual cycle. A student of gorilla sexual behaviour must be a very patient character indeed.

In one more respect the chimpanzee is somewhat exceptional among the primates, and indeed among the mammals. The males are not only comparatively sexually tolerant, but also cooperative. They can form a kind of male brotherhoods when associating with the group mates with whom they have been familiar from early youth onwards. In many other social species, by contrast, the females spend their whole life in the group in which they were born. Consequently they form strong affiliative relationships with their female relatives. Now the males are more individualistic. Often they leave their natal group at late adolescence, venture in the wide world and try to settle in other groups. There they meet females that are much more interesting than their dull sisters and female cousins. In chimpanzees it is the other way around. The males stay in their natal group in their natal territory. The females may come from elsewhere and join males who possess a productive territory. The bondedness of the males facilitates tolerance and cooperation. For instance, together they hunt other primates. Their cooperation also finds a grim expression. With the human the chimpanzee is the only primate species where systematic and organised intertribal war exists (e.g. Wrangham, 2004). Occasionally a "band of brothers" ventures into neighbouring territory and in a gruesome manner attacks and sometimes kills conspecifics that it encounters there. In so doing the band can expand its territory and even stimulate females to switch to the territory of the winners.

Comparing the Hominoids

When we compare the different hominoids, the taxon to which we humans belong we notice three main types of social organisation. These are clearly reflected in physical and behavioural features.

We noted already that both chimpanzees and bonobos are polygynandrous; they are only slightly sexually dimorphic and have huge testes. Matings are a quick affair, a matter of seconds, and these occur rather frequently. In addition the females show large conspicuous genital swellings just before and during the days of fertility. As is the case in a number of other polygynandrous taxa in both chimpanzees and bonobos the swollen labia broadcast the message to whoever is around that the female is in her fertile period, thus indiscriminately inviting male interest and instigating male (sperm) competition.

Gorillas mostly live in one-male polygynous groups. Strong male contest and monopolisation are reflected in an enormous degree of sexual dimorphism. Testes are small; matings are infrequent and a matter of minutes rather than seconds. Female genital swellings are absent: they possess a "cryptic" estrous.

Orangutans are a polygynous species as well. The fully developed adult males monopolise a territory in which several females roam about. These males are extremely hostile towards other fully developed adult males. Sexual dimorphism is enormous. Testicles are small. Matings are infrequent and are an elaborate and lengthy affair. There are no noticeable female genital swellings.

Gibbons and siamangs, the so-called lesser apes, mostly live in small monogamous family groups consisting of a parent pair and the occasional offspring. There is no sexual dimorphism, males and females being equally big. Both defend the family teritory and ward off members of the opposite sex. Testicles are comparatively small. No genital swellings. Mating is a comparatively lengthy indulgement.

Does the Human Species Fit in This Picture?

Putting our own species in this comparative perspective leads to some amazing conclusions. First of all we do not resemble our closest relatives, the chimpanzee and the bonobo, at all. True enough, we share with them a modest degree of sexual size dimorphism, and, remarkably, a comparatively great intermale tolerance. With the chimpanzee (but not with the bonobo), we share male association in cooperative bonds. However, we manage with small testicles and even "quickies" last longer than in our closest cousins. We also lack sexual swellings as signals of fertility ("Thank heavens", is that what you said?). In these respects we bear some resemblance, on the one hand, to the monogamous gibbons, and, on the other hand, to the polygynous gorilla and orangutan (except for the large sexual dimorphism).

In 1949 the anthropologist George Murdock published a cross-cultural data set, extended in later years (e.g. 1981) in which he reviewed the "official" systems of cohabitation of the sexes in 849 cultural groups. He categorised the majority (706) as mildly polygynous. More than a quarter (136) but not the least important ones, were monogamous. Only a handful of cultural groups, and very small ones at that, were classified as polygynandrous (4) or polyandrous (3). Note, however, how such classifications depend on the methods and criteria applied, as illustrated by the controversy between Freeman (1989) and Shankman (e.g. 2000) about Margaret Mead's (e.g. 1935) inference of promiscuous tolerance, supposed to exist in some Polynesian societies.

There clearly is quite some variation in socio-sexual organisation especially between, but also within species. Attempts to consider these variations as adaptively related to specific environments have certainly met with some success. In considering the human species the emphasis has traditionally been on impressive cultural variations. However, with the broader perspective that is revealed when we compare the knowledge about our own species with the recent socio-ecological studies of our primate relatives it is difficult to maintain that the human socio-sexual pattern is a set of arbitrary cultural attributes that can vary without restraint. We as a species fit in a grand global scheme of evolutionarily regulated adaptations. We weave a different texture, but we do it following the same laws. In so doing we have realised a limited set of possible options. This is brought home most pertinently by the fact that we do resemble our closest relatives, the chimpanzees and the bonobos socio-sexually only to a limited extent. In stead we occupy, in terms of the parameters listed above, a position in between the polygynous gorillas and the monogamous gibbons and siamangs. But unlike these, we humans do possess a high degree of between-male tolerance, as do chimpanzee and bonobo.

At first sight one is inclined to see this between-male tolerance as a characteristic that we share because it developed in our common ancestor, i.e. before the phylogenetic branches leading to chimpanzees and to humans diverged some 7 million years ago – a homology, as evolutionary biologists call this. However, it could also be an analogy, a characteristic which has developed independently in both branches after the split. There is fossil evidence supporting the latter. Prehumans and earlier species of *Homo* show a much greater sexual dimorphism than *Homo sapiens*, the species that exists since about 150,000 years. This suggests that these earlier species have lived under a regime of more intense male competition. They may have lived in small one-male family groups, much more like present day gorillas.

In chimpanzees the male cooperative bondedness is not hindered by an excessive sexual competition and intolerance. Sure, there is some, but it is part of a system of "political negotiation" (De Waal, 2001). By contrast a severe intolerance towards other males infringing on acquired pair bonds manifests itself clearly in almost all human cultures. Yet humans have overcome the obstacle that sexual competition between males forms for cooperative male bonding. In stead of accepting a chimpanzee type of sexual promiscuity, the human has hidden sex. In all human cultures sexual intercourse is normally banned from the public domain and hidden behind the curtain of privacy that shields off the sleeping domain. Humans have reinforced this by means of formulas of cohabitation, marriage rules that are officially recognised and validated by society.

Friedl (1994) has argued against the generally accepted idea that the hiding of sex is a product of recent civilisation, i.e. of certain cultural and arbitrary religious developments. He regards it more probable that the hiding of sex is an old and universal human adaptation. Putting out of sight the jealousy fuelling signals of sexual interaction not only allowed cooperative male bonds to develop and be maintained in our species. It also facilitated by an increasing paternal commitment within more or less durable pair bonds that are not constantly threatened by destabilising sexual provocation. This paternal commitment to communal brood care is generally present in the human species and greater than in any other primate species with the exception of the monogamous or polyandrous(!) callitrichids. We shall return to this below, but will first consider the tense relation between sexual rivalry and male bonding.

A certain respect for the established pair bonds of other male group members exists in one other primate species, where it is associated with male cooperation as well. This fascinating analogon is found in the hamadryas or sacred baboon. This species of baboon lives in the arid highland steppes of the Ethiopian region and near South-west Arabia. Its social organisation differs strikingly from that of the savanna baboon species elsewhere in Africa which live in large multi-male multi-female groups. The hamadryas baboon has a remarkable four-level social organisation. The basic unit is the "harem", an association of an adult male with one or more females. Several harems of closely related males form a clan. The clans form part of a band. These in turn form the group. Clans coordinate some of their behaviours. The clan males, for instance, vote in the early morning, before splitting up for their day-long foraging trips, about places where they meet at noon to drink (Stolba, 1979). With clever field experiments the Swiss primatologist Hans Kummer could show that a male respected the pair bond of another member of the same clan. A male was put in a cage from where he could watch how in another cage a male clan mate acquainted a female that was introduced to him. This female was caught at a far away location and was strange to both clan members. When the observer male was introduced into the cage of the now settled pair, he not only went out of their way, but also behaved in an inhibited way, avoiding all behaviours that might betray an interest in the pair; he turned his back on them and avoided looking at them. This was in striking contrast with the behaviour of an observer male who did not come from the same troup as the other male. On being introduced to the pair he would fight the other male and try to appropriate his female, provided he was not smaller than the pair male (Kummer, 1992). Male cooperative bondedness clearly is irreconcilable with sexual rivalry in a multi-male society.

Care Giving Fathers

Our species does have something special by which it differs from practically all other monkey species, in particular from its nearest relatives, the chimpanzee and the bonobo. This is paternal bonding.

When some 7 million years ago the pre-chimpanzees and the pre-humans split away from one another, the pre-chimpanzees stayed in what is thought to be the more ancestral habitat, the forest. We have very good reasons to believe that the pre-humans became adapted to life in more open savanna landscapes. Life was different there and required special adaptations. The prehumans differentiated in a number of different species and even genera. Some of these (e.g. the paranthropines or robust australopithecines) specialized in a herbivorous direction. They fed from hard vegetation elements. Others, the gracile australopithecines and early species of Homo incorporated scavenging and hunting in their way of life. Meat as a source of proteins gradually became more important than it is for present-day chimpanzees, and than it had been, presumably, for the common ancestor. There are indications that, if not the prehumans, then at least the developing humans began to hunt larger prey cooperatively.

Thus a situation arose which bears some resemblance to that of the wolf. As in this socially living and cooperative carnivore, the females of early humans with their helpless infants were restricted more in their movements and bound more closely to a "home location", as in present day hunter-gatherer societies. They could raise their infants more successfully if they could rely on a male provider. Such a "bonded" male, restricting his paternal investment largely to one or at the most a few females, would be rewarded by a more or less exclusive sexual access to "his" female(s). Not only would his paternal investment be irreconcilable with a strategy that maximizes his opportunities to fertilize as many females as possible, he would also meet the constraints imposed on him by other males facing precisely the same predicament. Other "bonded" males would invest considerably in warding off attempts of rival males who would corrupt their paternity. A situation of "free sex" and promiscuity, as we see in our nearest relatives, the chimpanzee and the bonobo, would inhibit paternal care, since it is difficult to imagine how a situation could develop and be evolutionarily stable in which a male provides care to youngsters which have a low likelihood of being his own.

The only monkey species that show exclusive pair bonding and substantial paternal care are found among the callitrichids. These species are very small animals living from insects and plant juices and resins. In adapting to this life style they have become dwarfs, but they still bear comparatively large babies. Once the mother has carried the burden of pregnancy and still has to carry the burden of lactation, then a male can make a difference by carrying the young. Indeed he takes over the load, and she is attached to him for that. But she also displays the most extreme jealousy, leading to expulsion, suppression and even psychological castration of other females, older daughters included (e.g. Abbott, 1993).

We are a primate species where it is in the interest of the female to secure the commitment of cooperative care from a male which is not diluted (or at least not too much) by a distracting interest in other females. It is in the interest of the male to achieve certainty of paternity for the offspring that are the objects of his cooperative care. This will stimulate a tendency on part of both sexes to monopolise and defend established pair bonds. It leads to the fascinating sociosexual dynamics that many people like watching in the soaps on the screen every night: monopolisation on the one hand and not waive opportunities for other "profits" on the other. As we noted above, the latter forms a temptation especially to males. Primarily dominant and otherwise attractive males can more easily score reproductive success on a broader front. But also females can on occasion profit from the sexual interest of more men and, although this is not to the delight of a possible established partner, they can follow more promiscuous strategies (e.g. Gangestad & Simpson, 2000). An advantageous consequence of being attracted to successful men is undoubtedly that good quality genes for a possible offspring come by even though the offspring care is provided by another male. This is reflected in changes in females' sexual preferences that depend on the phase of the menstrual cycle. Thus females' preference shifts from more feminine types of men outside the fertile period to more masculine types of men in the fertile period (Penton-Voak & Perrett, 2001). This resembles the variation in partner preferences found in monogamous birds. A number of studies have shown that females which have formed a pair bond may nevertheless actively seek secret extra-pair copulations. In these matings high-quality dominant males are preferred, thus enabling the females to have "proven" genes for (part of) their offspring whilst not jeopardizing the paternal dedication of their mate, which has also vested interest in maintaining the bond.

Even taking into account these variations we have become more "wolf-like" than almost any other primate (but note the callitrichid exception) with a tendency for pair bonding. We tend to fall in love with that one person (or this one now, and another sometime later, but there is a clear fixation on a particular partner). Chimpanzees do not show signs of suffering from such mono-mindedness. We are also extremely jealous. Males do not easily tolerate sexual avances to their partner. That is nothing special; we share this characteristic with many species where there is male contest competition for females. But also human females can be jealous. Psychological studies show that it is for them about something else. They may be forgiving with respect to a sexual excursion of their male. However, they get extremely concerned when that male engages in an affectionate relationship with another female (e.g. Buunk & Dijkstra, 2004). Then they run the risk of losing his caring dedication for themselves and the offspring.

In humans these sex differences appear to be large and a universal characteristic. This is demonstrated impressively by a world-wide and comprehensive census study by David Smith that has been discussed extensively in an issue of Behavioral and Brain Sciences (2005). His team collected Sociosexual Orientation Inventories, self-report measures indicative of the degree of restricted versus promiscuous mating orientations, from more than 14,000 subjects across 48 nations. It revealed some interesting results regarding fundamental patterns and cultural variations in human mating patterns. Sex differences in sociosexual orientations were universal, males scoring considerably higher in promiscuous orientation than females in all nations studied. There were, however, variations in patterns of sociosexuality across nations and in relation to economic and ecological patterns. For instance, relational, economic and political equality was associated with a shift of the mating patterns towards a less restricted sociosexuality. In addition the differences between the sexes became more moderate. The difference was smaller also in environments where the reproductive efforts were less exacting and burdensome, a finding that is not surprising in view of the parental investment models presented above. In high-stress and taxing ecological conditions, moreover, a shift towards monogamy was found. In other words, the variation shows clear cultural adaptations to the local ecology. When ecologically determined cultural pressures relax, when the valuation of women independence is greater and treatment becomes more equitable, then less restricted sociosexual attitudes and behaviours manifest themselves. Short term sexual preferences and desires, such as described above, may be revealed. However, as is noted as a conclusion of this study, although the attitude and behaviour of women is often more constrained by cultural values and institutions than of men, women never precisely match the sociosexual psychology of men. It is obvious that any explanation of these differences between the sexes in terms of the controversial alternatives of either phylogenetic adaptation or cultural adaptation is spurious and misleading. On the one hand the influence of socioenvironmental factors is obvious. However, these often work in similar directions as the evolutionary selective pressures that are deduced in evolutionary models and that are found in empirical studies in a wide range of taxa. At predictable moments also human females are fascinated by male macho styles, at other moments they rather fancy manifestations of male dedication and helpfulness.

References

Abbott, D.H. (1993). Social conflict and reproductive suppression of in marmoset and tamarin monkeys. In W.H. Mason & S.P. Mendoza (Eds.), *Primate Social Conflict* (331–372). Albany, NY: State University of New York Press.

Buunk, B.P., & Dijkstra, P. (2004). Gender differences in rival characteristics that evoke jealousy in response to emotional versus sexual infidelity. *Personal Relationships*, 11, 395–408.

Darwin, C.R. (1859). *On the Origin of Species by Means of Natural Selection, or the Preservation of Favoured Races in the Struggle for Life*. London: John Murray.

De Waal, F.B.M. (1997). *Bonobo: The Forgotten Ape*. Berkeley, CA: University of California Press.

De Waal, F.B.M. (2001). *The Ape and the Sushi Master*. Harmondsworth: Penguin.

Freeman, D. (1989). *The Fateful Hoaxing of Margaret Mead: A Historical Analysis of Her Samoan Research*. New York, NY: Westview Press.

Friedl, E. (1994). Sex, the invisible. *American Anthropologist*, 96, 833–844.

Gangestad, S.W., & Simpson, J.A. (2000). The evolution of human mating: trade-offs and strategic pluralism. *Behavioral and Brain Sciences*, 23, 573–587.

Hill, R.A., & Dunbar, R.M. (2002). Climatic determinants of diet and foraging behaviour in baboons. *Evolutionary Ecology*, 16, 589–593.

Kummer, H. (1992). *Weiße Affen am Roten Meer: Das soziale Leben der Wüstenpaviane*. München: Piper.

Malthus, T.R. (1798). *An Essay on the Principle of Population, as It Affects the Future Improvement of Society, with Remarks on the Speculations of Mr Godwin, M. Condorcet and Other Writers*. London: J. Johnson.

Mead, M. (1935). *Sex and Temperament in Three Primitive Societies*. New York, NY: William Morrow.

Murdock, G.P. (1949). *Social Structure*. New York, NY: Macmillan.

Murdock, G.P. (1981). *Atlas of World Cultures*. Pittsburgh, PA: University of Pittsburgh Press.

Penton-Voak, I.S., & Perrett, D.I. (2001). Male facial attractiveness: perceived personality and shifting female preferences for male traits across the menstrual cycle. *Advances in the Study of Behavior*, 30, 219–260.

Schmitt, D.P. (2005). Sociosexuality from Argentina to Zimbabwe: a 48-nation study of sex, culture, and strategies of human mating. *Behavioral and Brain Sciences*, 28, 247–311.

Shankman, P. (2000). Culture, biology and evolution: the Mead-Freeman controversy revisited. *Journal of Youth and Adolescence*, 29(5), 539–556.

Smuts, B.B. (1985). *Sex and Friendship in Baboons*. New York, NY: Aldine.

Smuts, B.B. (1987). Sexual competition and mate choice. In B.B. Smuts, D.L. Cheney, R.M. Seyfarth, R.W. Wrangham, & T.T. Struthsaker (Eds.), *Primate Societies* (385–399). Chicago: University of Chicago Press.

Stolba, A. (1979). *Entscheidungsfindung in Verbänden von Papio hamadryas*. Dissertation. Universität Zürich.

Wrangham, R. (Fall, 2004). Killer species. *Daedalus*, 133, 25–35.

Chapter 4
Sexual Differentiation of the Human Brain and Male/Female Behaviour

Dick F. Swaab

My brain? It's my second favourite organ.
(Woody Allen in Sleeper, 1973)

Organization and Activation of the Human Brain

Sexual differentiation of our brain shows how the interaction of the developing neurons with the environment brings about permanent changes in brain and behaviour. The environment of a neuron is formed by the nerve cells surrounding it and further by the child's circulating hormones, nutrients, hormones and medication, as well as chemical substances from the environment, that enter the foetal circulation by the mother via the placenta. All these factors may have a lasting effect on the process of sexual differentiation of the brain.

The testicles and ovaries develop in the sixth week of pregnancy. This happens under the influence of a cascade of genes, of which the presence or absence of the sex-determining (SRY) gene on the Y chromosome of the father plays an important role. If present, the sex organ will develop into a testis, if absent an ovary is formed. The production of the androgens testosterone and dihydrotestosterone by a boy's testes is necessary for the formation of a penis, prostate and scrotum. Without androgens the vagina and uterus of a girl will be formed.

Once the differentiation of our sexual organs into male or female is settled, the next thing to be differentiated is the brain – for an important part by the influence of sex hormones on the developing brain cells. As this concerns permanent changes, we call this an "organizing" effect of the sex hormones on brain development. During puberty the brain circuits that developed in the womb are "activated" by sex hormones, and sexual behaviour becomes overt (Swaab, 2004). Although various genetic factors are also involved in the sexual differentiation of the brain

D.F. Swaab (✉)
Emeritus Professor of Neurobiology, University of Amsterdam, Amsterdam, The Netherlands
e-mail: d.f.swaab@nin.knaw.nl

G. Beets et al. (eds.), *The Future of Motherhood in Western Societies*,
DOI 10.1007/978-90-481-8969-4_4, © Springer Science+Business Media B.V. 2011

(Mayer et al., 1998; Dewing et al., 2003), sex hormones are very important for the development of our gender identity and sexual orientation.

The developing brain is protected against the effect of circulating oestrogens (from the mother and from the girl's own ovaries) by α-fetoprotein, a foetal protein which strongly binds oestrogens but not testosterone and which is only produced before birth (Bakker et al., 2006).

Sex Hormones and Brain Development

> We must remember that all our provisional ideas in psychology will one day be explained
> on the basis of organic substrates. It seems then probable that there are particular chemical
> substances and processes that produce the effects of sexuality and permit the perpetuation
> of individual life. (Sigmund Freud, *On Narcissism*)

From the earliest stages of foetal brain development on, many neurons throughout the entire nervous system already have receptors for testosterone and oestrogens and thus are influenced by these hormones. The prenatal development of boys shows two periods during which the testosterone levels are especially high: between weeks 12 and 18 of pregnancy (Finegan et al., 1989) and between weeks 34 and 41 of pregnancy. During this last period testosterone levels are 10 times higher than those of girls (De Zegher et al., 1992).

During the first 3 months after birth the testosterone levels in boys are as high as they will be in adulthood. In girls there is a peak in oestrogen levels which does have an effect on the brain now because the oestrogen binding α-foetoprotein is not produced any more after birth (Quigley, 2002), while testosterone levels remain low. The behavioural effects of the neonatal oestrogen peak in girls is not yet clear. The two peaks of testosterone levels in boys are assumed to fix the development of structures and circuits in the brain for the rest of their lives (= programming or organizing). The rising hormone levels during puberty "activate" circuits that were built during foetal development, and behavioural patterns and disorders that originated much earlier in the development are then expressed.

The difference in brain structures resulting from the interaction of sex hormones and developing brain cells, are thought to be the basis of sex differences in behaviour, in whether we feel like a man or a woman (gender identity), in the way we behave as man or woman in society (gender role), in our sexual orientation (hetero-, bi- or homosexuality) and in the obvious sex differences in cognition and aggressive behaviour. Factors that interfere with the interaction between hormones and the developing brain systems during foetal growth may permanently influence our behaviour later in life. As the sexual differentiation of the genitals takes place during the first 2 months of pregnancy and the sexual differentiation of the brain mainly in the second half of pregnancy, these two processes may be influenced independently of each other. This explains why it is possible to have persons who behave like females but genetically are normal males, why some individuals have female sexual organs but feel as being males and why there may be a discrepancy between the degree of masculinization of the genitals at birth and the degree of masculinization of the brain. For example, in the complete androgen insensitivity syndrome – caused by mutations in the receptor gene for androgens – genetically normal XY-males are not sensitive for testosterone and develop therefore as phenotypically normal women including normal female heterosexual orientation, fantasies and experiences (Wisniewski et al., 2000). This abnormality may only be discovered when "she" appears to be sterile later in life. A more complicated situation arises when a boy has a mutation of the gene for the enzyme that allows testosterone to be transformed into dihydrotestosterone which is the hormone responsible for the development of the male sexual organs. A normal "girl" with a normal or slightly enlarged clitoris is then born. However, when the testosterone production rises during puberty, the "clitoris" grows to penis size, the testicles descend and the child's build begins to masculinize. Despite the fact that these children have been raised as girls, the majority develop into normal heterosexual males (Wilson et al., 1993; Hughes et al., 2006; Imperato-McGinley et al., 1979; Cohen-Kettenis, 2005), apparently due to the organizing effect of testosterone on early brain development.

Transsexuality

Re: new phalloplasty technique proposal: seeking surgeon. P.S. I am interested in a neophallus uncircumcized in appearance. So I am looking overseas, since a natural uncircumsized penis is more common in Europe than in the U.S. (From a letter of a female-to-male transsexual to me, D.F. Swaab)

It is not right for a woman to be dressed in man's clothing, or for a man to put on a woman's robe: whoever does such things is disgusting to the Lord, your God (Deuteronomy XXII, 5)

Transsexuality is characterized by a conviction to be born in the wrong body, and thus by a total discrepancy between the feeling of belonging to one gender when the physical reality is the opposite. The best solution in individuals having this rare condition is to change the physical sex by many operations. This radical action is hardly ever regretted afterwards. Gender problems often crop up early in development. Little boys for example insist on wearing their mother's clothes and only show an interest in girls' toys.

Genetic factors are involved (Coolidge et al., 2002; Henningsson et al., 2005; Hare et al., 2009). Intrauterine exposure to abnormal testosterone levels may play a role, as suggested by the high frequency of female-to-male transsexuals in girls the mothers of whom had high testosterone levels because of having congenital adrenal hyperplasia (CAH). Epileptic women who are given phenobarbital or diphantoin during pregnancy also have an increased risk of giving birth to a transsexual child (Dessens et al., 1999). Both these substances change the metabolism of the sex hormones and can interfere with sexual differentiation of the brain of the child.

Between 1939 and 1960 some 2 million pregnant women in the USA and in Europe were prescribed the oestrogen-like substance diethylstilboestrol (DES) with the intention to prevent miscarriage. DES turned out not to prevent miscarriage at all, but, if the pregnancy continued to term, gave rise to an increased risk of vaginal cancer and of transsexuality in children exposed to DES. There are no indications that social factors after birth are responsible for the occurrence of transsexuality (Cohen-Kettenis & Gooren, 1999).

The theory on the origin of transsexuality is based on the fact that the sexual differentiation of our sexual organs takes place during the first couple of months of pregnancy, before the sexual differentiation of the brain. As these two processes have different timetables it is possible that they take different routes under the influence of factors mentioned earlier. If that is the case, we would expect female structures in the male brain of male-to-female transsexuals and vice verse. And indeed, we found female differentiation of the central nucleus of the Bed Nucleus of the Stria Terminalis (BSTc) – a brain structure that is involved in many aspects of sexual behaviour – in otherwise normal male brains of male-to-female transsexuals. Until now we have only been able to study one female-to-male transsexual, but her BSTc indeed turned out to have all the male characteristics. Our observations thus support the above-mentioned neurobiological theory about the origin of transsexuality. The size of the BSTc and the number of neurons match the gender that transsexuals feel they belong to and not the sex of their sexual organs, birth certificate or passport. Unfortunately, the sex difference in the BSTc volume does not become apparent until early adulthood (Chung et al., 2002), and this neuroanatomical sex difference therefore cannot play a part in the early diagnosis of transsexuality.

Sexual Orientation: Heterosexuality, Homosexuality and Bisexuality

Thou shalt not lie with mankind, as with womankind: it is an abomination (Leviticus XVIII, 22)

If a man has intercourse with a man as with a woman, both commit an abomination. They must be put to death (Leviticus XX, 13)

Our sexual orientation is determined during early foetal development, under the influence of our genetic background and of factors that affect the complex interactions between sex hormones and the developing brain. The importance of genetic factors has become apparent from twin studies and family research, indicating that the heritability of homosexuality in both sexes is more than 50% (Bailey & Bell, 1993; LeVay & Hamer, 1994). Which genes are involved is, however, not yet clear. As homosexuals do not tend to procreate, it is amazing that such genes have been maintained in the population throughout evolution. Apparently they also have a beneficial effect on the procreation of the group as a whole as has been demonstrated by Camperio-Ciani et al., (2004).

Abnormal hormone levels from the child itself during intrauterine development may influence sexual orientation, as appears from the large percentage of bisexual and homosexual girls with CAH (Meyer-Bahlburg et al., 1996; Zucker et al., 1996; Dessens et al., 2005). Intrauterine exposure to DES also increases the chance of bisexuality or homosexuality in girls (Ehrhardt et al., 1985; Meyer-Bahlburg et al., 1995; Titus-Ernstoff et al., 2003). The chance that a boy will be homosexual increases with the number of older brothers. This phenomenon is assumed to be an immunological response of the mother to a product of the Y-chromosome of the sons, which increases with every pregnancy (Blanchard, 2001; Bogaert, 2003). Prenatal exposure to nicotine, amphetamine or thyroid gland hormones raises the chances of giving birth to lesbian daughters (Ellis & Cole-Harding, 2001; Ellis & Hellberg, 2005). Finally, a stressed pregnant woman has a bigger chance of giving birth to a homosexual son (Ellis et al., 1988; Ellis & Cole-Harding, 2001) or a lesbian daughter (Bailey et al., 1991).

Although it has often been postulated that postnatal development is also important for the direction of our sexual differentiation, any solid proof for this is lacking. For example, children who were born after artificial insemination with donor sperm and raised by a lesbian couple, have not a higher probability of becoming homosexually oriented (Green, 1978). There is also no proof for the suggestion that homosexuality results from deficient upbringing nor that it is a "lifestyle choice" or would be brought about by social learning. This latter idea is also refuted by the fact that even an English boarding school education, does not lead to a higher frequency of homosexuality in adulthood (LeVay, 1996). Nevertheless, the idea that the social environment matters with respect to the development of our sexual orientation, has led to massive persecution. The belief of Nazi Germany – articulated by Hitler himself – that homosexuality was as contagious as the plague, resulted in the inconceivable: first voluntary then compulsory castrations and eventually the systematic murdering of homosexuals in concentration camps.

Clinical observations have shown the involvement of a number of brain structures related to sexual orientation. For some patients with the Klüver-Bucy syndrome, with lesions of the temporal lobe, it has been reported that their orientation changed from heterosexual to homosexual. Shifts in sexual orientation (to homosexual or paedophilic) have also been reported in connection with tumours in the temporal lobe and hypothalamus. Lesions in the pre-optic area of the hypothalamus in experimental animals also show shifts in sexual orientation (Swaab, 2004).

A number of structural and functional differences in the brain have been described in relation to sexual orientation. We found the first brain difference in relation to sexual orientation in the suprachiasmatic nucleus (SCN), the clock of the brain, which turned out, in homosexual men, to be twice the size of that of heterosexual men (Swaab & Hofman, 1990). A similar difference could also be induced in rats, by pharmacologically disturbing the interaction between testosterone and the developing brain around their time of birth. This experiment yielded bisexual adult rats, which had a larger number of cells in their SCN (Swaab et al., 1995).

In 1991, LeVay reported that homosexual men, just like heterosexual women, have a smaller area in the frontal part of the hypothalamus (INAH-3). In 1992, Allen and Gorski reported that the anterior commissure of homosexual men is larger than that of heterosexual men. This structure, which is also larger in women than in men, takes care of left-right connections of the temporal cortex and in this way is involved in sex differences related to cognitive abilities and language.

Functional MRI scanning of the brain has recently also pointed out differences in the hypothalamus in relation to sexual orientation. Savic et al., (2005) did experiments with scent, a pheromone excreted in our perspiration and urine in concentrations that are 10 times higher in men than in women and demonstrated that it activated parts of the hypothalamus of heterosexual women and homosexual men, but not of heterosexual men. A follow-up study (Berglund et al., 2006) showed that it elicited an activation in the frontal part of the hypothalamus of heterosexual women but not in lesbian women. Moreover, when lesbian women were exposed to a pheromone derived from female hormones (oestrogens), they responded with an activation of the frontal part of the hypothalamus in a way that partly matched the pattern seen in heterosexual men. Showing a female face made the medial prefrontal cortex of heterosexual men and homosexual women react more strongly, whereas the same structures reacted more strongly to the face of a man in homosexual men and heterosexual women (Kranz & Ishai, 2006). Neurobiological research in relation to sexual orientation in man is only just beginning, but already an overwhelming array of brain differences has become apparent, not only in relation to gender-identity (Kruijver et al., 2000; Garcia-Falgueras & Swaab, 2008), but also in relation to sexual orientation (Kinnunen et al., 2004).

Society's Response to My Research into the Sexual Differentiation of the Brain

When, in the early 1970s, I gave my first university lectures on sexual differentiation of the brain, the broadly accepted view on the importance of the social environment was extensively put into words by Simone de Beauvoir and others, and offered guidelines for feminist thinking: all the differences between the sexes with regard to behaviour, profession and interests, were thought to be forced upon women by the male-dominated society. During those first university lectures I became aware of the first row of the lecture hall, filled with female medical students busy knitting and crocheting. It was obvious that they did not want to hear what I was discussing. When I switched off the lights to show my slides there was a loud protest: they couldn't see their needlework! From that moment on I decided to show my slides spread out over the entire lecture, with very dim lighting throughout. The ladies of the front row sent a delegation to the Rector of the university to insist on a non-chauvinist lecturer. Apparently such a person was not available: the matter never came up again.

When we first reported on a sex difference in the hypothalamus of man (Swaab & Fliers, 1985) we heard some disapproving noises from the feminist movement, because a sexual difference in the brain did not fit their philosophy that every difference in behaviour, and therefore in the brain, had been forced upon women by society. For example in an interview in the Dutch magazine HP (17/1/87) biologist Joke 't Hart responded to our publications with: "If I were to accept that there are sex differences in such fundamental aspects as the structure of the brain, I might as well stop being a feminist."

Since then many observations have been done that question the dominant importance of the environment on our differentiation into men and women.

After our report of the first difference in the brain between homosexual and heterosexual men (Swaab & Hofman, 1990) the response was unexpectedly massive and negative. It began in December 1988, with an interview in the Academy News (the monthly organ of the Royal Netherlands Academy of Arts and Sciences (KNAW) read by almost nobody) when I told something about our studies on sexual orientation and gender identity. This story was picked up by the journalist Hans van Maanen, who wrote two scientifically sound articles that caused an unbelievable riot. After all these years, the exact reason for this violent emotional and completely wrongly directed massive reaction is still not clear to me: apparently the taboo of the biological background of our sexual orientation at a time when everything was considered makeable, was extremely strong. There was a group of homosexual men who almost religiously believed that all men were gay but that only some had the courage to come out of the closet. They called being gay a political choice. My response was that I did not see what was political about it and that the choice of your sexual orientation is made for you, in the womb of your mother. There was great anger and in 3 weeks' time many hundreds of articles appeared in the press. The COC (the Dutch Lesbian, Gay, Bisexual, and Transgender Organization) was "amazed" when they learned of the research. Professor Rob Tielman was one of my fiercest antagonists at the time. He publicly vilified the research by calling it "in bad taste", which set the tone, and said that I should have first asked him for permission to research and publish, which of course was utter nonsense. But in the mean time the editor of the Gay Newspaper, Henk Krol, had also given his two cents' worth: "This kind of research feeds the idea that homosexuality is a disease. This supports once again the discrimination of gays."

There were questions in Dutch Parliament by Peter Lankhorst, a member of the PPR party. His questions ended via the desks of the Minister and the President of the KNAW on my desk, and my answers took the same route back. We endured phone terror at home, day and night, and I received threats per post, addressed "To the SS-doctor Dr. Mengele-Swaab" that informed me, often in sentences full of spelling mistakes: "Nazi, seen you on the TV. Villain's face. We homophiles will kill you. As example the Spiritual leader Khomeini-Iran about the Englishman" and "You probably would have liked to be able to work under Mengele in Auschwitz".

Committees reviewed my work and security measures were taken for a lecture in the Amsterdam University Hospital. There were bomb scares at the institute, our children were harassed about the matter at school and one Sunday morning I awoke to a demonstration right outside my door, an occurrence that the late Gerard Reve (famous Dutch gay author) wrote about in his inimitable way: "Only then Professor Swaab's serious omission became clear: he had neglected to ask for permission for his research from the gay union, the C.O.C. Well, the consequences showed up and made themselves heard: on a Sunday morning a large group of motivated individuals appeared at Professor Swaab's house in Amstelveen, chanting all together and loudly: "Dick, cut into your own pr(...)!" Most peculiar, when you think that, although Professor Swaab was investigating sexuality, he studied the brain, and not the sexual organs. However, as the followers of this union do not have brains, but do possess sexual organs, it did make sense in a way."

It took 3 weeks for the ruckus to die down. Ayatollah Khomeini pronounced a fatwah against Salman Rushdie, because of his book *The Satanic Verses*, and instantly the entire focus shifted to the British-Indian author.

When the dust around my "affair" had settled and I had remained standing, the President of the KNAW, David de Wied, gave an interview to *De Telegraaf* newspaper, in which he supported me and said that such an affair should never happen again.

But there were nice reactions too, such as Peter van Straaten's cartoon and some personal ads in the weekly *Vrij Nederland*, such as the one that said: "Nice guy (37, 1.87, 87 kg, blonde and blue) with large hypothalamus seeks. . ." and "LARGE suprachiasmatic nucleus, PO Box 654 Wageningen". However, it took 17 years before the *Gay Journal* changed its view of that period and published an article entitled "Angry gays got it all wrong".

When we then published the first sex reversal in the transsexual brain (Zhou et al., 1995) we only received positive reactions. Transsexuals pounced upon this paper to enforce a change of sex in their birth certificate or passport in countries where that had not been possible. The paper was also used in the European Court of Justice for this purpose and played a role in bringing about legislation about this issue in England. After our last study on reversed sex differences in the brain of transsexual people (Garcia-Falgueras & Swaab, 2008), there was no public reaction whatsoever.

Sex Differences in Cognition and Aggression: Little Effect of the Social Environment

Many factors and mechanisms are involved in sexual differentiation of the brain, resulting in our gender identity (the feeling of being a man or a woman) and in our sexual orientation (heterosexual, bisexual or homosexual). In the 1960s and 1970s it was postulated that a child was born as a tabula rasa and that it was forced into the male or female direction by society's conventions. John Money, a famous American psychologist, put this as follows (1975): "Gender identity is sufficiently incompletely differentiated at birth as to permit successful assignment of a genetic male as a girl. Gender identity then differentiates in keeping with the experience of rearing." This concept has had devastating results (see later).

One of the stereotypical behavioural differences between boys and girls, which has often been said are forced upon us by our upbringing and social environment, is our behaviour in play. Boys are more active and wilder and they prefer to play with cars, whereas girls prefer dolls. Thirty years ago my wife and I systematically offered our children, a boy and a girl, both types of toys, but our daughter only played with dolls and our son was only interested in toy cars. Two children are not sufficient for a publication. However, the idea that it is not society that forces these choices upon children but a sexual difference in the early development of their brains and behaviour was supported by a study by Alexander & Hines (2002), who offered dolls, toy cars and balls to Green Velvet monkeys. The female monkeys preferentially chose the dolls started to show maternal behaviour and examined the dolls ano-genitally, whereas the male monkeys were more interested in playing with the toy cars and with the ball. "Neutral" toys, such as a picture book and a toy dog, did not show sex differences in either humans or monkeys. Our preference for certain toys can thus be traced back tens of millions of years in our evolutionary history. Girls who are exposed to too high testosterone levels in the womb, in the case of congenital adrenal hyperplasia (CAH), tend to choose boys as playmates, play preferentially with boys' toys and are generally wilder than other girls and are called tomboys (Nordenström et al., 2002). The sexual differences in play behaviour apparently originate early on in our evolution and are imprinted in our brains during intrauterine development under the influence of sex hormones.

A similar conclusion can be drawn with respect to sex differences in spontaneous drawings. Japanese research shows that subject matter, choice of colour and composition of drawings by boys and girls show clear sex differences. Girls tend to draw human figures, mainly girls and women, flowers and butterflies. They use bright colours, such as red, orange and yellow. Their subjects tend to be peaceful and arranged in a row on the ground. In contrast boys prefer to draw more technical objects, weapons and fighting, and means of transport, such as cars, trains and airplanes, in bird's-eye view compositions and in dark, cool colours such as blue. Drawings by girls who had been exposed to too high testosterone levels in the womb due to CAH show male drawing characteristics some 5–6 years later, even when they were treated immediately after birth (Iijima et al., 2001). Apparently, the sex differences that are revealed through play or drawings are determined by exposure to hormones in the womb rather than by what society demands later on.

The well-known story of John-Joan-John (a pseudonym of David Reimer, see Colapinto, 2001) means that the concept of sexual neutrality at birth, as introduced by John Money in the 1950s, may be seriously questioned. According to Money, gender imprinting did not start until the age of 1 year and its development would be far advanced by the age of 3–4 years (Money & Erhardt, 1972). This was the basis for the decision to make a girl out of an 8-month old boy who lost his penis due to a mistake during a phimosis operation. The testicles were removed before the age of 17 months in order to facilitate feminization. The child was dressed in girl's clothes, received psychological counselling and was given oestrogens in puberty. Money described the development of this child as normal female. However, later on it became clear that this had not at all been the case. In adulthood the child changed back to male, married, and adopted a few children (Diamond & Sigmundson, 1997). Unfortunately, he lost money on the stock exchange, got divorced and eventually committed suicide in May 2004. The sad story of David Reimer shows that even removing the penis and testicles, psychological counselling and oestrogens in puberty failed to change the gender identity of this child. Gender imprinting occurs already in the womb and a boy's testosterone is of great importance for this process, whereas there does not seem to be an overriding influence of the social environment after birth, as was assumed a few decades ago.

Many sex differences have been described in adult behaviour. Also aggressive behaviour shows clear sex differences. Men commit 5 times more murders than women and 80% of their victims are not intimates, whereas women tend to aggress against intimates (Kellermann & Mercy, 1992). Women are better able to read faces and are quicker than men when it comes to detecting universal emotions – disgust, fear, joy, sadness and surprise – with one exception: anger. Anger is picked up quickest by both men and women, but men are quicker than women (Williams & Mattingley, 2006). This may have been an evolutionary advantage – in fact it may still be that, as can be seen from the sex difference regarding murder: men run the highest risk of getting murdered, and anger in the face of the other is your last warning.

The apparent impossibility to get someone to change their sexual orientation is a major argument against the importance of the social environment in the emergence of homosexuality, as well as against the idea that homosexuality is a lifestyle choice. The mind boggles at what has been tried to achieve this: hormonal treatments, such as castration, administering testosterone or oestrogens, treatments that appeared to affect libido but not sexual orientation, psychoanalysis, apomorfine injections serving as an emetic during exposure to homo-erotic pictures, psychosurgery (lesions in the hypothalamus), electroshock treatment, chemical induction of epileptic insults and imprisonment. As none of these interventions have led to a well-documented change in sexual orientation (LeVay, 1996), there can be little doubt that our sexual orientation is fixed during prenatal and early development and is beyond influencing in adulthood. Changes in sexual orientation in adulthood have been described, e.g. from heterosexual to paedophile, but only in cases of brain tumours in the hypothalamus and prefrontal cortex (Miller et al., 1986; Burns & Swerdlow, 2003). However, such devastating changes in the hypothalamus cannot be interpreted in terms of functional changes in particular neuronal circuits. There are also claims of a change from paedophiles and homosexual men into heterosexual behaviour through stereotactical psychosurgery by means of lesions in the nucleus ventromedialis (Dieckmann & Hassler, 1977), but these interventions are not only of questionable ethical quality but they also do not meet any scientific standard and can thus not teach us anything. There are also claims of conservative religious organizations that they are capable of changing a homosexual orientation into a heterosexual one. The 2009 Report of the American Psychological Association Task Force on Appropriate Therapeutic Responses to Sexual Orientation is clear about this claim: the efforts to change sexual orientation are unlikely to be successful and involve some risk of harm. One should not aim at changing sexual orientation (www.apa.org/pi/lgbc/publications/).

The sexual differences between men and women regarding the allocation of tasks have also proved remarkably resistant to change. Despite all attempts instigated by the feminist movement, the past 50 years have seen only marginal shifts in the male-female role pattern. The outcome of a questionnaire in the Dutch feminist magazine *Opzij* in 2006 speaks for itself: only 6% of the Dutch males share work and care equally with women. Only 18% of care leave is taken up by men. Feminism claims that the feminist movement is responsible for the fact that women can nowadays enjoy further education and take jobs outside the home, but forgets the important role of the emergence of smaller families. That became possible through the introduction of the contraceptive pill, thanks to the work of pioneers such as Gregory Pincus and in the Netherlands my father (Swaab, 1964), both man.

More Dutch mothers work part-time than any other mothers in Europe. The media go on and on about it. Studies have shown that there is almost nothing that will stimulate these women to start working fulltime, not even better childcare facilities, because they want to look after their children. And what is wrong with taking care of children you deliberately chose to have? Apparently, and despite the feminist ideals, we tend to choose what best fits our programmed (by natural sexual selection developed) brains. The male discussion groups of the 1970s and 1980s failed as well. It was a brave attempt of men to try and meet the demands of feminists to behave in a less masculine way. Feminism also hoped for an equal division of jobs between men and women, but a female plumber is still an exception. In the field of science, too, this principle of equality is not doing as well as was hoped: it is unlikely that 50% of the professors in physics or mathematics will soon be women.

Women do not only dominate the home, they are also overrepresented in home-care and nursing. Interestingly, it is not just gender, but also sexual orientation that affects our choice of profession. More homosexual men than heterosexual men tend to be nurses, air stewards, hairdressers, dancers and fashion designers. Of course equality is, in principle, a valuable achievement and it is praiseworthy that everyone is allowed any education or profession, but anyone hoping for a completely equal division of tasks between men and women in the family or in the various disciplines will be sadly disappointed. Our sexually differential brains will not lend themselves to it.

Conclusions

- During our intrauterine period the brain develops in male direction through a direct action of a boy's testosterone on the developing nerve cells, and in female direction through absence of this hormone in a girl. In this way our gender identity (the feeling of being a man or a woman) and our sexual orientation are programmed into our brain structures when we are still in the womb.
- Sex differences are not only found in relation to gender and sexual orientation, but also in cognition, aggression, and many other behaviours.
- Our gender and sexual orientation are influenced by many biological factors. There is no proof that our social environment after birth has an effect on the development of our gender or sexual orientation.
- Differences in brain structures and brain functions have been found that are related to sexual orientation and gender.
- There is great public interest in research of the brain and in research of our sexual behaviour. However, the combination of these two subjects has turned out to be dynamite.

Acknowledgement I want to thank Mrs. Wilma Verweij for her professional help with the English.

References

Alexander, G.M., & Hines, M. (2002). Sex differences in response to children's toys in nonhuman primates (Cercopithecus aethiops sabaeus). *Evolution and Human Behavior*, 23, 467–479.

Allen, L.S., & Gorski, R.A. (1992). Sexual orientation and the size of the anterior commissure in the human brain. *Proceedings of the National Academy of Sciences of the United States of America*, 89, 7199–7202.

Bailey, J.M., & Bell, A.P. (1993). Familiality of female and male homosexuality. *Behavior Genetics*, 23, 313–322.

Bailey, J.M., Willerman, L., & Parks, C. (1991). A test of the maternal stress theory of human male homosexuality. *Archives of Sexual Behavior*, 20, 277–293.

Bakker, J., De Mees, C., Douhard, Q., Balthazart, J., Gabant, P., Szpirer, J., & Szpirer, C. (2006). Alpha-fetoprotein protects the developing female mouse brain from masculinization and defeminization by estrogens. *Nature Neuroscience*, 9, 220–226.

Berglund, H., Lindström, P., & Savic, I. (2006). Brain response to putative pheromones in lesbian women. *Proceedings of the National Academy of Sciences of the United States of America*, 103, 8269–8274.

Blanchard, R. (2001). Fraternal birth order and the maternal immune hypothesis of male homosexuality. *Hormones and Behavior*, 40, 105–114.

Bogaert, A.F. (2003). The interaction of fraternal birth order and body size in male sexual orientation. *Behavioral Neuroscience*, 117, 381–384.

Burns, J.M., & Swerdlow, R.H. (2003). Right orbitofrontal tumor with pedophilia symptom and constructional apraxia sign. *Archives of Neurology*, 60, 437–440.

Camperio-Ciani, A., Corna, F., & Capiluppi, C. (2004). Evidence for maternally inherited factors favouring male homosexuality and promoting female fecundity. *Proceedings of the Royal Society B: Biological Sciences*, 271, 2217–2221.

Chung, W.C., De Vries, G.J., & Swaab, D.F. (2002). Sexual differentiation of the bed nucleus of the stria terminalis in humans may extend into adulthood. *The Journal of Neuroscience*, 22, 1027–1033.

Cohen-Kettenis, P.T. (2005). Gender change in 46, XY persons with 5α-Reductase-2 deficiency and 17β-hydroxysteroid dehydrogenase-3 deficiency. *Archives of Sexual Behavior*, 34, 399–410.

Cohen-Kettenis, P.T., & Gooren, L.J.G. (1999). Transsexualism: a review of etiology, diagnosis and treatment. *Journal of Psychosomatic Research*, 46, 315–333.

Colapinto, J. (2001). *As Nature Made Him. The Boy Who Was Raised As a Girl*. New York, NY: Harper Collins Publishers Inc.

Coolidge, F.L., Thede, L.L., & Young, S.E. (2002). The heritability of gender identity disorder in a child and adolescent twin sample. *Behavior Genetics*, 32, 251–257.

Dessens, A.B., Cohen-Kettenis, P.T., Mellenbergh, G.J., Van de Poll, N.E., Koppe, J.G., & Boer, K. (1999). Prenatal exposure to anticonvulsants and psychosexual development. *Archives of Sexual Behavior*, 28, 31–44.

Dessens, A.B., Slijper, F.M., & Drop, S.L. (2005). Gender dysphoria and gender change in chromosomal females with congenital adrenal hyperplasia. *Archives of Sexual Behavior*, 34, 389–397.

Dewing, P., Shi, T., Horvath, S., & Vilain, E. (2003). Sexually dimorphic gene expression in mouse brain precedes gonadal differentiation. *Molecular Brain Research*, 118, 82–90.

De Zegher, F., Devlieger, H., & Veldhuis, J.D. (1992). Pulsatile and sexually dimorphic secretion of luteinizing hormone in the human infant on the day of birth. *Pediatric Research*, 32, 605–607.

Diamond, M., & Sigmundson, H.K. (1997). Sex reassignment at birth. Long-term review and clinical implications. *Archives of Pediatrics & Adolescent Medicine*, 151, 298–304.

Dieckmann, G., & Hassler, R. (1977). Treatment of sexual violence by stereotactic hypothalamotomy. In W.H. Sweet, S. Obrador, & J.G. Martin-Rodriguez (Eds.), *Neurosurgical Treatment in Psychiatry, Pain, and Epilepsy* (451–462). Baltimore, MD: University Park Press.

Ehrhardt, A.A., Meyer-Bahlburg, H.F.L., Rosen, L.R., Feldman, J.F., Veridiano, N.P., Zimmerman, I., & McEwen, B.S. (1985). Sexual orientation after prenatal exposure to exogenous estrogen. *Archives of Sexual Behavior*, 14, 57–75.

Ellis, L., Ames, M.A., Peckham, W., & Burke, D. (1988). Sexual orientation of human offspring may be altered by severe maternal stress during pregnancy. *Journal of Sexual Research*, 25, 152–157.

Ellis, L., & Cole-Harding, S. (2001). The effects of prenatal stress, and of prenatal alcohol and nicotine exposure, on human sexual orientation. *Physiology & Behavior*, 74, 213–226.

Ellis, L., & Hellberg, J. (2005). Fetal exposure to prescription drugs and adult sexual orientation. *Personality and Individual Differences*, 38, 225–236.

Finegan, J.-A., Bartleman, B., & Wong, P.Y. (1989). A window for the study of prenatal sex hormone influences on postnatal development. *The Journal of General Psychology*, 150, 101–112.

Garcia-Falgueras, A., & Swaab, D.F. (2008). A sex difference in the hypothamaic uncinate nucleus: relationship to gender identity. *Brain*, 131, 3132–3146.

Green, R. (1978). Sexual identity of 37 children raised by homosexual or transsexual parents. *The American Journal of Psychiatry*, 135, 692–697.

Hare, L., Bernard, P., Sánchez, F.J., et al. (2009). Androgen receptor repeat length polymorphism associated with male-to-female transsexualism. *Biological Psychiatry*, 65, 93–96.

Henningsson, S., Westberg, L., Nilsson, S., Lundstrom, B., Ekselius, L., Bodlund, O., Lindstrom, E., Hellstrand, M., Rosmond, R., Eriksson, E., & Landen, M. (2005). Sex steroid-related genes and male-to-female transsexualism. *Psychoneuro endocrinology*, 30, 657–664.

Hughes, I.A., Houk, C., Ahmed, S.F., Lee, P.A., & LWPES/ESPE Consensus Group. (2006). Consensus statement on management of intersex disorders. *Archives of Diseases in Childhood*, 91, 554–563.

Iijima, M., Arisaka, O., Minamoto, F., & Arai, Y. (2001). Sex differences in children's free drawings: a study on girls with congenital adrenal hyperplasia. *Hormones and Behavior*, 40, 90–104.

Imperato-McGinley, J., Peterson, R.E., Gautier, T., & Sturla, E. (1979). Male pseudo-hermaphroditism secondary to 5αReductase deficiency – a model for the role of androgens in both the development of the male phenotype and the evolution of a male gender identity. *Journal of Steroid Biochemistry*, 11(1B), 637–645.

Kellermann, A.L., & Mercy, J.A. (1992). Men, women, and murder: gender-specific differences in rates of fatal violence and victimization. *The Journal of Trauma*, 33, 1–5.

Kinnunen, L.H., Moltz, H., Metz, J., & Cooper, M. (2004). Differential brain activation in exclusively homosexual and heterosexual men produced by the selective serotonin reuptake inhibitor, fluoxetine. *Brain Research*, 1024, 251–254.

Kranz, F., & Ishai, A. (2006). Face perception is modulated by sexual preference. *Current Biology*, 16, 63–68.

Kruijver, F.P.M., Zhou, J.N., Pool, C.W., Hofman, M.A., Gooren, L.J.G., & Swaab, D.F. (2000). Male-to-female transsexuals have female neuron numbers in a limbic nucleus. *The Journal of Clinical Endocrinology and Metabolism*, 85, 2034–2041.

LeVay, S. (1991). A difference in hypothalamic structure between heterosexual and homosexual men. *Science*, 253, 1034–1037.

LeVay, S. (1996). *Queer Science. The Use and Abuse of Research into Homosexuality*. Cambridge, MA: The MIT Press.

LeVay, S., & Hamer, D.H. (1994). Evidence for a biological influence in male homosexuality. *Scientific American*, 270, 44–49.

Mayer, A., Swaab, D.F., Pilgrim, C., Reisert, I., & Lahr, G. (1998). Genes involved in male sex determination are expressed in adult human brain. *Neurogenetics*, 1, 281–288.

Meyer-Bahlburg, H.F.L., Ehrhardt, A.A., Rosen, L.R., Gruen, R.S., Veridiano, N.P., Van, F.H., & Neuwalder, H.F. (1995). Prenatal estrogens and the development of homosexual orientation. *Developmental Psychology*, 31, 12–21.

Meyer-Bahlburg, H.F.L., Gruen, R.S., New, M.I., Bell, J.J., Morishima, A., Shimshi, M., Bueno, Y., Vargas, I., & Baker, S.W. (1996). Gender change from female to male in classical congenital adrenal hyperplasia. *Hormones and Behavior*, 30, 319–332.

Miller, B.L., Cummings, J.L., McIntyre, H., Ebers, G., & Grode, M. (1986). Hypersexuality or altered sexual preference following brain injury. *Journal of Neurology, Neurosurgery, and Psychiatry*, 49, 867–873.

Money, J. (1975). Ablatio penis: normal male infant sex-reassigned as a girl. *Archives of Sexual Behavior*, 4, 65–71.

Money, J., & Erhardt, A.A. (1972). *Man and Woman, Boy and Girl: The Differentiation and Dimorphism of Gender Identity from Conception to Maturity*. Baltimore, MD: Johns Hopkins University Press.

Nordenström, A., Servin, A., Bohlin, G., Larsson, A., & Wedell, A. (2002). Sex-typed toy play behavior correlates with the degree of prenatal androgen exposure assessed by *CYP21* genotype in girls with congenital adrenal hyperplasia. *The Journal of Clinical Endocrinology and Metabolism*, 87, 5119–5124.

Quigley, C.A. (2002). The postnatal gonadotropin and sex steroid surge – insights from the androgen insensitivity syndrome. *The Journal of Clinical Endocrinology and Metabolism*, 87, 24–28.

Savic, I., Berglund, H., & Lindstrom, P. (2005). Brain response to putative pheromones in homosexual men. *Proceedings of the National Academy of Sciences of the United States of America*, 102, 7356–7361.

Swaab, L.I. (1964). Enige resultaten bij de toepassing van orale ovulatieremmers (orale anticonceptie). *Nederlands Tijdschrift voor Geneeskunde*, 108(22), 1070–1076.

Swaab, D.F. (2004). *The human hypothalamus. Basic and Clinical Aspects. Part II: Neuropathology of the Hypothalamus and Adjacent Brain Structures*. Handbook of Clinical Neurology. M.J. Aminoff, F. Boller, & D.F. Swaab. (Series Editors). Amsterdam: Elsevier, 596 pp.

Swaab, D.F., & Fliers, E. (1985). A sexually dimorphic nucleus in the human brain. *Science*, 228, 1112–1115.

Swaab, D.F., & Hofman, M.A. (1990). An enlarged suprachiasmatic nucleus in homosexual men. *Brain Research*, 537, 141–148.

Swaab, D.F., Slob, A.K., Houtsmuller, E.J., Brand, T., & Zhou, J.N. (1995). Increased number of vasopressin neurons in the suprachiasmatic nucleus (SCN) of 'bisexual' adult male rats following perinatal treatment with the aromatase blocker ATD. *Developmental Brain Research*, 85, 273–279.

Titus-Ernstoff, L., Perez, K., Hatch, E.E., Troisi, R., Palmer, J.R., Hartge, P., Hyer, M., Kaufman, R., Adam, E., Strohsnitter, W., Noller, K., Pickett, K.E., & Hoover, R. (2003). Psychosexual characteristics of men and women exposed prenatally to diethylstilbestrol. *Epidemiology*, 14, 155–160.

Williams, M.A., & Mattingley, J.B. (2006). Do angry men get noticed? *Current Biology*, 16, R402–R404.

Wilson, J.D., Griffin, J.E., & Russell, D.W. (1993). Steroid 5a-reductase 2 deficiency. *Endocrine Reviews*, 14, 577–593.

Wisniewski, A.B., Migeon, C.J., Meyer-Bahlburg, H.F.L., Gearhart, J.P., Berkovitz, G.D., Brown, T.R., & Money, J. (2000). Complete androgen insensitivity syndrome: long-term medical, surgical, and psychosexual outcome. *The Journal of Clinical Endocrinology and Metabolism*, 85, 2664–2669.

Zhou, J.N., Hofman, M.A., Gooren, L.J.G., & Swaab, D.F. (1995). A sex difference in the human brain and its relation to transsexuality. *Nature*, 378, 68–70.

Zucker, K.J., Bradley, S.J., Oliver, G., Blake, J., Fleming, S., & Hood, J. (1996). Psychosexual development of woman with congenital adrenal hyperplasia. *Hormones and Behavior*, 30, 300–318.

Chapter 5
On the Societal Impact of Modern Contraception

Dirk J. van de Kaa

The Mastering of Childbirth

One of the greatest achievements of mankind is the mastering of childbirth. It is essential for its own survival as a species and also essential for the survival of many other animal species and plants. That in the absence of birth control the whole globe would become endangered as a result of runaway population growth is, of course, patently nonsensical: the earth will continue to circle the sun for millions of years to come. But that the impact of the mastering of childbirth on the future of mankind is tremendous cannot be disputed. If from the end of the eighteenth and the beginning of the nineteenth centuries some form of birth control would not have become established our world would even now have been in a much more perilous condition and certainly far less attractive than it currently is.

Declines in the numbers of births born per woman were first observed in France and Hungary. Early writers attributed the onset of fertility control mainly to value change. Writing in 1890 French author Arsène Dumont introduced a new principle of population, which he called "capillarité sociale" or "l'attraction capillaire". In his view the wish to improve one's position politically, economically, and educationally led to an excessive dominance of "individual tendencies". He noted an inverse relationship between the level of fertility and social mobility. People avoided having too many children to give these a good start in life. They invested in quality rather than quantity. For most of his long career in public life and population another Frenchman, Adolph Landry (1909/1934) defended the thesis that the control of fertility gave rise to a demographic "revolution". A new demographic regime came to be established that was quite distinct from those preceding it. This modern regime recognized that, given the gradual declines in mortality in modern societies, fewer births were needed to give each family the desired number of surviving children (Festy, 1971). The means and methods to achieve that reduction in fertility

D.J. van de Kaa (✉)
Emeritus Professor of Demography, University of Amsterdam, Amsterdam, The Netherlands;
Honorary Fellow, Netherlands Interdisciplinary Demographic Institute (NIDI), The Hague,
The Netherlands
e-mail: vandekaa@nidi.nl

G. Beets et al. (eds.), *The Future of Motherhood in Western Societies*,
DOI 10.1007/978-90-481-8969-4_5, © Springer Science+Business Media B.V. 2011

are now commonly described as ineffective, primitive, or traditional. They include coitus interruptus, sponges, douches, pessaries, condoms, (periodic) abstinence and, usually illegal, abortion. In addition people tried to reduce the years "at risk" by insisting on virginity before marriage, marrying late, and ending regular sexual intercourse at an early age.

During the Second World War a group of American scholars began wondering what the future of fertility in the various countries of the world, and particularly those of the Third World, would be. They adapted Landry's concept to formulate the so-called theory of the demographic transition. Part of its attractiveness is that it is a good, easily understandable story. It appeals to our common sense. As their social and economic development progresses all societies will see their demographic equilibrium change from one based on the combination of high mortality and a high fertility level to match that, to one resulting from the combination of low levels of both mortality and fertility. During that transition process countries will experience a period of rapid population growth, but fortunately that is just a temporary phenomenon. In due course all countries will reach a new, stable balance between the two determinants of natural population growth: deaths and births.

The Perfection of Contraception

It was generally assumed that around the mid-1960s the industrialized societies were close to having completed that transition process. Indeed, if thereafter the number of children born per woman had stabilized at roughly the level needed to ensure the replacement of generations – an average of 210 births per 100 women – interest in the study of fertility would have waned. But it did not. On the contrary, since then almost everywhere in the developed world fertility has fallen way below replacement level. Of the 46 European countries covered by the Council of Europe 18 had a total fertility rate at or below 1.3 per woman in 2003 (Council of Europe, 2005). The lowest levels were observed in the Ukraine (1.17) and the Czech Republic (1.18), but extremely low levels also occurred in countries one would not immediately associate with it, such as Greece (1.29), Italy (1.29), Poland (1.22) and Spain (1.30). Even the highest figure reported in 2003 – 2.43 in Turkey – is not particularly high by pre-1965 standards. This unprecedented and drastic drop in fertility[1] has dramatically altered the demographic prospects in all European, and even more general, in all industrialized societies. It would be absurd to attribute this change in demographic perspective entirely to the discovery of "the pill" and the perfection of contraception. Even so, during the last decades the development of oral contraceptives has had a much more profound impact on our societies than its proponents ever envisaged. Without "perfect" contraception we would live in a very different society. It has profoundly influenced the relation between partners. This was neither

---

[1] After 2003 the total fertility rates slightly increased in many European countries.

expected nor intended. The pill allowed couples and individuals to make choices hitherto unheard of. One could have sexual relations outside marriage without fear of experiencing an unwanted pregnancy and could begin cohabiting as a couple instead of marrying. It is interesting to note that some of its effects have been in diametric opposition to expectations. For example, the number of extra-marital births has, quite paradoxically, increased instead of declined.

The Development of the Pill

By 1954 Gregory Pincus (1903–1967) had developed an oral contraceptive that could be tested clinically. As he was a chemist he could not undertake that clinical-medical research himself. He was lucky to find John Rock (1890–1984), another pioneer in the history of family planning in the USA, willing to do it. Only 2 years later, the new "pill", called Enovid, could be submitted for approval to the Food and Drug Administration. Another 3 years later, in 1959, half a million American women were using the new invention to regulate what was prudently called "serious menstrual disorders". The speed of developments thereafter is truly amazing. The numbers of users reached 2.3 million in 1963. The decision of the American High Court in the famous case of Griswold versus Connecticut that prohibiting contraceptives should be regarded as a "violation of a couple's right to privacy" gave the important signal that legal provisions were not immutable. By 1967 world wide 12.5 million women already relied on the pill.

Intentions of the Protagonists

The protagonists of the pill had relatively straightforward intentions: they wanted to liberate women from the burden of unwanted pregnancies. It was also assumed that good contraception would help combat poverty amongst the least privileged groups in society. It was expected to reduce the number of illegal, and hence very dangerous, abortions. It would, further, increase the status of women as they would acquire greater control over their destiny. There is no doubt that in the thinking of one of the great driving forces behind the development of oral contraception, Margaret Sanger, ideational factors played a significant role. Nevertheless, practical considerations held center stage: there was an unmistakable need for a safe, efficient, and effective contraceptive that could replace the not very reliable method of Ogino/Knaus, spermicidal pastes, and the many other "traditional means and methods" listed before. The basic aim was to make sexual relations, particularly inside marriage, less risky and more fulfilling at a time when most couples already tried to limit the size of their families. Illustrative in this regard is that membership in the Netherlands Association for Sexual Reform (NVSH), the association providing its members with information on the various methods of contraception, and if desired, provided the means and gave personalized instruction on their use, had risen from just 26,800 in 1947 to precisely 136,249 in 1959 (Kooy, 1980).

The Demographic Consequences as Foreseen

The pill was not accepted equally well in all industrialized countries. In a few the medical professions resisted its diffusion, partly on medical grounds. In fact, out of fear for its possible long-term side effects, the use of oral contraception has not been officially accepted in Japan until very recently. But that were exceptions rather than the rule. Elsewhere the pill was received most warmly. In the Netherlands, for example, the pill was embraced particularly enthusiastically. By the early 1970s no less than 18% of all women not intending to become pregnant used the pill even at first intercourse; a figure that increased to an amazingly high 67% for later sexual contacts. And, if women did not want to become pregnant because they considered their family completed only 33% used some inefficient method or no method at all, while the remainder had switched to a modern, highly efficient method (Cyrus-Gooswit et al., 1976).

In cases such as the Netherlands the demographic consequences as foreseen quickly materialized. Figures illustrate that a large number of unintended, if not unwanted, pregnancies could be prevented by it. The number of births with a rank number of three or more declined spectacularly. While in 1965 about eight such births were recorded per 1,000 of the population, 10 years later it was no more than two. Evidently couples succeeded in preventing the birth of further children once they considered the family completed. For them it was, of course, easiest to consult a physician and to receive a prescription. However, soon the risks of having an unwanted pregnancy before marriage also declined. In the Netherlands in 1965 about 20% of all brides were pregnant at the time of marriage if one considers as such all women who had a first child within the first 7 months of marriage. By 1974 the proportion of these so-called "shotgun-marriages" had been halved. This should have led to an increase in the average age of marriage. But, at least in the Netherlands, this was not the case; in the first instance the mean age at marriage continued its downward course. This presumably because parents no longer saw reason to counsel their sons and daughters intent on marrying to wait a while: after all they could easily prevent the birth of children within their marriage if they so wanted! They were right. Survey research conducted in the 1970s amongst persons who married for the first time in 1963 and 1968 has revealed that important changes in family planning behaviour were taking place. Amongst the 1963 marriage cohort no more than 4% aimed at postponing a first birth for 1.5 year or more by means of contraception. This proportion had increased to 15% amongst couples marrying 5 years later (Moors, 1974). However in the longer term the mean age at first marriage did rise; that phenomenon did in fact become a hallmark of the new planning behaviour.

Consequences for Contraceptive Practices and Legislation

One of the great advantages of the pill aside from providing almost risk free contraception is that it is such a simple term free of sexual connotations. One may well wonder what its reception would have been had a less fortuitous term been selected for it. Now family planning could be discussed under almost all circumstances. There was no suggestion of something quasi legal, best sold from under the counter and associated with prostitution and improper behaviour. The perfectly legal prescription of the pill to couples choosing to plan their family through birth control within or before marriage, contributed to a wider and more profound discussion. If people were free to make that particular choice, or to have an IUD inserted, why were they, if the circumstances were right and it was the course of action they preferred, not free to choose options such as abortion, sterilization, and later on, the "morning after pill"? The idea that women should be free to decide whether to have children or not, to have them early or late in life, to have them in or outside marriage, and to have the full say over their bodies gradually gained ground and led to the rapid abolishment of restrictive provisions in national legislations.

The pill had amply demonstrated that there was a huge market for easy to use, safe, and reliable contraception. This, no doubt, spurned further research and developments in that area. As a result the arsenal of means widened to include improved versions of the pill, several types of IUDs such as "Lippes loop" and the "Copper T", injectables, implants, and abortifacients. Taken together the means and methods of birth control now available enable couples and individuals if they so wish to plan childbirth perfectly and not to have children if they do not want them.

The World Population Conference held in Bucharest in 1974 enshrined this basic right of all couples and individuals to decide freely and responsibly on the number and spacing of their children in the World Population Plan of Action adopted by consensus. And although not legally binding as an internationally adopted "basic human right", it reflects the intention of governments to leave the choice to the people themselves and to facilitate that decision process. In most European countries freedom of reproductive choice is well nigh complete. Couples having difficulty in conceiving a child frequently can count on highly specialized medical support to help them overcome their problems through in vitro fertilization, surgery, and fertility enhancing drugs.

Unforeseen Demographic Consequences

Before the pill and other efficient means of birth control came on the market people had to make a conscious decision during or before each sexual intercourse to try and prevent a conception. Moreover, success was not guaranteed. It is also true that the means and methods then available suited experienced couples better than young lovers. Thus, sexuality and marriage were very closely linked. The pill, inadvertently one must assume, broke that narrow link. When one relies on the pill in a partner relation, and this applies equally to other modern means such as the IUD or an implant, contraceptive protection is constant. Consequently contraception, rather than the coitus, has to be interrupted deliberately if a conception is desired. Partners have to feel that having a (additional) child would enrich their lives. In a sense this makes the choices for children a "derivative". A choice in favor of a (further) child presupposes that the pair has weighed a large number of factors and perceives the outcome as positive. The time that having children was the "natural" outcome of being married and that becoming married implied the willingness and readiness to have children was over. As Philip Ariès (1980) expressed it in his famous essay on the two successive motivations for the decline of the birth rate in the West, the days of the King-Child (l'enfant roi) have passed. Now the interests of the couple hold central stage. One "takes" a child rather than "have or receive" one, and that child is expected to provide the parent(s) with a great deal of satisfaction. Ideally, it should help to deepen and cement their relationship, should contribute to their personal development, and should give them an exceptionally rewarding human experience only to be gained by this route. The child is expected to do them proud and to be worthy of all the love and affection they intend to lavish on it.

Understandably, fulfilling the many pre-conditions necessary to reach a positive decision is no simple or easy matter. The marriage or relationship should be stable enough to make becoming a parent a responsible decision. Employment should be sufficiently secure (Liefbroer, 2005). Many competing priorities are encountered. Is the need to care for a child compatible with completing a study, holding a demanding job, or remaining part-time employed in the for women highly attractive service sector (Klijzing, 2005)? Can that care be arranged satisfactorily? Can it be paid for? Are the opportunity costs not too high? After all, you only live once and there still are a great many pleasurable things to do and an endless number of attractive places to pay a visit to. Would it, on mature reflection, not be wiser to forego the possibility of becoming a father or mother? Aren't there enough children in the world already? In summary: amongst large sections of the population taking an active part in its demographic renewal is no longer a matter of course. Procreation has become a matter of personal preferences. And the drive to procreate apparently is much weaker than long assumed. The proportion of women remaining childless tends to increase and, reportedly, may come close to 25% in Germany (BFSFJ, 2005), a country characterized by a remarkably low desired mean family size. According to Dorbritz (2004) that average now is well below the level required for the replacement of generations: the average desired number of children only is 1.74 amongst German women and is even lower, 1.57, amongst German men. This suggest, that the commonly held idea that the almost always encountered average ideal desired family size of around two children is indicative of a situation in which couples find they are unable to fulfil their stated desire, may not be a correct interpretation. Perfect contraception may well have revealed a new societal truth: wherever this becomes a matter of personal values, preferences and choice, the wish to procreate may not be strong enough to assure the replacement of generations.

An equally important finding may be that where perfect contraception allows near perfect planning of conceptions, recorded births tend to occur at more advanced ages of fertile women. From the mid-1960s to the first years of the twenty-first century the mean age at first birth has increased everywhere in Europe to reach 27–29 years in most of Western and Southern Europe and somewhat lower figures in the eastern parts of the continent. It may be argued that to a substantial degree this reflects the novel, unforeseen, and enabling role of modern contraception: it allows women and couples to postpone childbirth to the later ages of childbearing. To the extent that this phenomenon is taking place it will also be implicated in the very low levels of fertility currently observed. However, for biological and other reasons a full "recovery" is highly unlikely. Better medical support notwithstanding, part of the attempts to assure a late conception will remain fruitless. Moreover, unions may break up and/or people may have difficulty in finding a (new) mate before they are ready to have the child they would like to have.

Effect on Sexual Relations and Marriage

As the song says, for many generations love and marriage went "together like a horse and carriage". Sexual relations were supposed to be limited to those within marriage. Where a pregnancy revealed that this ideal had not been adhered to the couple was quickly forced into marriage and, if religious, had to confess their sin in church in front of the whole congregation before receiving the church's blessing.

Effective contraception, slowly but surely, demolished societal control over sexual behaviour and marriage. The mean age at first intercourse decreased after the 1960s by 2–3 years in all Western European countries. A survey carried out in the Netherlands in 1989 revealed that the median age was between 21 and 22 years for both men and women born in 1932–1941; it had declined to below 18 for men and women born in 1962–1966 (Kontula, 2003, p. 80). In Europe the mean age remained more or less stable after the 1980s but Kontula (2004, p. 16) reports that in the first part of the 1990s a further decline occurred. The lowest average age recorded – just over 13 years – now is reported for less educated men, aged 20–39 in Greece; amongst women average ages below 18 are common (Kontula, 2004, p. 29). Newspapers and weeklies abound with stories about teenage girls having sex with a boy for the price of a mixed alcoholic drink known as a "breezer", or the entry fee to a discothèque. Sexual practices long hushed up – oral or anal sex, for example – appear to form part of contemporary petting practices. Frequently a certain degree of affection for the sexual partner is no longer considered to be a precondition for having sexual relations. To reduce the high risks of contracting a STD during sexual relations a so-called "dental dam" has been developed that is supposed to provide the necessary protection during oral-vaginal or oral-anal intercourse. The behavioural variations within the industrialized countries are considerable. But according to Kontula (2004) in those of Western Europe the age at first sexual intercourse was "almost completely unrelated to marriage" while in Eastern Europe the ages at sexual initiation, marriage, and childbirth were closer linked. Survey data from around 1990 clearly show that education is an important determinant of age at sexual initiation. The proportions of women and men younger than 39 having their first sexual intercourse below age 18 invariably are noticeably higher amongst the poorly educated than amongst those with a high level of education. As against that the prevalence of contraception at first intercourse tends to be higher amongst the better-educated young women aged 20–24. A fair assumption is that everywhere in Europe young people entering marriage, a cohabiting union even, will be much more experienced lovers and users of contraceptive means and techniques than the newly weds of earlier generations.

When managing their lives successive generations with access to modern contraception saw themselves confronted by a whole series of new behavioural options. To some extent these followed each other in a logical sequence. For example, if one could have well-protected sexual relations with the partner of one's choice before marriage, why rush into it? Wouldn't it be much simpler and more sensible to start cohabiting? After all, why should one formalize a relationship by marriage if, at least for the time being, one didn't plan to have children? Why accept societal control over an arrangement that, to some at least, appeared to be an outdated, bourgeois institution? Such an arrangement, at first opted for by a defiant few, quickly gained popularity to become readily acceptable to parents and peers alike. Initially, the cohabiting couple may have been planning to marry as soon as the birth of a child announced itself. Later on the need to enter into marriage, as a means of legitimizing a recent or impending birth, was no longer felt and over time the numbers of births formerly called "illegal" rose. The stigma long attached to children born out-of-wedlock frequently was formally removed and marriage became an option the un-married were free to choose or to reject. A more general phenomenon is that the life course of men and women became less predictable and conformed less and less to precise standards and sequences. The NKPS-survey in the Netherlands has revealed that 22% of the 18–29 year olds were living together with a partner while another 20% maintained a "living-apart-together"- relation. Some may opt for a marriage later, but even amongst 30–39 year old respondents 20% reported to be cohabiting (Dykstra & Komter, 2004).

Understandably, the breaching of the narrow link between sexuality and marriage has resulted in a substantial increase in the mean age at marriage and the proportions of men and women ever concluding a first marriage. The Council of Europe (2005) reports a mean age at first marriage (of women before age 50) of 29 years and more for Iceland, Norway, Sweden, Denmark and Liechtenstein, and in excess of 27 for the rest of the countries that form part of Western or Southern Europe (Council of Europe, 2005). In the Netherlands a value of below 23 years was recorded in the early 1970s; in 2002 it reached 28.2 years. Since 1960, the total first marriage rate below age 50 of women in Europe declined from close to unity to frequently not much more than half of that (Council of Europe, 2005). This implies that from 30 to 50% of all women will never marry unless behavioural patterns change. Cohabitation appears to have become a realistic alternative to marriage. It has also been argued (Santow & Bracher, 1997) that it may be precisely because people expect so much of the other as a sexual partner, companion, mate, and contributor to the household, that they have difficulty identifying the man or woman they would like to share their life with.

Paradoxical Effects

A rather funny, and for scholars also somewhat unsettling finding, is that the new options successive generations found themselves confronted with, did on occasion bring them to choices that are diametrically opposed to what demographers initially expected. A, certainly at first sight, quite reasonable expectation was, for example, that much improved contraception would lead to a decline in extra-marital fertility. Indeed, at first that effect could frequently be observed. But now, the proportion of births born to unmarried parents is higher than ever before. It reaches 63.6% in Iceland and values in excess of 40% are reported for a whole range of countries: Bulgaria, Denmark, Estonia, Finland, France, Georgia, Latvia, Norway, Slovenia, Sweden, and the United Kingdom. Clearly, extra-marital fertility no longer is simply indicative of failed contraception. It reflects that the breaching of the strong link between sexuality and marriage had also broken the even stronger link between procreation and marriage. Now a whole series of alternative ways of arranging legal partnerships commonly is available to couples, whether of the same sex or not.

By the same token it was commonly assumed that vastly improved contraception would reduce the proportion of brides pregnant at the time of the wedding. While this effect can be documented in the initial phase, it is quite evident that at a later stage couples continued to cohabit until such time as a desired conception occurred, all this upon the understanding that they would then marry to assure that the child would be born within that specific legal union. Now it is quite common for couples not to marry before their family is completed and they have been able to accumulate sufficient funds to throw a lavish party.

A further rather peculiar and unexpected effect is that in terms of marriage behaviour the older generations appear to have begun copying the young. As cohabitation has become such a well-accepted arrangement older men and women who, for whatever reason, see their first marriage come to an end, now commonly refrain from marrying a second time. As De Jong Gierveld (2004) reported, older men and women who divorce or become widowed, prefer to cohabit or to maintain a LAT-relation with a new partner rather than entering into a second or further marriage. In fact, such a solution may be more acceptable to their adult children than a new marriage that would result in these suddenly having a stepmother or stepfather.

Another interesting and unforeseen sequel of improved means and methods of contraception is that access to fertility regulation has become a right. When it was proclaimed that all individuals and couples had the freedom to decide on the number and spacing children, it was generally assumed that this would help reduce the numbers of children born. Improved contraception and the right to have the information and means to use that would, it was thought, help mightily in bringing population growth under control. And indeed, it has helped. But rights can be used in various ways. As noted in the introductory paragraph, in many countries the perfection of contraception has brought fertility down to levels substantially below replacement. To the dismay of many governments, improved contraception has created serious population problems that appear to be extremely difficult to resolve and to require a restructuring of the approach to reproduction in welfare states. Do governments, that consider a higher fertility rate necessary to counteract the ageing process so characteristic of industrialized countries, really have the means to raise fertility without violating the individual freedoms solemnly agreed upon in international forums?

A final effect that may be referred to as paradoxical, is that the greater freedom of choice the new means of contraception offered, has evolved into a right to have medical assistance if it is felt that the waiting time to a conception, once desired, is too long or attempts to conceive in the natural way appear unlikely to be successful.

Couples and individuals who strongly desire to have a child are prepared to go to almost any length, and to use all the means available to them, to realize that objective. Evidently, people don't want to have many children and some don't want to have them at all. But, on occasion, the wish to have a child is more strongly expressed than ever before.

By Way of Conclusion

The pill and other effective means of contraception that came on the market around the mid-1960s have had a, what can best be termed, catalytic influence on subsequent societal developments in industrialized countries. They not only have provided highly efficient and easy to use means and methods of birth control, but have spurned all sorts of legal changes that afforded populations greater control over their family life and size: abortion, sterilization, divorce, union formation, IVF, and so on. One of the most important effects of this development has been that the narrow link between sexuality and marriage has been broken. In turn, this has severed the strong traditional link between formal marriage and procreation. The number of options for arranging their lives the young can now choose from has vastly increased. There are fewer behavioural standards to conform to: each individual and couple has to structure its course through life.

The breadth of the societal impact of modern contraception can best be gauged by asking oneself a rhetorical question. Just as in the early twentieth century Adolphe Landry asked himself: "Would this have been possible if people would have had to rely entirely on abstinence?" one should ask: "Could this development have occurred in the absence of modern birth control?" In an amazingly large number of cases one can only conclude that while it might not have been entirely impossible, it really is highly unlikely.

The tenor of this essay is not that modern contraception is the cause of all the demographic changes indicated. Rather, it should be interpreted as an attempt to highlight its important role in the process of social change industrialized societies experienced since the mid-1960s. As I have argued elsewhere, social change has three dimensions: structural/economic change, cultural change, and technological change (Van de Kaa, 1996). The first dimension is invariably referred to in the demographic literature. It comprises the development of the welfare state, the rise in personal income and standard of living, improved education, and so on. And, to explain the currently low levels of fertility, reference is usually made to the difficulties people experience in becoming parent in Europe (Hobcraft & Kiernan, 1995). Combining the role of parent and active participant in the labour force is far from easy, the costs of childcare are high and good facilities are scarce, the levels of unemployment are high, and the young encounter great difficulties on the housing market (Sobotka, 2004). The second dimension also is frequently discussed. Ron Lesthaeghe and I have drawn attention to the effect of the changes in value system – move towards post-materialism and post-modernism – on demographic behaviour. We have identified it as a "second demographic transition"; which implies the emergence of a new demographic regime, of a new set of interrelations between demographic variables, and our late-modern or "reflexive modern" society.

More recently Arland Thornton has in a very stimulating book provided a much more penetrating analysis of the value changes that have affected the family in Europe for centuries. His argument is that, what he calls, the developmental paradigm has given rise to developmental idealism. Four fundamental propositions constitute the notion of developmental idealism: "(1) modern society is good and attainable; (2) the modern family is good and attainable; (3) the modern family is a cause as well as an effect of modern society; and (4) individuals have the right to be free and equal, with social relationships based on consent" (Thornton, 2005, p. 136).

This essay focuses on the third, the technological dimension of social change. It should be easy to see that the invention and marketing of highly effective modern contraception was directly relevant for all of the propositions of developmental idealism. But, it enabled in particular the further realization of its fourth proposition. In my view, this has been why the principles of "perfect contraception" were so rapidly and warmly embraced even in countries where specific forms of it were only adopted belatedly.

References

Ariès, P. (1980). Two successive motivations for the declining birth rate in the West. *Population and Development Review*, 6(4), 645–650.

BFSFJ – Bundesministerium für Familie, Senioren, Frauen und Jugend and FamilienForschung Baden-Württemberg (2005). *Familie ja, Kinder nein. Was ist los in Deutschland?* Monitor Familiendemographie, Ausgabe 1-3, Berlin/Stuttgart.

Council of Europe. (2005). *Recent Demographic Developments in Europe*. Strasbourg: Council of Europe Publishing.

Cyrus-Gooswit, L., Faberij, I., & Harmsen, J. (1976). *Anticonceptiegedrag bij voltooide gezinnen*. NISSO-onderzoeksrapport 15. Zeist: NISSO.

De Jong Gierveld, J. (2004). Remarriage, unmarried cohabitation, living apart together: partner relationships following bereavement and divorce. *Journal of Marriage and the Family*, 66, 236–243.

Dorbritz, J. (2004). Demographische Trends und Hauptergebnisse de deutschen Population Policy Acceptance Study (PPAS). *Zeitschrift für Bevölkerungswissenschaft*, 29(3–4), 315–328.

Dumont, A. (1890). *Dépopulation et civilation. Étude démographique*. Paris: Lecrosnier et Babé.

Dykstra, P., & Komter, A. (2004). Hoe zien Nederlandse families er uit?'. *Demos*, 20, 74–78.

Festy, P. (1971). Évolution de la nuptialité en Europe Occidentale depuis la guerre. *Population*, 26(3), 137–151.

Hobcraft, J., & Kiernan, K. (1995). Becoming a parent in Europe. In *Evolution or Revolution in European Population*. European Population Conference, Milano. Milano: FrancoAngeli, 27–61.

Klijzing, E. (2005). Globalization and the early life course: a description of selected economic and demographic trends. In H.-P. Blossfeld, E. Klijzing, M. Mills, & K. Kurz (Eds.), *Globalization, Uncertainty and Youth in Society* (25–49). Abingdon: Routledge.

Kontula, O. (2003). Trends in teenage sexual behaviour: pregnancies, sexually transmitted infections and HIV infections in Europe. In N. Bajos, A. Guillaume, & O. Kontula (Eds.),

Reproductive health behaviour of young Europeans. Volume 1. *Population Studies, No. 42.* Strasbourg: Council of Europe Publishing, 77–131.

Kontula, O. (2004). Reproductive health behaviour of young Europeans. Volume 2. *Population Studies, No. 45.* Strasbourg: Council of Europe Publishing.

Kooy, G.A. (1980). Ontwikkelingen met betrekking tot de intieme levensfeer. In *Nederland na 1945, Beschouwingen over ontwikkeling en beleid.* Deventer: Van Loghum Slaterus. 40–63.

Landry, A. (1909/1934). *La révolution démographique.* Paris, INED (1982). The 1909 contribution appeared in *Scientia,* it was included in his 1934 volume with the same title and published in the 1982 INED-edition introduced by Alain Girard.

Liefbroer, A.C. (2005). Transition from youth to adulthood in the Netherlands. In H.-P. Blossfeld, E. Klijzing, M. Mills, & K. Kurz (Eds.), *Globalization, Uncertainty and Youth in Society* (83–105). Abingdon: Routledge.

Moors, H.G. (1974). *Child Spacing and Family Size in the Netherlands.* Leiden: Stenfert Kroese.

Santow, G., & Bracher, M. (1997). *Whither Marriage? Trends, Correlates, and Interpretations. In IUSSP General Conference, Being.* Volume 2. Liège: IUSSP. 919–941.

Sobotka, T. (2004). *Postponement of Childbearing and Low Fertility in Europe.* Amsterdam: Dutch University Press.

Thornton, A. (2005). *Reading History Sideways. The Fallacy and Enduring Impact of the Developmental Paradigm on Family Life.* Chicago, IL: Chicago University Press.

Van de Kaa, D.J. (1996). Anchored narratives: the story and findings of half a century of research into the determinants of fertility. *Population Studies,* 50, 389–432.

Chapter 6
The Demography of the Age at First Birth: The Close Relationship between Having Children and Postponement

Gijs Beets

Introduction

Over the past few decades the significant increase in the age at *first* motherhood represents a major change in demographic behaviour. Later motherhood than before is not only observed now in Western, but also in several non-Western countries. The contraceptive pill, introduced in the 1960s, gave increasingly larger numbers of women and their partners the possibility to prevent becoming pregnant at younger ages and to have their first child not before they felt prepared to provide it with a warm place.

Evidence suggests that the age at first birth used to be somewhat higher in the first half of the previous century than after the Second World War (see Fig. 6.1 with data from the Netherlands). Around 1970 many Western countries showed a tendency towards having the first child increasingly later in their parents life. Ups and downs in the curve over the past century reflect the age at first marriage, economic prosperity, uncertain prospects, and separation of married partners during war periods. Since the 1970s modern contraceptives, rising educational levels and new (non-marital) life styles led to an unprecedented rise in the age at first birth.

Although the post-war trend is similar in many Western societies, variation exists in the levels and timing (Fig. 6.2). The age of the mother at first birth started to rise in the Scandinavian countries in the 1960s, followed by Western Europe in the 1970s, by Southern Europe in the 1980s, and by Central and Eastern Europe after the fall of the Berlin Wall, i.e. in the 1990s. Specifically Italy and Spain showed strong increases and most likely[1] Spain is the current "world champion in late motherhood". However also in Denmark, Finland, France, Germany, Greece, Ireland, the Netherlands, Sweden and Switzerland as well as in for example Japan the first

G. Beets (✉)
Senior Demographic Researcher, Netherlands Interdisciplinary Demographic Institute (NIDI), The Hague, The Netherlands
e-mail: beets@nidi.nl

[1] Not all countries have reliable and comparable fertility statistics on the age at first birth.

G. Beets et al. (eds.), *The Future of Motherhood in Western Societies*,
DOI 10.1007/978-90-481-8969-4_6, © Springer Science+Business Media B.V. 2011

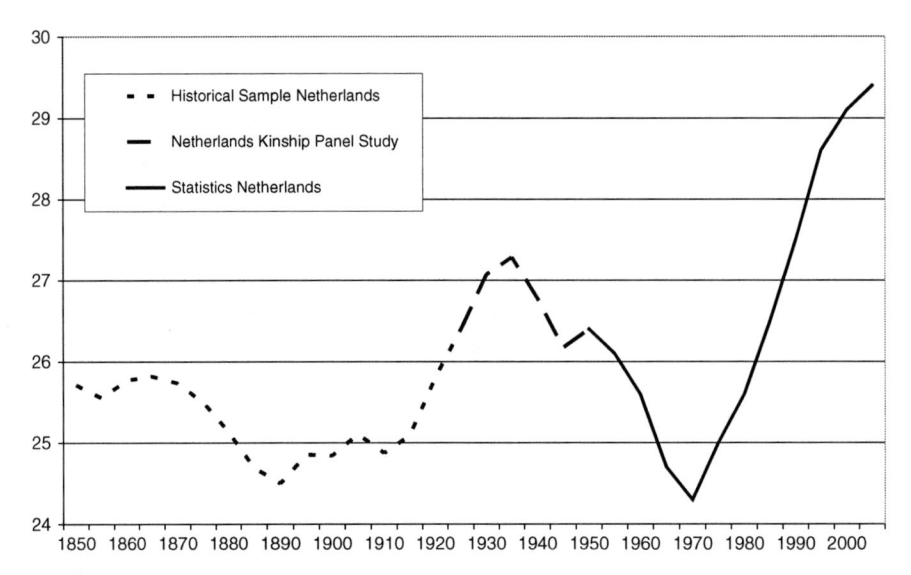

Fig. 6.1 Mean age of the mother at first birth, the Netherlands, by year of births of her first child (data based on various sources) (Van Gaalen & Van Poppel, 2007)

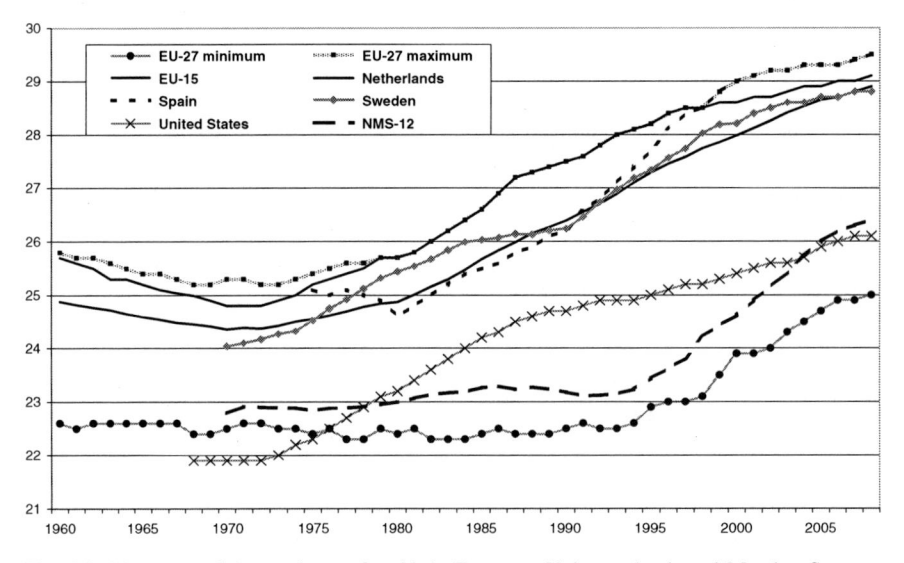

Fig. 6.2 Mean age of the mother at first birth, European Union and selected Member States + United States (EU-15 = the "old" EU; NMS-12 = 12 new Member States that entered the EU since 2004) (Source: Eurostat) (See Annex 1 with country specific details)

child arrives at the age of 28 years or above. In Northern America the change to a higher age of mothers at first birth occurred from the mid-1970s onwards, but due to substantial numbers of teenage pregnancies the mean age at first birth is still relatively low, in the USA more pronounced than in Canada. Also the United

Kingdom, Australia and New Zealand have a substantial share of teenage mothers, which reduces the rise of the average figure on the age at first birth.

In Western societies the 1960s mean age of the mother at first birth typically ranged between 22 and 26 years, currently between 25 and 29. This of course indicates that increasingly larger shares of first-born babies have mothers who are 30 years or over at their delivery, even though teenage pregnancies have not disappeared. Although everywhere the trend is in the same upward direction the underlying country-specific patterns have become more diversified.

Not only the age of the *mother* shifted, also the age at first fatherhood rose, although evidence is scarcer. As one of the few countries with annually published statistics Sweden registered a rise in the mean age at first fatherhood from 26.6 (1970) to 31.2 years (2006). This increase almost perfectly follows the rise of the mean age at first motherhood in Sweden, with a difference of about 2.5 years. Obviously we can, when using the term *late motherhood* in this book, easily exchange this term with *late fatherhood*, or even with *late parenthood*. *Late motherhood* is defined here as having a *first* child when the woman is 30 years or over. However, the term *late motherhood* does not easily fit individual behaviour as people may not have a strict reference point in time to which they personally are scheduling a delay. It corresponds to macro level behaviour: on average people born in a certain year make a later start with having children than women born earlier. It coincides with higher levels of childlessness, with higher shares of small families, and changes in birth intervals. At the micro level women often have their first baby at a higher age than their mothers did.

The shift to later parenthood is part and parcel of the so-called *Second Demographic Transition* (SDT) (Lesthaeghe & Van de Kaa, 1986; Van de Kaa, 1994). SDT has profoundly influenced research on family and fertility[2] behaviour and presently constitutes "the" mainstream concept among population scholars dealing with demographic change in European societies. "SDT entails on the one side a macro-level view of societal development that stresses the importance of ideational changes in bringing about certain demographic behaviours such as single living, pre- and post-marital cohabitation, delayed fertility, high prevalence of non-marital fertility and high rates of union disruption."[3] One can debate this view, for example on the persistence of variation across Europe, and more specifically on the cradle of "new" family patterns in Northern Europe versus more traditional patterns elsewhere.

"On the other side, on the micro level the diffusion of the SDT concept has focussed attention on the importance of subjective evaluations – especially of values." This is of course connected with the emergence of new family values and behaviour. Persistence of old behavioural patterns or acceptance of new behaviour

---

[2]In the social sciences among which demography, the term "fertility" is mainly used as an indication for the number and timing of having (live-born) children.

[3]Quotes and arguments in the sections on SDT are from http://www.eaps.nl/activities/wgcurr/2ndtransition.html

may vary across contexts, and is reflected in the variation in reproductive behaviour and the values of the next generation.

This chapter overviews and clarifies various demographic aspects of fertility postponement: what are the circumstances and restrictions, and how do they relate to smaller families? What are the main causes and consequences? The chapter shows that young adults have become much more autonomous in making decisions. However making rational decisions about irreversible life events is far from easy. And more often than before union dissolution interferes before people have realised the number of children they want to have.

The Demography of Late Parenthood: Circumstances and Consequences

Having the First Child Later than in Previous Generations

Biologically the optimal period in life for women to have children is from about 18 to 30 years (see Chapter 2 by Te Velde elsewhere in this book). However, from a social point of view having children "too early" (specifically teenage motherhood) is viewed as an "abnormality" because the mother (and possibly also the father) are not yet seen as adult enough to satisfactorily manage their lives with respect to education, work and income, let alone raising a child. Teenagers also may not have much stability in their partner relationship. The United Kingdom, Poland, Canada and even more so the USA, still happen to have relatively large shares of teenage mothers. Many of the children to teenage mothers grow up in low-income one-parent (often: lone mother) families which make their future prospects grim. These youngsters are confronted with high levels of social deprivation (Daguerre & Nativel, 2006). From that perspective later childbearing is to be encouraged. But the increase of the mean age at first birth is but partly explained by a drop in teenage fertility; childbearing rates beyond 30 years have much more increased than the rates for teenage mothers have decreased.

As mentioned, in Europe first children arrived as a "standard" when women were in between 22 and 26 years in the 1960s while that is now in between 25 and 29 years. When in the 1960s and before women gave birth to a baby while in their 30s or 40s almost all of them already had one or more children. Having a first baby when in their 30s used to be exceptional, while it has become more or less normal nowadays. For example in the Netherlands, almost half of all first-born babies are born now to mothers of 30 years or over, as against just over only 10% around 1970. Nowadays, 12% of first children have a mother of age 35 or over and that is up from 3% around 1970. From studies looking at *all* children born, irrespective of birth order, one may observe that relatively large shares of them have, even used to have a mother of 30 years or above. We should keep in mind that data on *all* children born are very sensitive for the declining family size. That is a major reason to focus here on first born children, which represent the major life course transition from

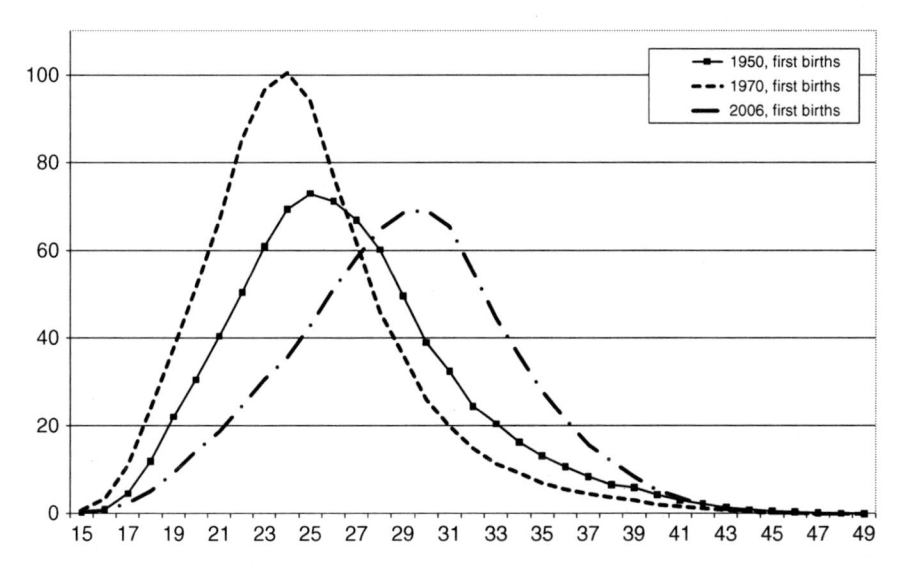

Fig. 6.3 Age-specific fertility rates for *first* motherhood (per 1,000 women at each age), 1950, 1970 and 2006, the Netherlands (Source: Statistics Netherlands)

childlessness to motherhood. For this reason the timing of first born children is the best indicator of postponement.

For a closer look at the age of women at delivering their first babies Fig. 6.3 gives the so-called age-specific fertility rates in the Netherlands indicating per age which share of women deliver their first baby at that age. We notice the recent shift from left to right, i.e. the *ageing of fertility*: more recently lower shares of women become first time mothers at younger ages and higher shares at older ages. Around 1970 the peak of having a first baby lay at age 24 (about 100 per 1,000 women of that age = 10%), by 2006 the peak was lower and had shifted upwards to age 30 (about 70 per 1,000 women of that age had their first baby = 7%). The 1950 peak was at age 25 (73 per 1,000 women), telling us that for Dutch standards first motherhood arrived relatively early around 1970. From the graph one can see the enormous shift in the mother's age at first childbearing. This shift is related to (1) the disappearance of the wish (and the economic necessity) for having a "large family" with three or more children, and (2) the extension of the period of early adulthood committed to exploring the "world" or other "exciting business" than raising children. The idea behind this is that if people only want to have one or two children they think they can easily start somewhat later in life with realising their wish.

The Netherlands is one of the countries characterised by having the first child "late". This country used to be the "world champion in late motherhood" in the 1980s and 1990s but Spain currently has taken over that position. The Spanish curves resemble those of the Netherlands but are nowadays, if they had been shown in Fig. 6.3, lower and more to the right, i.e. to higher ages. Other Western countries have similar curves or a bit more to the left than the Netherlands, i.e. to slightly

Table 6.1 Mean age of women at first birth in selected countries, calendar years 1970–2006 (ages at 1st January[a])

	Calendar years				
	1970	1980	1990	2000	2006
EU-27[b]	24.1	24.6	25.9	27.4	27.7
EU-15[b]	24.4	24.9	26.4	28.0	28.4
NMS-12[b]	22.8	23.0	23.2	24.6	25.9
Czech Republic	22.5	22.4	22.5	24.9	26.9
Denmark	23.8	24.6	26.4	27.7	28.4
Finland	24.4	25.7	26.5	27.4	28.0
Hungary	22.8	22.5	23.1	25.1	26.9
Italy	25.1	25.0	26.9	28.4	28.7
Netherlands	24.8	25.7	27.5	28.6	28.9
Poland	22.8	23.4	23.5	24.5	25.9
Romania	22.3	22.6	22.4	23.6	25.1
Spain		24.6	26.2	29.0	29.3
Sweden	24.0	25.5	26.3	28.2	28.8
United States	21.4	22.7	24.2	24.9	25.7

Source: Eurostat; VID et al., 2009

[a]Ages shown in this table are on average half a year lower than the exact age at delivery. Some countries, for example the Netherlands are used to present statistics on the exact age of the mother at having her first baby, i.e. for example 29.4 in 2006.

[b]Estimates, as data are not available for all Member States. For example, data on first birth in Belgium, France, Germany, Luxembourg, Switzerland and United Kingdom deviate as they refer to the first child in the marriage, and not to the biological first child to the mother.

lower ages. All follow the same trend with increasingly higher ages over the past decades. Even in Eastern Europe the *pattern of early fertility* is (gradually) being replaced by a *pattern of late fertility*. Within Europe, Albania, Bulgaria, Romania and the Russian Federation still stay somewhat behind although the trend moves into the same direction: the age-specific peak has become much lower, shifts to higher ages, and the curve also widened. The obvious conclusion is that in Europe less people choose for early motherhood, postponement is massive, and first deliveries nowadays do not take place concentrated in a narrow "early age range" but in a much broader "later age range" (see Table 6.1 with the mean age of women at first birth in various EU Member States).

The pattern towards later childbearing has several faces: some countries show significant increases in first children born to mothers after she turned 30, others only minor increases or even declines in the over 30 fertility rates as the first child may arrive more frequently when mothers are in the 25–29 age range. In general one can say that the later one starts with having the first child the lower the ultimate life time family size, because the remaining reproductive life span is reduced: late fertility goes hand in hand with increasing rates of childlessness, and a lower ultimate number of children than intended (at the individual level: 1 child instead of 2 children, 2 instead of 3, etc.). This is partly due to declining fecundity with increasing age (the biological ability to procreate), but also voluntary and involuntary factors contribute to this trend such as changing personal circumstances (having a partner or not) or changing personal preferences (wish for children). Also the level of education and labour market commitments play a role here (see later in this chapter). The tendency towards later fertility coincides with increasing demands for and supply of Assisted Reproductive Technology (ART). However, the impact of ART on family size is low and so are success rates although these have been increasing over time (Leridon, 2004; Habbema et al., 2009).

Postponement and the Increased Risk of Childlessness

Ending up life without children is a serious risk of postponement behaviour. A positive statistical correlation exists between late fertility and childlessness: the later a population starts with having the first child the larger the ultimate percentage (voluntarily and involuntarily) childless women (Beets, 1996). On average over half of the EU-15 women who nowadays turn 28 years are still childless. (Projected) ultimate childlessness is still fairly low in Central and Eastern Europe (around 13% for birth cohort 1960, which is also the level in the United States), more elevated in the EU-15 (around 16%) and as high as 20% in Austria, England & Wales, Finland, Germany, Ireland, and Italy, and just under 20% in the Netherlands (Dorbritz, 2005; Sobotka, 2004).

Figure 6.4 shows first fertility rates for selected female birth cohorts, in the Netherlands. Birth cohort 1945 represents the *early* Dutch age pattern of women having their first child, 1965 the *late* pattern. Later birth cohorts show even further postponement behaviour but women from birth cohorts 1975 en 1985 are still in their reproductive life span, and we are not sure yet where they will end up. The bottom graph shows the cumulative effect and therefore also informs us about childlessness. In successive birth cohorts we see a decreasing share of women having a first child, i.e. an increase of childlessness. As said, birth cohort 1965 ends up just below 20%.

Table 6.2 shows for some selected EU Member States what numbers of women born in 1945 and in 1960 ever gave birth to a first child, and at what mean age. In all mentioned countries, except Finland and Sweden, the average (cohort) number of children diminished. Childlessness increased everywhere, but Finland and Sweden stand out as countries where the one-child family diminished and the three-or-more children family increased. The age at first birth increased everywhere in this selection of countries – with more than $1\frac{1}{2}$ years on average – and is for birth cohort 1960 (women who currently are already 45+) lowest in Italy and Spain and highest in the Netherlands. So, a rising age at first birth does not automatically lead to a lower family size.

It is difficult to assess whether in a period of fertility decline, determined by several societal factors, the increasing age at first birth has a separate effect on the ultimate birth cohort family size. It may be the other way around: the wish for lower family sizes provoked postponement. From studies in natural fertility (non-contracepting populations) we know that women who delay the birth of their first

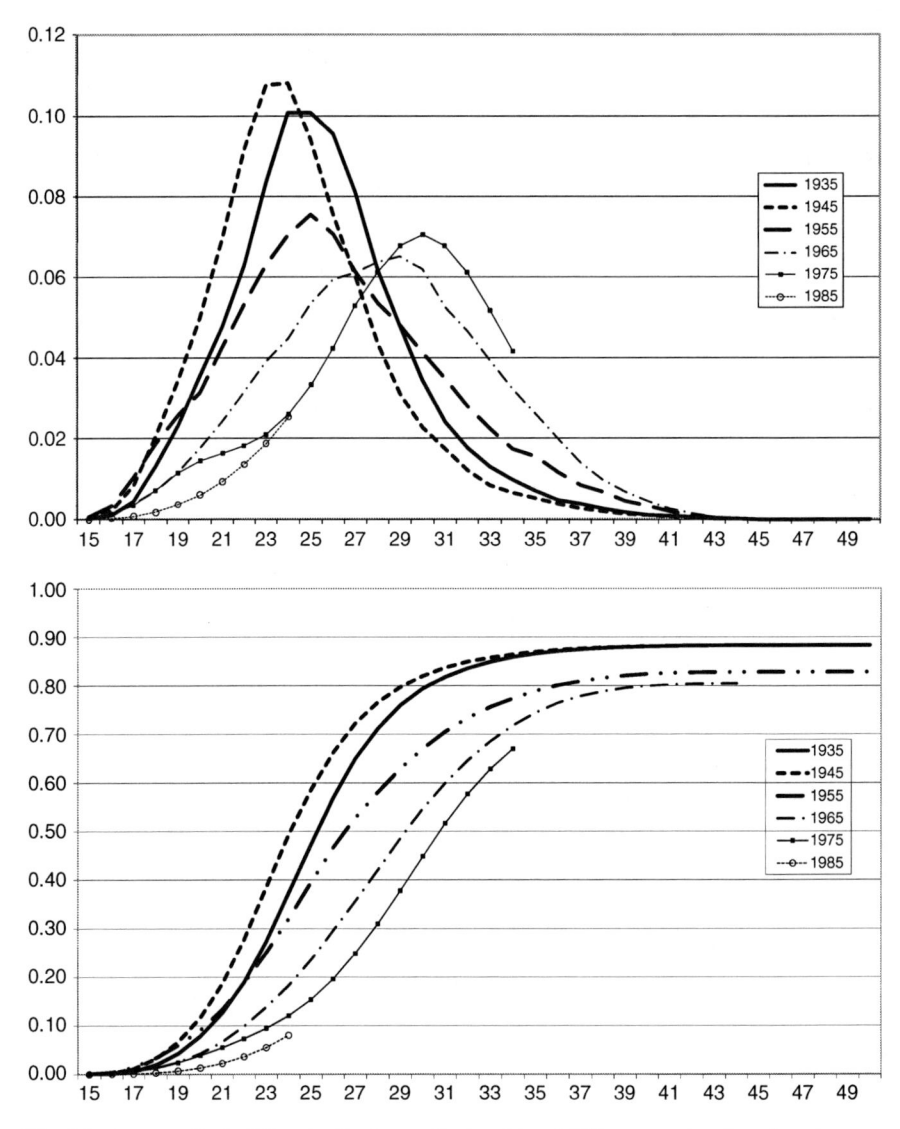

Fig. 6.4 Age-specific fertility rates for *first* motherhood (per 1,000 women at each age), and cumulative rates (*bottom panel*), selected years of birth, women, the Netherlands (Source: Statistics Netherlands)

child ultimately have a lower number of children than those who started earlier (Larsen & Vaupel, 1993; Wood, 1994). However in the modern contraceptive world such a relationship may be much more difficult to assess as the wish for children intervenes.

Table 6.2   Women by final family size (%), cohort total fertility rate (CTFR) and mean age of the mother at first birth per birth cohort (1945 and 1960), selected countries

	0		1		2		3+		CTFR		Mean age at first birth	
	1945	1960	1945	1960	1945	1960	1945	1960	1945	1960	1945	1960
Denmark	8	10	16	22	47	43	28	24	2.06	1.90	23.3	26.2
Finland	14	19	21	14	40	36	25	31	1.87	1.96	24.4	26.5
Italy	10	15	19	25	41	43	30	17	2.06	1.68	24.4	26.0
Netherlands	12	18	13	16	49	42	25	25	1.99	1.85	24.5	27.5
Spain	6	10	10	26	36	47	48	17	2.43	1.76	25.4	26.0
Sweden	12	13	17	15	45	41	27	31	1.96	2.04	24.0	26.5

Source: Eurostat

The Relation Between Age at First Birth and Family Size

Postponement behaviour contributes to the decline of the Total Fertility Rate (TFR), the average number of children per woman. This is immediately visible in the so-called period Total Fertility Rate (PTFR), an easily produced annual statistic. It summarises the number of children born in a certain period (usually a calendar year) to women per age.

Of course, having babies in a calendar year occurs to women of various ages. Some do so for the first time, others already have earlier born children. As these women stem from various birth cohorts and have different reasons and considerations to have a (first or higher order) child in that particular calendar year, fertility research based on period indicators is surrounded with flaws, specifically when age groups behave differently than previous generations did at similar ages. From its onset postponement behaviour results then in a lower PTFR (a "baby bust"), while "advancing" behaviour (the opposite of postponement) results in a higher PTFR (a baby "boom").

However, we can also look at these issues from the life course perspective, i.e. per *birth cohort*: the so-called *cohort Total Fertility Rate* (CTFR). This way of looking is much to be preferred, as it provides "a unifying framework" (Sobotka, 2004). Women born in the same year experienced at the same age moments of societal change, whether from a policy, economic, cultural or value perspective. And also in their life course they experience transitions to education, labour market as well as union formation in about the same period, i.e. at about the same age. They watch movies, listen to music, go sporting or have fun with their peers. This may have an important effect on life time decisions, much more important than information they most likely gathered from their parents on their decisions and behaviour a generation ago.

In Fig. 6.5 the relationship between postponing the first birth, the PTFR and the CTFR is presented (simplified from Sobotka, 2004). The general idea behind this is that if a new birth cohort of women starts postponing to have a baby the age at first birth will rise while the number of children born will initially drop and after a

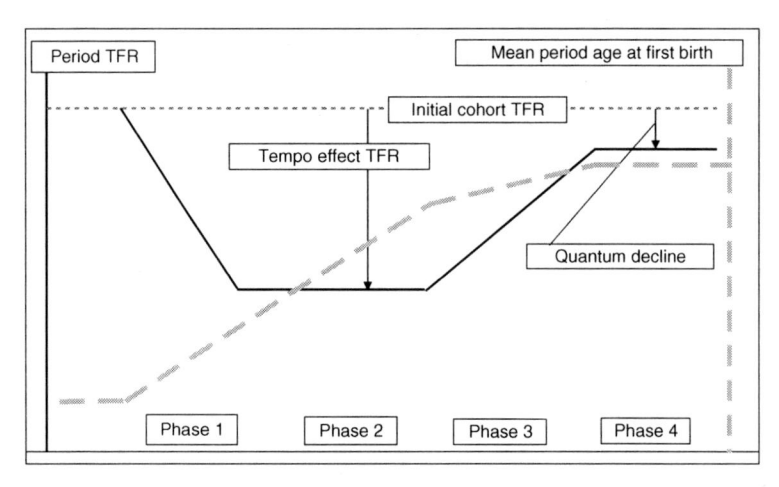

Fig. 6.5 A simplified model of fertility postponement, together with the period and cohort total fertility rates for first births (based on: Sobotka, 2004)

while stall at a lower level. Later on, the rise of the age at first birth will diminish creating a rise in the number of births again, namely when women start to recuperate having the children they postponed up until then. Sobotka distinguishes four phases starting from a situation where it is normal for women to have a first child at a specific (early) mean age. The *first* phase shows the onset of the rise in the (period)[4] mean age at first birth (MAFB) which rises for example from 24 to 25 years (right axis). Since in that year due to this postponement process a much lower number of women will get their first child the PTFR will show a significant drop (left axis). In the *second* phase the MAFB continues to rise (for example from 25 to 28 years), but the PTFR stays more or less constant because the forerunners have gone for a first child now since they stopped to postpone further. In the *third* phase recuperation behaviour prevails making the MAFB start to bend towards stabilisation and the PTFR to rise further. In the *final* phase the MAFB and both the PTFR and CTFR will stay constant again. If all delayed births would be recuperated then CTFR equals the initial PTFR. However a later start normally leads to a decrease in fertility due to fecundity decline and other reasons like union dissolution: the CTFR will end up somewhat lower than the initial PTFR, the so-called "quantum decline" (the effect on the fertility level). The initial significant fall in the PTFR can be labelled as the "tempo effect" (the effect on the timing of fertility). In an opposite situation when the MAFB would start to fall the effects would be the other way round: the PFTR would first start to rise (and create a baby boom) and become stable and equal to the CTFR again as soon as the MAFB does not drop any further. Likely, the CTFR would then end up slightly higher than the initial PTRF. This situation was apparent in many European regions in the 1950s.

---

[4]A cohort mean age at first birth exists as well, which self-evidently also rises in periods of postponement.

Recuperation has been most advanced in several of the countries that are at the end of the postponement process (like the Netherlands or Sweden). In the Netherlands for example fertility rates for first children at age 30 or shortly after that age recently increased substantially, but in other countries (Germany, Italy, Spain) these rates hardly changed or only moderately so that the PTFR has only risen modestly there up until now. The extent of recuperation varies widely and "is not strongly associated with the pace of previous first birth postponement" (Sobotka, 2004, p. 78).

Will Fertility Behaviour Change in the Future?

In the past century the CTFR has dropped, first rather rapidly, of late at a slower pace. What can we say about the near future: will the CTFR of more recent birth cohorts stall or continue to fall? Of course we do not exactly know whether the CTFR would also have fallen if over the past decades the MAFB had remained constant. We have to wait up until women per birth cohort are 50 years of age before we can observe their final reproductive data and know for sure. However, if we compare the fertility behaviour of women from various birth cohorts up until specific ages (at for example 25, 30, 35 years) we get an idea of what is happening in younger female birth cohorts. Several quantitative methods have been developed as well as scenario building, informing us about out what may happen under various conditions. But only the future will definitively learn what trend the CTFRs of those born in the 1970s, 1980s, 1990s and further will follow: whether the age at first birth will stall and if so at what age, whether childlessness will rise further, whether women will fully recuperate postponement behaviour (Kravdal, 2001; Rendall & Smallwood, 2003). And to what extent the financial crisis will lead to another wave in postponement behaviour? Sobotka (2004, p. 79) concludes that "obviously, late timing of first birth is not necessarily associated with very low completed cohort fertility."

Period and cohort rates relate like the weather versus the climate, and their trends contain some information about the future: future European PTFRs may be higher to substantially higher. As we just saw, in periods of a rising MAFB the CTFR of still reproducing birth cohorts of women is underestimated, indicating that PTFRs may rise. Specifically in Central and Eastern Europe many 1965 born women already had their children before the onset of the rise in the age at first birth there, which onset started after the fall of the Berlin Wall. The socio-economic situation there has changed fundamentally since then, and the fertility patterns of females born in the 1970s and 1980s reflect that (the MAFB is rising significantly leading to a drop in the PTFR but that may likely be only temporarily).

An advanced demographic exercise to allow for the tempo-effect, i.e. to calculate the PTFR free from the tempo-effect, is the so-called "tempo-adjusted TFR" (Bongaarts & Feeney, 1998). It uses fertility data by birth order, if available, and corrects the PTFR for changes in the mother's age pattern of having children. Countries amidst the transition of fertility postponement have a higher to substantially higher life-time fertility level than is suggested by the PTFR, usually 0.2–0.4 higher.

Table 6.3 Some summary indicators on the age at first birth and family size, selected European countries

| | Mean age of the mother at first birth | | | Total fertility rate (number of children per woman) | | | | | |
| | | | | Period | | | | Cohort | Adjusted |
	1970	1990	Latest[a]	1970	1990	Latest[a]	2050[b]	1965	Latest[a]
Czech Republic	22.5	22.5	26.9	1.90	1.90	1.33	1.49	1.93	1.76
Denmark	23.8	26.4	28.4	1.95	1.67	1.85	1.85	1.89	2.00
France[c]	*23.9*	*26.5*	*27.8*	2.47	1.78	1.98	1.94	2.03	2.07
Germany[c]	*24.0*	*26.6*	*28.7*	2.03	1.45	1.33	1.49	1.55	1.59
Hungary	22.8	23.1	26.9	1.98	1.87	1.34	1.50	1.97	1.75
Italy	25.1	26.9	28.7	2.37	1.33	1.35	1.52	1.50	1.48
Netherlands	24.8	27.5	29.0	2.58	1.62	1.72	1.76	1.78	1.82
Norway	23.6	26.1	27.7	2.51	1.93	1.90	1.89	2.07	2.01
Poland	22.8	23.5	25.9	2.20	2.05	1.27	1.49	2.04	1.58
Spain	*24.8*	26.2	29.3	2.87	1.36	1.38	1.52	1.61	1.39
Sweden	*24.2*	26.3	28.8	1.92	2.13	1.85	1.85	2.00	1.96
United Kingdom[c]	*23.9*	*25.8*	*27.4*	2.41	1.83	1.84	1.84	1.96	1.98

Source: partly based on Eurostat Statistics, partly on http://www.oeaw.ac.at/vid/datasheet/download/European_Demographic_Data_Sheet_2008.pdf

NB. *Figures in italics* are estimates based on own calculations by Gijs Beets.

[a]Latest=around 2006.

[b]Based on the 2008 medium variant EU population forecasts (Eurostat).

[c]Estimates for first biological child to the mother.

Relatively low tempo-adjusted TFRs (below 1.6) are currently observed in Belarus, Germany, Greece, Italy, Latvia, Malta, Poland, Russia, Slovenia, Spain, Ukraine, and also in Japan (VID et al., 2009). For a selection of countries Table 6.3 shows an overview of the MAFB, the PTFR and CTFR for birth cohort 1965 as well as the tempo-adjusted TFR (around 2006). These corrected rates are supposed to indicate much better what the future fertility level will be. Where the 1965 cohort rates and the adjusted rates do not deviate much, the future PTFR will end up more or less similarly (see the period numbers of children that EUROSTAT, the EU Statistical Office, expects for the various countries by 2050). Where the deviation is much larger the future may be more uncertain, and that feeds concerns about the low to very low fertility levels to remain there for a longer period (Czech Republic, Germany, Hungary, Italy, Poland, Spain). And these concerns go together with uncertainty about the future course of the age at first birth: will it rise further or level off, and if levelling off, at what age?

Other evidence for a likely future PTFR rise, although remaining below the replacement level[5], comes from a recent study by Myrskylä et al. (2009). The

---

[5]The replacement level: the number of children per woman needed to exactly replace the previous generation, currently around 2.1 children per woman. A population with replacement level fertility does not change in size.

authors claim that some fertility rise is glimmering in developed countries, even when controlled for a rise in the age at first birth. Up until now the unprecedented increases in economic and social development coincided with substantial fertility declines. But in the most advanced countries further development seems to reverse the declining trend in fertility.

Population forecasts do not contain variants according to age at first birth. The basic reason behind is that the variation in the timing at first birth normally only has a minor extra effect on population size and its age structure, the most important output data.

We can only speculate about whether there is a certain natural ceiling to a population's mean age at first birth. In a few countries the rate of increase in the age at first birth seems to stabilise, in between 29 and 30 years. It will still take a while before such a stable level could be valid for larger shares of the world population, also given the persistence of teenage pregnancies in several regions. If pregnancies before the age of 25 years are to disappear it could become common practice that first motherhood starts at maybe a mean of 32 years. Whether it would ever rise to, say, 35 years remains to be seen. That may become feasible in a very few countries, regions or subpopulations when educational expansion is high and early childbearing rare, or in case of a major medical breakthrough that makes healthy first childbearing possible in the late 30s, or even later, for example via freezing eggs.

The Wish for Children

The current low and late fertility indicators do not suggest that children are not appreciated nowadays. Fokkema and Esveldt (2008, p. 154) argue that "Europeans still value children highly. (. . .) Children are especially regarded as a source of private, parental and family joy; they are considered less as an essential element in personal happiness or an obligation towards society." High values of children are also observed in many European countries that currently have low PTFRs. Normally highly-educated people have comparatively low values of children, while people for whom religion is important have relatively high values. It is during early adulthood that people, next to investing in education, making a start on the labour market as well as searching for an intimate relationship, develop ideas on having children in the future. Some never had doubts and already know for a long time that a life with children is one of their aims; others weight the pros and cons.

The wish for children (the ultimate number of children one would like to have) is initially relatively high due to selection[6], and maybe also to overestimation and unrealistic optimism, but gradually declines when people get older. In surveys,

---

[6]Due to the fact that it is initially only those with a relatively high wish that have made up their mind and answer numerical survey questions on this issue. Those weighting pros and cons make up their mind much later and usually answer "does not know (yet)" earlier in life.

women give more precise (numerical) answers to the question on the wish for children than men. That the wished number of children is not stable and diminishes over the life course – before having the first child women generally have a higher (wished) ultimate number of children than after the first child is born – is probably related to getting experienced with what parenthood really means (Liefbroer, 2008). Currently the average number of children women wish to have when they are in their 20s is somewhat above the replacement level in several European countries (Van Peer & Rabusic, 2008), but after the first child is born it drops below that level. Due to union break up and fecundity problems the final realised number of children is even lower. Data show geographical variation: the lowest wish for children is currently visible in Austria and Germany where even at relatively young ages women already have below replacement wishes (Lutz et al., 2005; Van Peer & Rabusic, 2008). Since there is no good theory telling us whether fertility rates in low fertility countries will recover in the future the finding that the early adulthood wish-for-children is already below replacement has led these authors to formulate the so-called "low fertility trap"-hypothesis assuming that fertility rates might not easily recuperate because young adults are not acquainted to a society in which children are visible and play an important role. Self-reinforcing mechanisms keep fertility low or may even have a further lowering effect: (1) the fact that youngsters themselves belong to small birth cohorts and have not many brothers and sisters, (2) that they have only seen fertility rates drop in the previous generations, and (3) that they are so much oriented at self-fulfilment that they envisage a life with a small family, also due to dropping expected income levels for younger cohorts. These three factors "would work towards a downward spiral in" future births (Lutz et al., 2005).

Relatively high wishes for children are expressed in Scandinavia. Western Europe has levels in between, while the wishes in Eastern and Southern Europe are fairly low (Van Peer & Rabusic, 2008). Together with the declining wish for children "the ideal age at first birth" (based on respondent's answers in surveys) has increased in Europe (Van Nimwegen et al., 2002). In countries with a relatively low observed age at first birth the ideal age is slightly higher than the observed. That seems to indicate that there still is some room for a further rise in the age at first birth. As most people also want a second child many nowadays plan to have the second at a relatively short interval from the first.

According to a large majority of Dutch survey respondents the best age range for women to have the first child is 25–29 years (Esveldt et al., 2001). And many are indeed successful in having the first baby in that age group. It is normal that mothers turn out to be content with the age at which they themselves had their first baby, but several who had their first child early (under 25) indicate later on that it would have been better if they had waited. And, the reverse, several who had their first baby late (over 30) state that they had preferred to have it earlier. The higher the age at first birth the larger the share that perceives that age as "too late". And, the higher the educational level the more women prefer to have the first baby at 30 or over. Although several admit that it was not optimal others most likely defend their own behaviour. Obviously people judge that one should not be too old nor too young when having a first child; preferably one should be in the late-20s.

The Road Towards Childlessness

Initially everyone is childless but when people start getting children the childless group gets smaller and smaller quickly. Ultimately the group of people without children consists of two clear opposites: those who do not want to have children (voluntarily childless) and those who unsuccessfully tried to have children (involuntarily childless). The group that is truly unable to have children due to biological reasons is small, and so is the opposite group of those who do not want to have children right from childhood onwards. But that is not all there is: from surveys we know that respondents have difficulties in assigning themselves as belonging to either the first or the second group as many childless men and women may find themselves somewhere in between (Van Balen et al., 1995): for example several are still doubting about having children or not, others are still so "young" that they have not made any decision yet and are just postponing in order "not to cut one's own throat", and other others actually had wanted to have children but did not have them due to various circumstances, like illness, not having a partner (anymore), or having a partner who already has children from an earlier union. And one may change ideas over the life course: those who always wanted to have children, may have postponed for a while and decided then to remain without, versus those who wanted to stay without but ultimately had one or more children (Liefbroer, 2008).

Childlessness as wilful goal requires both an explicit choice and a permanent commitment to that choice (Miettinen & Paajanen, 2005). The choice may alter with increasing age. Up to age 30 people may doubt about having children or not, about the advantages and disadvantages of a life with or without children. A definite choice often does not come easily. And a commitment to a life without children may be regretted later on, sometimes not until after retirement when the work career fades away and peers are blessed with grandchildren (Alexander et al., 1992). Childless people turn out to be at greater risks for social isolation in late life than parents as the networks of the childless elderly become smaller more rapidly, as they have more network ties with age peers who are dying out and less so with people from the next generations (Dykstra, 2006). But this may change over time when the new generations with larger shares of childlessness grow older.

Data on the size of each childless subgroup are only vaguely known; the topic is generally under-researched (Dorbritz, 2005). From medical sources it is known that on average 2–4% of the couples are permanently involuntarily childless because of biological causes (Te Velde & Beets, 1992). Childlessness is unexplained for another only small share of the population. But sterility increases with age: from about 4% for women who married around the age of 20, via 6% when marrying at 25, 10% at 30, 16% at 35 to 33% at the age of 40 years (Wood, 1994). At age 45–49 it is becoming very unlikely that a woman will easily conceive at all. The main reason for the decline of female fecundity is the decline of both the quantity and quality of the oocyte/follicle pool (Te Velde & Pearson, 2002).

There are reasons to believe that a substantial share of women from more recent birth cohorts remaining childless throughout their life (with access to perfect contraception) did not opt voluntarily for childlessness. Toulemon (1995) estimated that

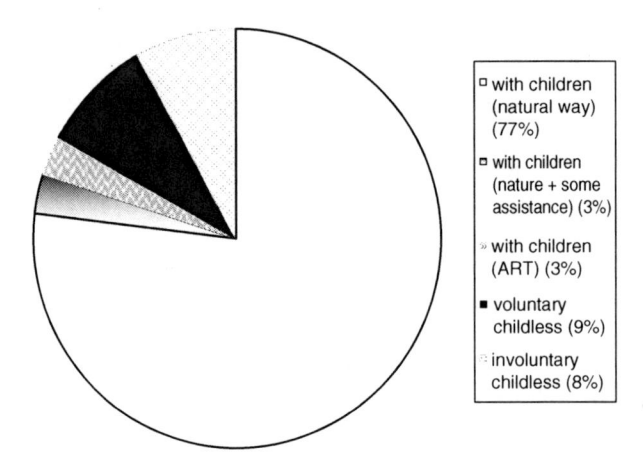

Fig. 6.6 Fertility status of women born in 1960, at age 42, the Netherlands (author's estimates mainly based on data from Statistics Netherlands)

about half of all couples without children in France are "more or less" involuntary childless, i.e. they had preferred to have children. This is in accordance with Dutch research (De Graaf & Loozen, 2005). Testa and Toulemont (2006) also showed that involuntary postponement of the first child increases with age.

There are reasons to believe that women (and men) may not be "fully aware" of decreasing fecundity with age. Surveys show that women easily overestimate their own fecundity (Lampic et al., 2006; RVZ, 2007). Also ART success rates are generally overestimated. Starting a pregnancy is not always as easy as preventing one, certainly not at women's ages above 30 years.

Figure 6.6 shows that 82% of Dutch women born in 1960 had one or more children, the majority of them conceived in the most natural way. A small share was medically assisted, either by medication or by ART. Voluntary and involuntary childlessness were estimated at about equal. We assume that a similar graph for birth cohort 1945 would show that 88% of the women have children, with in the remaining share of the childless slightly more voluntarily than involuntarily childless women. ART was not yet widespread available to help 1945 born women to raise their family size. It is difficult to exactly assess how much extra involuntary childlessness was "caused" by the 3 year rise in the age at first birth towards birth cohort 1960. Without ART involuntary childlessness would definitively have been higher.

The Optimal Timing of Parenthood

If people only want to "take" and raise a small number of children in a relatively short period of their life it would be helpful to dispose of an obvious "optimal pattern of timing" for realising such wishes. From a health perspective it is apparent that *too late* childbearing is beyond the optimum as it is associated with long-term negative health consequences, for both the mother and the child (see Chapter 2 by

Te Velde elsewhere in this book). Mirowsky and Ross (2002) estimated the "optimal age from a health perspective" for becoming first time mother to be 30.5 years. Most likely, the socio-economic optimum is different. Economic theories about fertility search for the "economic optimum" and talk about "utility" and "rationality": how to schedule life in such a way that family life becomes optimal from an economic perspective, i.e. how to minimise consumption losses due to child-related expenses and lost income (see for an overview: Sobotka, 2004). But next to an optimal socio-economic career one also looks for an optimal partner and optimal living arrangements/housing accommodation; at least it would be nice if all these essentials are suitable and adequate. Moreover if one happens to suffer from some setback: stress is not the best associate of starting a pregnancy. Most likely the optimal plan for family building does not exist, as it differs per person.

The Limits to Late Parenthood

Becoming a parent obviously has an age limit, but how late can late fertility be? On the individual level women have shown to be able to reproduce up to late in their 40s. However already these women are exceptions. Stories in the popular press that women delivering a baby in their 50s or 60s as some have been able to do with the assistance of Italian gynaecologist Severino Antinori rarely inform the reader that these women were using egg donation.

According to the on-line encyclopaedia Wikipedia "the average age of menopause is 51 years, and the normal age range for last period ever is somewhere between age 45 and 55. Age 55–60 for last period ever is described as a 'late menopause', an 'early menopause' may already occur between age 40–45." Several years before entering menopause reproduction is unlikely (Te Velde & Pearson, 2002).

In non-contraception populations the average age at last birth has been registered at around 41 years (Te Velde & Pearson, 2002). Since these populations usually had large families it may be remarkable that this (more or less natural) age at last birth is not higher. In current Western societies with small families the age at last birth is self-evidently much lower, probably somewhere in the mid-30s. Quantitative information on the age at last birth can only arrive from special surveys, as birth registration never establishes immediately whether a specific birth will be the last one.

We can only speculate about the maximum mean age at first birth. Significant and acceptable medical breakthroughs may have a profound effect – for example via freezing eggs technology. But it is unlikely that all countries will follow the same path.

The Age at First Birth among Immigrants

Immigrant populations normally bring the pattern of childbearing prevailing in the country of origin. Currently in many Western low-fertility societies immigrants arrive from countries with substantially higher fertility rates. The fertility patterns among recently arrived immigrants resemble what had happened to them if they had not migrated. However, the longer their duration of stay in the new home country before the start of family formation, the more the fertility pattern will start to deviate from that in the country of origin. It converges towards what is normal in the country of arrival. The fertility pattern of the second generation (children born in the country of arrival to first generation immigrants) does not differ much anymore from the native population's pattern. This transition is not only related to the habits in the country of arrival but also to the changes in the country of origin (where the age at first birth also rises and fertility rates drop). This transition is also visible in union selection and marriage patterns (see for the Dutch example of immigrant fertility: Garssen & Nicolaas, 2008).

Population Growth and Population Ageing

A population characterised by an early pattern of childbearing will have higher population growth than a population with a late pattern (Beets et al., 2001, pp. 51–56). As shown before in this chapter a rising age at first birth makes the PTFR temporarily drop, as the yearly numbers of children born are lower. Postponement results in an increase of the intergenerational distance between parents and children, and eventually also the age at first grandparenthood will rise. Specifically if postponement results in a lower lifetime number of children than otherwise had been the case, population increase will lower and population ageing will be strengthened: the population age pyramid shrinks at the bottom and broadens at higher ages. The process of population ageing is of course also dependent on mortality and migration trends, but generally the PTFR is the most important determinant of the ageing process.

Late Parenthood: Non-Demographic Consequences

These decades we witness a coincidence of late parenthood with a much stronger position of women in the labour market. Better education, growing individualism and emancipation have created completely different generations of women than previously. Unintended pregnancies are disappearing, but the search for the best suitable partner has become a more difficult and time-consuming process.

Without postponement behaviour fewer women would have been economically active before family formation. In that sense postponement has been very advantageous for economies: higher productivity and tax incomes, less maternity leaves, less costs for pre- and post-natal health care, even less costs for child care in general, just due to lower numbers of children born. But the coincidence in the health sector with a larger demand (and supply) of ART, which are relatively costly, leads to rising costs in this field. If these treatments involve more hospitalisations of labour market employees extra sickness leave will be taken up. Children born from ART are surrounded with extra pre- and post-natal health care costs (more miscarriages;

more multiple births; more Caesarean deliveries; more children in various needs of lifelong care; higher later in life risks for "late mothers" on developing breast cancer). The medical consequences of ART are in general much more costly than the treatment itself (Habbema et al., 2009).

Late parenthood also has social advantages as parents are more mature both physically and emotionally, and more experienced in coping with complex situations. Parents may have more union stability, and more financial resources. This could for a while outweigh the health disadvantages (Stein & Susser, 2000; Van Balen, 1997). However parents who are unable to easily manage all careers simultaneously may end up in divorce. Later in life, children from divorced parents have more difficulties in bonding themselves in a stable union and in choosing to have children. Having children themselves normally occurs relatively late in their lives.

Children with older parents show some jealousy towards children with younger parents. Although older parents are more mature and have more financial resources they may easily be perceived by peers as grandparents rather than parents. Children may even develop fears about becoming an early orphan. However such ideas are more pronounced if parents and children differ more than 40 years than only around 30–35 years. No evidence exists about possible negative impacts of late parenthood on child development and the upbringing of children. Finally it should be mentioned that involuntary childlessness usually is emotionally very straining and difficult to accept (Van Balen, 1997).

The Determinants of Late Parenthood

For what (main) reason do current generations have their children later in life than previous generations did? Individual behaviour is conditioned by various social actors on the micro- as well as the meso- and macro-level, which determine the options from which people make a final choice (Willekens, 1999). People are rational decision makers using all available relevant information to achieve their goals. This may lead to different strategies for people in different settings. We no longer "get children" like our ancestors did, but carefully make decisions now whether or not (yet) to "take children". Making such decisions is a hazardous undertaking: one is afraid to make this step of no return because it requires giving up at least part of a nice and independent life, and it is never fully clear when the setting for having children is optimal (see also Chapter 10 by Beck-Gernsheim elsewhere in this book). For the moment postponement is an easy way out then.

Partner Selection and Fertility Control

As often more than one reason is mentioned for having children late it is not always easy to determine their separate effects on postponement. However, a most important precondition for becoming a parent is of course to have a partner. Although it is possible to have children without a partner, hardly anyone wishes or plans to do so. Partner selection and union formation have fundamentally changed over the past decades: later marriage; more often non-marital cohabitation before or in stead of direct marriage; more union instability. More women and men than previously are without a partner in their late 20s, early 30s. Singlehood has become a trend. Most singles have had a partner before, but the relationship broke up, also because not all unions are even meant to be long-lasting: increasingly unions are seen as temporary or experimental (Sobotka, 2004, p. 36). When getting older some realise that the current partner may not be the perfect or even a suitable person to share parenthood with. The increased likelihood of being without partner at the peak of adulthood and the fact that relationships between partners are becoming shorter due to divorce/separation may help explain the low fertility rates. Keizer et al. (2008) show that the larger the number of relationships a man has had the larger the chance he will remain without children. Women more often seize new opportunities with both hands. The longer one is without union the larger the chance of remaining childless, both for men and women. The age at which the first union started does not have an effect.

Another important factor of course is birth regulation, (almost) perfect since several decades. Modern contraceptives have been instrumental in childbearing postponement, but not been a principle cause of contemporary low and late fertility (Frejka, 2008). Women (and men) can now enjoy sexual activities without having the fear of unintended pregnancies. The pill heads the list of things which most changed women's lives (De Guibert-Lantoine & Leridon, 1998). But paradoxically, writes Van de Kaa (see Chapter 5 elsewhere in this book), the pill also played a fundamental role in changing partner relationships – the spread of cohabitation; delayed marriages – and in the increases of non-marital fertility rates, as most experts had expected at the moment the pill was introduced that it would only have enabled people to time their pregnancies more effectively (within married life).

Women's Education is a Powerful Determinant of Late Motherhood

The shift towards the later timing of the first child is "an outcome of fundamental social, economic, and cultural transformations which altered the norms related to parenthood as well as the nature of decision-making on the timing of childbearing" (Sobotka, 2004). Multivariate analyses usually do not come up with one single determinant for change. Billari (2005) even prefers to portray "families of explanations" for the changes occurring in partnership, childbearing and parenting. According to Cleland (2003) education is one of the most powerful predictors for demographic behaviour. Although his research mainly focused on non-Western societies, much of the evidence is also valid for the demographic transition in Western societies.

Women usually do not have children while still in education. Being in education is not seen as compatible with family formation. As a higher educational level only arrives after a longer school career the higher educated have their first child several years later than lower educated women (Kravdal, 1994; Gustafsson & Kalwij, 2006). And more so than lower educated women, the higher educated are economically

Table 6.4 Number of children and mean age at first birth by educational level, Netherlands, selected birth cohorts for women (partly estimated)

Birth cohort	Level of education	Number of children (%)				CTFR per woman	CTFR per mother	Mean age at first birth
		0	1	2	3+			
1945–1949	Low	6	17	55	23	2.03	2.16	25
	Medium	13	15	50	22	1.88	2.16	27
	High	21	10	48	21	1.77	2.22	30
1960–1964	Low	16	14	46	25	1.89	2.24	27
	Medium	18	13	46	23	1.81	2.21	29
	High	29	11	38	22	1.60	2.25	33

Source: Statistics Netherlands

active for a substantial number of years between finishing education and having a baby (Mertens, 1998).

Due to educational expansion the shares of higher educated women have increased significantly over the past decades in Europe. This alone already had a rising effect on the age at first birth. But the age at first birth has also risen among women of each separate educational level (See Table 6.4). A study shows that in the Netherlands half of the increase in the age at first birth can be attributed to the rise in women's educational expansion[7]: if the educational levels of women had not changed over the past 3 decades then the mother's age at first birth would now have been around $26\frac{1}{2}$ years in stead of over 29 years (and up from around 24 years around 1970 (Beets et al., 2001). Similar findings were observed for other European countries but the real impact of education depends on the micro–macro level context, for example personal work experiences and the ruling welfare regime at the societal level (Billari & Philipov, 2004; Miettinen & Paajanen, 2005). Further, Testa and Toulemont (2006) report that "childless people with high education who consider themselves likely to start a family within the 5 years following the interview were significantly more likely to experience the transition to parenthood than childless people with low or medium education who had similar positive intentions". The better educated are seemingly better "planners", but this may be related with the finding by Esveldt et al., 2001, p. 61) that, controlled for age and other factors, the higher educated have a shorter time-to-pregnancy than the lower educated. The authors argue that this "easier start of a pregnancy" may be the result of a higher level of human capital among the higher educated and/or health and life style selection processes (which also may explain why the higher educated have a higher life expectancy than the lower educated). The higher level of human capital may (partly) be "inherited" as the higher educated are likely to have (had) higher educated parents as well, who may have paved a healthier life style for their children from birth onwards.

---

[7]The rising education of men hardly had any effect on the changing age at first birth.

Childlessness is more prominent among higher educated women, most likely because the opportunity costs of childbearing are much larger for them (see also Chapter 7 by Schippers elsewhere in this book). Childlessness has risen to 30, in some countries even 40% among the highest educated women, many of them being "workaholic" singles. But if higher educated women have children, they match up with mothers at other educational levels or even have a slightly higher CTFR as their shares of one- and two-child-families are lower and of three-plus-child-families higher. The variation in the number of children between highly educated women and other women stems basically from variation in (voluntary) childlessness.

Normative Pressures, Gender Equality and Uncertainty

As indicated the shift to a later childbearing regime is perceived as part of *the Second Demographic Transition* (see also Lesthaeghe & Neels, 2002). Overviews of the determinants of delayed parenthood mention several other factors which separately or jointly contribute towards later childbearing (see for example Sobotka, 2004). Some are related to higher education, as that enables people to develop distinct material and career values and preferences, less sensitivity to social pressure, and increased resistance to normative pressures. Women are increasingly joining the labour market. They often start in their 20s and that stimulates ambitions to make "some fun" and/or to acquire specific material goods before having children. It also strengthens doubts about having children as it involves such large responsibilities. The more one can reflect on whether or not having children the more having children may be perceived as a threat to career prospects and lifetime income perspectives. And that may coincide with another often mentioned obstacle for (soon) starting a family: the availability of too little child care facilities in the neighbourhood.

Gender equality is still lacking. Women want the best of both the family and the career world. Men still perceive their task mainly within the career realm – raising the (main) family income – and less so in that of the family. Over the past decades lives of women have become more similar to those of men (significant increases in female labour market participation) than vice versa (insignificant changes in men's participation in family and household chores). If both partners have different views on the number and/or timing of children as well as on how to share the child care commitments between the two, it may take a considerable amount of time to decide about the "optimal plan" towards having and raising children. Van Luijn (1996) reports that it takes on average about $2\frac{1}{2}$ years after high educated female partners decided to go for children before they made final arrangements with their partner on how to cope together with all the upcoming child care details. In that sense one could easily label this period as a "fertility loss" or the "male effect" (see also Chapter 11 by Henwood et al. elsewhere in this book).

Postponement is a likely outcome in periods of uncertainty (Sobotka, 2004). High levels of uncertainty are conducive to forgoing long-term commitments. Uncertainty may exist in the field of stable relationships, adequate housing accommodation, and/or basic income. Economic uncertainty like unemployment and non-standard employment contracts usually lead to postponement. However fertility reactions to economic uncertainty are likely related to the stage of family formation: unemployment at the beginning of a career (at younger ages) may enhance postponement, while unemployment later in the career (at higher ages) may speed up a conception (Van Bavel & De Wachter, 2007). In Central and Eastern Europe the political and economic transformations in the 1990s are thought to be responsible for much uncertainty in daily life and therefore for delays in family building.

Overall much remains unclear, for example whether having children is basically dependent on economic ambitions or whether economic activities depend on the number and timing of children? Although not specifically with a focus on later childbearing, Hakim (2003; see also Chapter 12 elsewhere in this book) developed her preference theory by confronting (1) women who are mainly work-centred or careerist (give priority to jobs, often remain childless even if married, and endorse the competitive, achievement-oriented values of the marketplace), with (2) home-centred or family-centred women (prefer not to work after marriage and childbearing, and espouse caring and sharing family values), and (3) adaptive women who seek a balance between employment and family life. Hakim's research finds that about 60% of the British women is adaptive, while both career and home centred women make up about 20%.[8] Hakim's preference theory predicts that men will retain their dominance in the labour market, politics and other competitive activities, because few women are prepared to prioritize their job (or other activities in the public sphere) similarly as men do. "This is unwelcome news to many feminists, who have assumed that women would be just as likely as men to be work-centered once opportunities were opened to them, and that sex discrimination alone has so far held women back from the top jobs in any society" (Hakim, 2003, p. 6).

To Sum Up

The educational expansion leads one to argue that increasingly fewer women will let things happen as they come. More women than before try to plan their future with "the best of all worlds", i.e. arranging their life course with everything they want to "enjoy" and without getting overburdened. They look for nice work, convenient income, nice living accommodation, "plenty" free time, nice kids, and foremost a "prince" who easily obeys her orders on sharing the various family and household commitments. Many women agree that the one-income breadwinner model belongs to the past, and that a labour market career is essential for their life. But how to find a better or even the optimal balance in life? Specifically higher educated women struggle with the dilemma of choosing between a labour or family career, as they prefer a combination of both. As long as they are undecided fertility postponement is an easy way-out and one has to take into account its multifaceted nature (Liefbroer,

---

[8]See also Vitali et al. (2007) who present data for in total 11 countries from various welfare regimes: on average 69% of all women is adaptive, 14% family and 17% career oriented. Family orientation is highest in Southern Europe, lowest in Social democratic countries (Scandinavia).

1999). However, are these women well informed: do they really know all the pros and cons of postponement?

"For most young adults, parenthood is an abstract possibility of the distant future. Their partnerships, employment, and living arrangements are marked by flexibility and impermanence, their life transitions have become non-standardised and less predictable" (Sobotka, 2004). Postponement is easy and one may add another rather easy rationale for a late start with childbearing: in times when people only want to realise a small family with often no more than two children it is not necessary to start early. Also a somewhat later start makes it possible for most people to realise the number of children one wishes and hopes to get. It also means that if one really wants to have three or more children one should not postpone too long. It would be advantageous if age-dependent healthy childbearing curves would be made available early to parents-in-spe.

Conclusion and Discussion

Compared with earlier generations current female life styles and fertility patterns are quite different: women are better educated, more often economically active, use contraceptives as long as they do not feel ready for having children and are not sure about having found the perfect partner. Teenage pregnancies are virtually disappearing, and postponement is easy and popular. Demographers can measure postponement by following the rising age at first birth. That leads, temporarily, also to a lower period Total Fertility Rate. That puts many on the wrong track if it suggests and is often interpreted as if women will have a lower life time number of children. This chapter shows that such a conclusion is wrong. In earlier days a later start with having children would result in a lower ultimate family size but since modern contraceptives are so effective and widespread one can also start somewhat later to realise the preferred small family size.

Postponement results in smaller families only if delayed childbearing is not fully recuperated, and if also ART does not make up for the wished number of children. Involuntary childlessness or a smaller than wished family size may turn out as an enormous grief. But postponement also has positive outcomes: because women currently are much better educated they are more often economically active and contribute to tax incomes with significantly larger sums than women from previous generations. As the interval between generations expands postponement behaviour also has an effect on the age at grandparenthood, but for societies probably more important are the effects on the smaller population size and some extra population ageing.

The onset of postponement started geographically at different moments. Everywhere within the Western world – and even in many countries outside – the age at first motherhood has risen but up until now in some areas more than elsewhere. It started in the 1960s in Northern and Western Europe, and gradually spread towards Southern Europe. The Nordic countries have "become more similar over time, with differences in cohort fertility patterns appearing to have diminished"

(Andersson et al., 2009). There seems to be a common Nordic fertility regime. Although postponement continues the Nordic countries distinguish because of the strong recuperation of fertility at older ages, and the weak role of educational attainment in completed fertility. "These patterns can, to some extent, be attributed to the impact of Nordic social policies that facilitate fertility recuperation and make social differences in behaviour small" (Andersson et al., 2009).

Only after the fall of the Berlin wall also Central and Eastern Europe joined postponement behaviour. So countries in this part of Europe made a much later start, are in an earlier stage of transition and not yet "so late" as is common now elsewhere in Europe also because they departed from a much earlier family building pattern (see Box *Stage of postponement in 2006*).

Stage of postponement in 2006

Early stage (woman's mean age at first (biological) birth <26 years)	Medium stage (woman's mean age at first (biological) birth 26–27 years)	Late stage (woman's mean age at first (biological) birth 28 years or over)
Armenia, Azerbaijan, Belarus, Bulgaria, Estonia, Georgia, Latvia, Lithuania, Macedonia, Moldova, Poland, Romania, Russian Federation, Serbia, Slovak Republic, Turkey, Ukraine, United States	Austria, Belgium, Canada, Croatia, Cyprus, Czech Republic, Hungary, Montenegro, Norway, Portugal, Slovenia, United Kingdom	Denmark, Finland, France, Germany, Greece, Iceland, Ireland, Italy, Japan, Netherlands, Spain, Sweden, Switzerland

Originally postponement behaviour started among the more highly educated and gradually became more popular among other women. The higher the education, the later the age at first birth. And, highly educated women with high labour market orientations often do not opt for children. Immigrants adapt to local circumstances: second generation immigrants have an almost similar fertility age pattern as natives.

There does not seem to be an ideal or optimal fertility (level and tempo) plan for those who want the best of both the family and labour market career. In survey research respondents suggest having children not too early, nor too late. As childbearing after the age of 30 years gradually is surrounded with more uncertainty around the healthy outcome, women preferably start family building not much later than around age 30, but obviously only if one aims at a family of two children, and has a nice partner, job and house by that time of their life. Children do not "arrive from God anymore", but are the result of a more or less rational decision making process. As long as that process is not finished, advanced and effective methods of birth control are available to postpone the birth of the first child. The weighting of pros and cons of having children is an essential new topic in the modern life course. If nothing is done to facilitate decision making, late fertility is there to stay.

Annex 1: Mean Age at First Birth, Selected Countries, Selected Years and in Birth Cohort 1965

	1960	1970	1980	1990	2000	2006	Birth cohort 1965
EU-27[a]		24.1	24.6	25.9	27.4	27.7	26.3
EU-15[a]	24.8	24.4	24.9	26.4	28.0	28.4	26.9
NMS-12[a]		22.8	23.0	23.2	24.6	25.9	23.2
Austria		23.7	24.3	25.0	26.3	27.5	25.3
Belgium[b]	*24.8*	*24.3*	*24.7*	*26.4*	*27.4*	*27.9*	
Bulgaria	22.1	22.0	21.9	22.0	23.5	24.9	22.1
Cyprus		23.8	23.8	24.7	26.2	27.9	
Czech Republic	22.9	22.5	22.4	22.5	24.9	26.9	22.5
Denmark	23.1	23.8	24.6	26.4	27.7	28.4	27.2
Estonia		24.1	23.2	22.9	24.0	25.4	
Finland	24.7	24.4	25.7	26.5	27.4	28.0	27.0
France[a]	24.8	23.9	24.5	26.5	27.9	28.4	26.3
Germany[b]	*25.0*	*24.0*	*25.0*	*26.6*	*28.2*	*29.0*	
Greece		24.0	23.4	25.1	27.5	28.5	25.4
Hungary	22.9	22.8	22.5	23.1	25.1	26.9	23.0
Ireland		25.3	25.5	26.6	27.8	28.7	27.4
Italy	25.8	25.1	25.0	26.9	28.6	28.7	27.0
Latvia			22.9	22.7	24.4	25.5	
Lithuania				22.9	23.9	25.2	
Netherlands	25.7	24.8	25.7	27.5	28.6	28.9	28.4
Norway		23.6	25.2	26.1	26.9	27.7	
Poland	25.0	22.8	23.4	23.5	24.5	25.9	23.3
Portugal	25.0	24.4	23.6	24.7	26.4	27.5	25.2
Romania		22.3	22.6	22.4	23.6	25.1	22.5
Russian Federation	24.3	23.3	22.9	22.9	23.7	24.2	
Slovak Republic	22.7	22.6	22.7	22.6	24.2	25.9	22.7
Slovenia		23.7	22.8	23.9	26.5	27.9	23.7
Spain			24.6	26.2	29.0	29.3	27.2
Sweden			25.5	26.3	27.9	28.8	26.8
Switzerland[b]	*26.1*	*25.3*	*26.4*	*27.6*	*28.7*	*29.3*	
Turkey			20.8				
United Kingdom[a]		23.9	25.1	25.8	26.5	27.4	26.3
United States		21.4	22.7	24.2	24.9	25.7	24.6

Sources: Council of Europe. (Various years) Recent demographic developments in Europe (various volumes). Strasbourg: Council of Europe

[a]Estimates.

[b]In *italics*: Age at first birth in the woman's marriage, which is not necessarily the first baby to the mother. Official data in Belgium, France, Germany, Switzerland and the United Kingdom are according to age at first birth in marriage, which are higher than age at first birth to the mother. For France and the UK corrected estimates are given for the biological first birth to the mother.

Annex 2: Fertility Rates, Independent of Birth Order (i.e. Sensitive for Changing Family Size): Percentage Distribution per Age Group of the Mother

	% before 25 years			% from age 30 onwards			% at 25–29 years		
	1970	1990	2006	1970	1990	2006	1970	1990	2006
Austria	43.6	32.9	20.7	30.2	31.0	47.2	26.2	36.0	32.1
Belgium[a]	36.7	23.6		30.2	33.2		33.1	43.2	
Bulgaria	59.7	62.4	41.7	14.7	12.9	26.8	25.6	24.7	31.5
Czech Republic[a]	58.2	52.3	19.2	15.0	16.9	45.4	26.8	30.8	35.4
Denmark	37.7	20.8	11.6	27.4	39.3	56.3	34.9	39.9	32.1
Finland	37.8	20.4	16.2	31.1	43.1	53.5	31.1	36.5	30.3
France	37.5	23.4	16.1	30.8	37.7	51.1	31.6	38.8	32.9
Germany	42.5	28.7	18.7	29.3	34.5	50.9	28.2	36.8	30.4
Greece[b]	35.2	34.0	17.5	32.8	30.8	53.8	32.1	35.2	28.6
Hungary	49.8	46.8	22.8	10.9	20.1	45.7	29.3	33.1	31.5
Iceland	40.7	32.1	20.8	32.6	36.3	47.9	26.7	31.5	31.3
Ireland	20.7	17.1	17.1	49.7	51.9	61.9	29.6	30.9	21.0
Italy	29.1	20.8	12.9	38.1	43.3	60.9	32.7	35.9	26.1
Luxembourg	37.4	25.6	17.1	29.5	35.5	54.1	33.1	38.9	28.7
Netherlands	27.2	14.8	11.3	36.4	48.0	59.5	36.3	37.2	29.2
Norway	38.8	25.1	15.9	30.3	37.7	52.0	30.9	37.3	32.1
Poland[a]	44.6	38.0	24.8	26.6	28.2	39.8	28.8	33.7	35.4
Portugal	26.9	32.9	20.6	42.4	32.2	51.8	30.7	34.9	27.7
Romania	46.3	49.8	36.4	27.5	21.7	32.1	26.2	28.5	31.5
Slovenia	45.8	44.7	13.8	27.2	21.0	50.4	27.0	34.2	35.8
Slovakia[a]	48.8	43.4	27.8	22.6	23.0	38.9	28.6	33.5	33.4
Spain	22.1	20.1	14.2	43.4	43.7	63.9	34.6	36.1	21.9
Sweden	36.1	22.7	12.8	29.6	41.0	58.4	34.3	36.3	28.9
Switzerland	31.5	17.4	12.8	34.6	43.6	59.3	33.9	39.0	28.0
United Kingdom[a]	42.8	27.9	24.3	24.7	42.5	49.4	32.5	29.5	26.4
United States	47.7	38.0		23.0	33.4		29.3	28.6	

Source: Eurostat
[a]Not 1990 but 1995.
[b]Not 1970 but 1972.

References

Alexander, B., Rubinstein, R., Goodman, M., & Luborsky, M. (1992). A path not taken: a cultural analysis of regrets and childlessness in the lives of older women. *The Gerontologist*, 32, 618–626.

Andersson, G., Rønsen, M., Knudsen, L.B., Lappegård, T., Neyer, G., Skrede, K., Teschner, K., & Vikat, A. (2009). Cohort fertility patterns in the Nordic countries. *Demographic Research*, 20(14), 313–352.

Beets, G. (1996). Does the increasing age at first birth lead to increases in involuntary childlessness? In EAPS/IUSSP, European Population Conference Milan (1995), *Evolution or revolution in European population, Volume II*. Milan: FrancoAngeli, 15–29.

Beets, G., Dourleijn, E., Liefbroer, A., & Henkens, K. (2001). *De timing van het eerste kind in Nederland en Europa*. (107 pp). NIDI rapport # 59. The Hague: Netherlands Interdisciplinary Demographic Institute.

Billari, F. (2005). Partnership, childbearing and parenting: trends of the 1990s. In M. Macura, A. MacDonald, & W. Haug (Eds.), *The New Demographic Regime: Population Challenges and Policy Responses* (63–94). New York, NY and Geneva: United Nations.

Billari, F., & Philipov, D. (2004). Education and the transition to motherhood: A comparative analysis of Western Europe. *European Demographic Research Papers 2004, No. 3*. Vienna: Vienna Institute of Demography. http://www.oeaw.ac.at/vid/download/edrp_3_04.pdf

Bongaarts, J., & Feeney, G. (1998). On the quantum and tempo of fertility. *Population and Development Review*, 24(2), 271–291.

Cleland, J. (2003). Education and future fertility trends with special reference to mid-transitional countries. In United Nations. *Completing the Fertility Transition* (187–202). New York, NY: United Nations.

Daguerre, A., & Nativel, C. (Eds.) (2006). *When Children Become Parents. Welfare State Responses to Teenage Pregnancy* (253 pp). Bristol: The Policy Press.

De Graaf, A., & Loozen, S. (2005). Door omstandigheden vaak geen of één kind. *Bevolkingstrends (CBS)*, 53(1), 42–45.

De Guibert-Lantoine, C., & Leridon, H. (1998). La contraception en France: un bilan après 30 ans de libéralisation. *Population*, 53(4), 785–812.

Dorbritz, J. (2005). Kinderlosigkeit in Deutschland und Europa – Daten, Trends und Einstellungen. *Zeitschrift für Bevölkerungswissenschaft*, 30(4), 359–407.

Dykstra, P.A. (2006). Off the beaten track; childlessness and social integration in late life. *Research on Aging*, 28(6), 749–767.

Esveldt, I., Beets, G., Henkens, K., Liefbroer, A.C., & Moors, H. (2001). *Meningen en opvattingen van de bevolking over aspecten van het bevolkingsvraagstuk 1983–2000* [Population policy acceptance issues 1983–2000]. Report #62. The Hague: Netherlands Interdisciplinary Demographic Institute, 137 pp.

Eurostat, Demographic and social statistics. See at: http://epp.eurostat.ec.europa.eu/portal/page/portal/statistics/search_database

Fokkema, T., & Esveldt, I. (2008). Motivation to have children in Europe. In C. Höhn, D. Avramov, & I. Kotowska (Eds.), *People, Population Change and Policies: Lessons from the Population Policy Acceptance Study* (141–155). Volume 1. Family change. European Studies of Population #16. Berlin: Springer.

Frejka, T. (2008). Birth regulation in Europe: completing the contraceptive revolution. *Demographic Research*, 19(5), 73–84.

Frejka, T., & Sardon, J.-P. (2007). Cohort birth order, parity progression ratio and parity distribution trends in developed countries. *Demographic Research*, 16(11), 315–374.

Garssen, J., & Nicolaas, H. (2008). Fertility of Turkish and Moroccan women in the Netherlands: adjustment to native level within one generation. *Demographic Research*, 19(33), 1249–1280.

Gustafsson, S., & Kalwij, A. (2006). *Education and Postponement of Maternity*. (325 pp). European Studies of Population #15. Dordrecht: Springer.

Habbema, D.J.F., Eijkemans, M.J.C., Nargund, G., Beets, G., Leridon, H., & Te Velde, E.R. (2009). The effect of in vitro fertilization on birth rates in western countries. *Human Reproduction*, 24(6), 1414–1419.

Hakim, C. (2003). Competing family models, competing social policies. Paper presented to the annual conference of the Australian Institute for Family Studies.

Keizer, R., Dykstra, P., & Jansen, M. (2008). Pathways into childlessness: evidence of gendered life course dynamics. *Journal of Biosocial Sciences*, 40, 863–878.

Kravdal, Ø. (1994). The importance of economic activity, economic potential and economic resources for the timing of first birth in Norway. *Population Studies*, 48, 249–267.

Kravdal, Ø. (2001). The high fertility of college educated women in Norway: an artefact of the separate modelling of each parity transition. *Demographic Research*, 5(6), 249–267.

Lampic, C., Skoog Svanberg, A., Karlström, P., & Tydén, T. (2006). Fertility awareness, intentions concerning childbearing, and attitudes towards parenthood among female and male academics. *Human Reproduction*, 21(2), 558–564.

Larsen, U., & Vaupel, J. (1993). Hutterite fecundability by age and parity: strategies for frailty modelling of event histories. *Demography*, 30(1), 81–102.

Leridon, H. (2004). Can assisted reproduction technology compensate for the natural decline in fertility with age? A model assessment. *Human Reproduction*, 19(7), 1548–1553.

Lesthaeghe, R., & Neels, K. (2002). From the first to the second demographic transition; an interpretation of the spatial continuity of demographic innovation in France, Belgium and Switzerland. *European Journal of Population*, 18(4), 325–360.

Lesthaeghe, R., & Van de Kaa, D.J. (1986). Twee demografische transities? In D.J. van de Kaa, & R. Lesthaeghe (Eds.), *Bevolking: groei en krimp* (9–24). Deventer: Van Loghum Slaterus.

Liefbroer, A.C. (1999). From youth to adulthood: understanding changing patterns of family formation from a life course perspective. In L.J.G. van Wissen, & P.A. Dykstra (Eds.), *Population Issues: An Interdisciplinary Focus* (53–85). Dordrecht/New York, NY: Kluwer Academic Publishers/Plenum Press.

Liefbroer, A.C. (2008). Changes in desired family size during the life course. *Demos*, 24(Special Issue), 3–5.

Lutz, W., Skirbekk, V., & Testa, M.R. (2005). The low fertility trap hypothesis: forces that may lead to further postponement and fewer births in Europe. *European Demographic Research Papers*, 2005/4. Vienna: Vienna Institute for Demography, 36 pp.

Mertens, E.H.M. (1998). *Loopbaanonderbrekingen en kinderen: gevolgen voor de beloning van vrouwen*. Utrecht: Universiteit.

Miettinen, A., & Paajanen, P. (2005). Yes, no, maybe: fertility intentions and reasons behind among childless Finnish men and women. *Yearbook of Population Research in Finland*, 41(2005), 165–184.

Mirowsky, J., & Ross, C. (2002). Depression, parenthood, and age at first birth. *Social Science a Medicine*, 54, 1281–1298.

Myrskylä, M., Kohler, H.-P., & Billari, F.C. (2009). Advances in development reverse fertility declines. *Nature*, 460, 741–743.

Rendall, M., & Smallwood, S. (Spring 2003). Higher qualifications, first birth timing, and further childbearing in England and Wales. *Population Trends*, 111, 18–26.

RVZ – Raad voor de Volksgezondheid en Zorg. (2007). *Uitstel van ouderschap: medisch of maatschappelijk probleem?* The Hague: Raad voor de Volksgezondheid en Zorg.

Sobotka, T. (2004). *Postponement of Childbearing and Low Fertility in Europe*. (298 pp). Amsterdam: Dutch University Press.

Stein, Z., & Susser, M. (2000). The risks of having children in later life (editorial). *British Medical Journal*, 320, 1681–1682.

Te Velde, E., & Beets, G. (1992). Are subfertility and infertility on the increase? *Tijdschrift voor fertiliteitsonderzoek*, 6(2), 5–8.

Te Velde, E., & Pearson, P. (2002). The variability of female reproductive ageing. *Human Reproduction Update*, 8(2), 141–154.

Testa, M.R., & Toulemont, L. (2006). Family formation in France: individual preferences and subsequent outcomes. *Vienna Yearbook of Population Research 2006*, 41–75.

Toulemon, L. (1995). Très peu de couples restent volontairement sans enfant. *Population*, 50(4–5), 1079–1110.

Van Balen, F. (1997). Met kunst en vliegwerk: laat ouderschap, vrijwillig of onvrijwillig. In G. Beets, A. Bouwens, & J. Schippers (Eds.), *Uitgesteld ouderschap* (65–74). Amsterdam: Thesis Publishers.

Van Balen, F., Verdurmen, J., & Ketting, E. (1995). *Zorgen rond onvruchtbaarheid, voornaamste bevindingen van het Nationaal Onderzoek naar Gedrag bij Onvruchtbaarheid*. Delft: Eburon.

Van Bavel, J. & De Wachter, D. (2007). Uitstel van ouderschap in het Vlaamse Gewest, 2002–2006: werkloosheid en werkonzekerheid vertragen de stap naar het moederschap bij de start van de 21e eeuw. In Jan Pickery (Red.), Vlaanderen gepeild! 2007. SVR-Studie 2007/2. Brussel: Studiedienst van de Vlaamse Regering, 359–397.

Van de Kaa, D.J. (1994). The second demographic transition revisited: theories and explanations. In Gijs B., et al. (Eds.), *Population and Family in the Low Countries 1993: Late Fertility and Other Current Issues* (81–126). Lisse: Swets & Zeitlinger (NIDI/CBGS Publication no. 30).

Van Gaalen, R. & Van Poppel, F. (2007). Leeftijd moeder bij eerste geboorte sinds 1850; stijging afgelopen 40 jaar blijkt zonder precedent. *Demos*, 23(4), 7–8.

Van Luijn, H. (1996). *Een vrouwelijk dilemma: besluitvorming van vrouwen met een ambivalente kinderwens*. Leiden: DSWO Press.

Van Nimwegen, N., Blommesteijn, M., Moors, H., & Beets, G. (2002). Late motherhood in the Netherlands: current trends, attitudes and policies. *Genus*, 69(2), 9–34.

Van Peer, C., & Rabusic, L. (2008). Will we witness an upturn in European fertility in the near future? In C. Höhn, D. Avramov, & I. Kotowska (Eds.), *People, Population Change and Policies: Lessons from the Population Policy Acceptance Study* (215–241). Volume 1. Family change. European Studies of Population # 16. Berlin: Springer.

VID (Vienna Institute for Demography), IIASA, & PRB (2009). *European Demographic Data Sheet 2008*. See at http://www.oeaw.ac.at/vid/datasheet/download/European_Demographic_Data_Sheet_2008.pdf

Vitali, A., Billari, F., Prskawetz, A., & Testa, M.R. (2007). Preference theory and low fertility: A comparative perspective. *European Demographic Research Papers*, 2007/2. Vienna: Vienna Institute for Demography, 36 pp.

Willekens, F. (1999). The life course: models and analysis. In L.J.G. van Wissen, & P.A. Dykstra (Eds.), *Population Issues: An Interdisciplinary Focus* (23–51). Dordrecht/New York, NY: Kluwer Academic Publishers/Plenum Press.

Wood, J.W. (1994). *Dynamics of Human Reproduction: Biology, Biometry, Demography* (653 pp). New York, NY: Aldine de Gruyter.

Chapter 7
The Economic Rationality of Late Parenthood

Joop Schippers

Introduction

At the beginning of the twenty-first century women in Dutch society tend to be subject of persistent concern. Some people, including policy makers, complain that Dutch women participate too little in paid work. They point to the low number of paid hours supplied by Dutch women, working primarily in parttime jobs, compared to the hours supplied by women in other European countries. Others worry about Dutch women having too little children and having their children too late. Once again, the Netherlands is at the edge of the spectre: for a long time Dutch women were considered to be the European champions in the field of postponement of motherhood. So, at first glance we are dealing with the contradictory situation that in a country where women have oceans of time available for care it takes them longer than most European women before they decide to be a mother. That is why the Netherlands constitutes a case that is worthwhile studying in the context of this book. If Dutch women can or will not opt for motherhood who else in Europe will?

Those in the Netherlands who support the view that women should increase their labour market participation – and this is also the official point of view of the Dutch government, as laid down in the so-called Lisbon targets of the European Union and the message the European Union keeps sending to The Hague year after year – usually do not pay much attention to fertility rates and the "timing" of children, that is the age at which mothers have their (first) child(ren). Yet, in the course of time increasingly more policy measures have been taken and facilities have been called into existence for a better and easier reconciliation of work and family life. In this respect the Netherlands have never been among the frontrunners, who can primarily be found among the Scandinavian welfare states (see Chapter 8 by Van Doorne-Huiskes & Doorten elsewhere in this book). Still, the Dutch government that came into office in 2007 shows a great concern for the well being of families and children

J. Schippers (✉)
Professor of Labour Economics and the Economics of Equal Opportunities, Utrecht University, Utrecht, The Netherlands
e-mail: j.j.schippers@uu.nl

over and over again. It has also made large budgets available for childcare and tax cuts for families.

Those who hold the opinion that Dutch women should have more children and should enter the process of family formation at an earlier age usually do not support the idea that women should engage in paid work *more*. On the contrary, many of them do not oppose the idea of working women or working mothers as such, but they often consider paid work as an obstacle for and too much of a restriction on (timely) motherhood. In this field the Dutch government abstains from expressing an explicit view, except for the idea that decisions concerning motherhood or parenthood in general are a personal matter and not subject to government interference. This holds for the number of children that parents would like to "take" as well as for the timing of any children. This neutral position is in line with international legal obligations to which the Netherlands has committed itself. For many people it also echoes the resistance to twentieth century nazi family policies and the longstanding Roman Catholic tradition, broadly practiced until the 1960s, that the local priest came by every year to "ask" whether parents had any plans for another baby.

If policy makers show any concern whatsoever with respect to developments around motherhood this usually relates to the number of children being born. Looking at annual birth rates and often disregarding figures on women's total fertility rate (see Chapter 6 by Beets elsewhere in this book) they conclude that women have too few babies to "live up" to the magic 2.1 baby per woman, i.e. the replacement level that is necessary for a stable population. Especially during the last few years this discussion is mingled with the discussion on ageing. A plea for more babies is then connected with the ageing of the labour force and the affordability of the social welfare state; in the final section of this chapter we will come back to this issue. But even within this framework policy makers consider parental/maternal decisions to have no children or only one child to be autonomous choices that should be respected and must be treated as firm and solid restrictions for government policies (see for instance CPB, 2006). If ever the "timing" of children is brought up in the discussion, this is only in a derived way, namely from the perspective that with respect to having a baby one of these days may be none of these days.

The formal abstinence of population policy does not wash away the fact that all kind of other policies, including specific measures that have been taken, may affect getting/having children: there are rules regarding pregnancy and birth leave, others regarding parental leave, children are fiscally supported and there are rules and arrangements concerning the quality and finance of different forms of childcare. Some rules and arrangements make it easier to have children; others may make it more difficult. Put in economic terms: different policies do influence the "price of children". This is a dimension of "implicit population policy" where there are huge differences between European countries. Some countries, like Sweden and Norway seem to be more family friendly than other European countries, even though it is difficult to bunch all dimensions of family friendliness into one mark for each country. Consider for instance a country like Switzerland where childcare is relatively expensive and many parents do not find it rewarding that both of them have a paid job. Public transport, however and the traffic system as a whole is much more family friendly than in most European countries. Moreover, as Den Dulk (2001) has shown countries do not only differ with respect to government policies, but there are also major differences with respect to the opportunities for the reconciliation of work and family life at the organisational level. And to some extent public arrangements and organisational arrangements or agreements between the social partners can be considered substitutes. We will come back to the role of these implicit prices of having children in the course of this chapter.

Could it be that both parties in the discussion are right and that women in the Netherlands should both participate more in paid work *and* have more children and have these children at an earlier age? Or do paid work and motherhood interfere so much that this will prove to be an illusion? This chapter investigates the validity of the hypothesis that women's labour market activities set a restriction to their number of children and can be hold responsible for the fact that women in the Netherlands who become a mother for the first time do so at a relatively high age (around the age of 30). Before we go deeper into these questions, however, we will demonstrate that the Netherlands constitutes a very particular case in Europe, because there is hardly any other country that leaves men and especially women so much time for family life.

More and More Women Participate, but "Parttime" Is the Watchword

Women's labour market participation in the Netherlands has been increasing for decades now. This becomes especially clear when we look at the participation behaviour of consecutive birth cohorts (see Fig. 7.1).

At the start it was primarily women who were not married (yet), childless women and especially high educated women who populated the labour market. During the 1990s mothers and women with secondary education caught up substantially. In the meantime, particularly for women with higher and secondary education entering the labour market and *staying* in the labour market has become the rule rather than the exception. The concept of "staying in the labour market" is especially illustrated by the gradual disappearance of the so-called "children's dip" in women's labour market participation, i.e. the period during which women from older cohorts interrupted their career, gave birth to their children and were fulltime involved in caring and bringing up the children. With younger cohorts these interruptions occur less frequent and they gradually disappear.

Looking from a European perspective the Dutch participation figures have moved up in the European bunch from a place at the back to the rows just behind the frontrunners (see Fig. 7.2).

Yet, on the occasion of motherhood many women change their fulltime job for a parttime job, or a large parttime job for a smaller one. Figure 7.3 shows the development of the number of weekly work hours for successive cohorts of women. In this respect there is hardly any difference between the generations. Parttime work was the watchword for the first generations of Dutch women who massively entered the

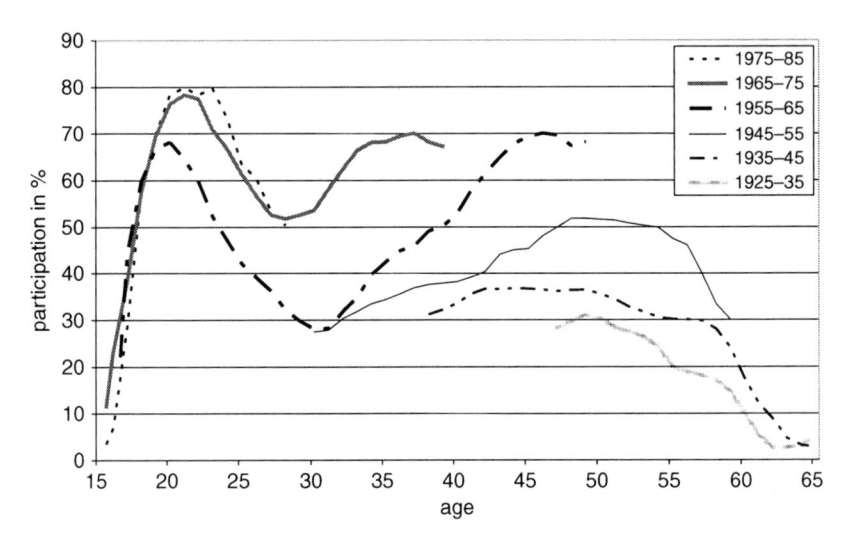

Fig. 7.1 Participation by age and cohort, all women as measured between 1980 and 2004. Source:
Román & Schippers (2007)

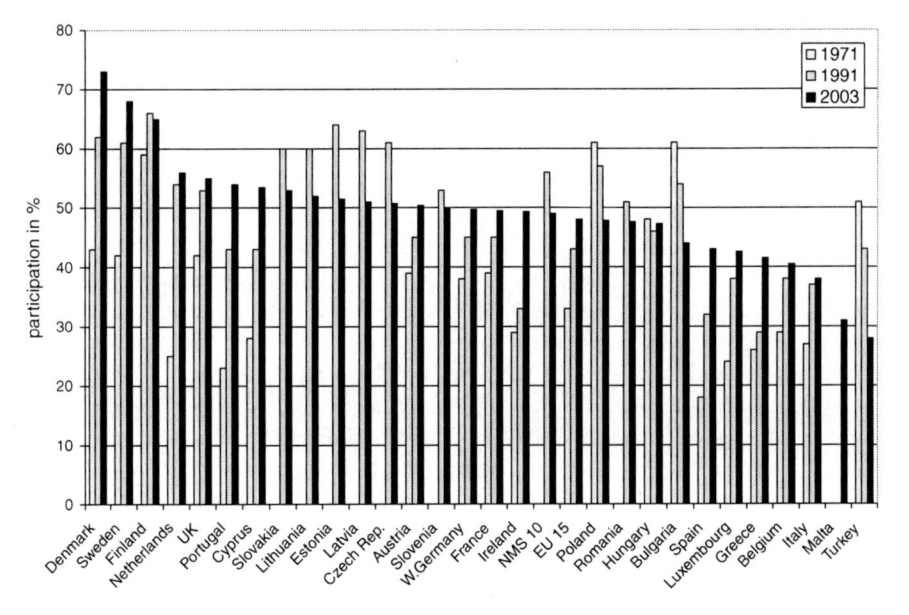

Fig. 7.2 Total labour force participation rates of women (15+) Source: Van Nimwegen & Beets
(2006, p. 120)

labour market and parttime work still is the watchword for "the" working woman in
the Netherlands.

A comparison of Figs. 7.4 and 7.5 shows, it is true, some difference between
women with and women without children, but this difference – about half a day to

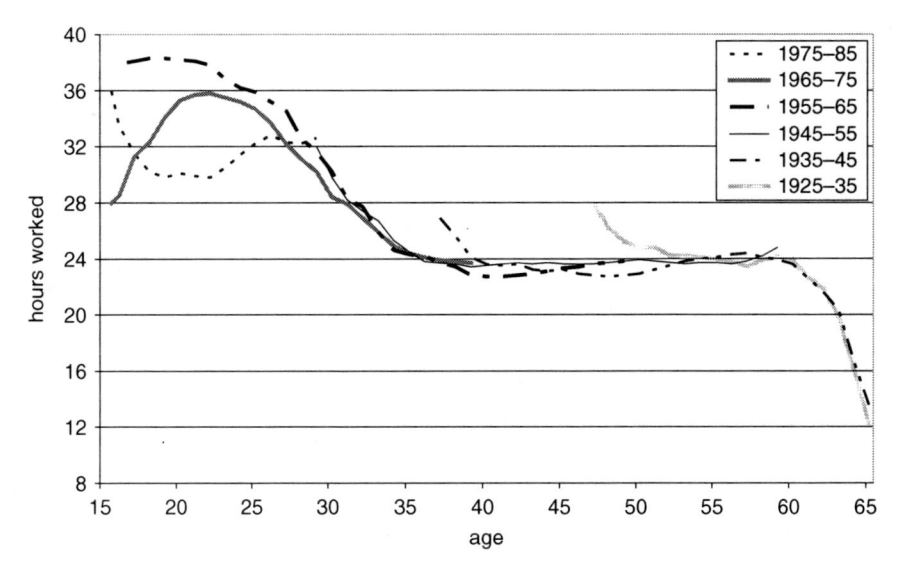

Fig. 7.3 Weekly hours by age and cohort, all women as measured between 1980 and 2004. Source: Román & Schippers (2007)

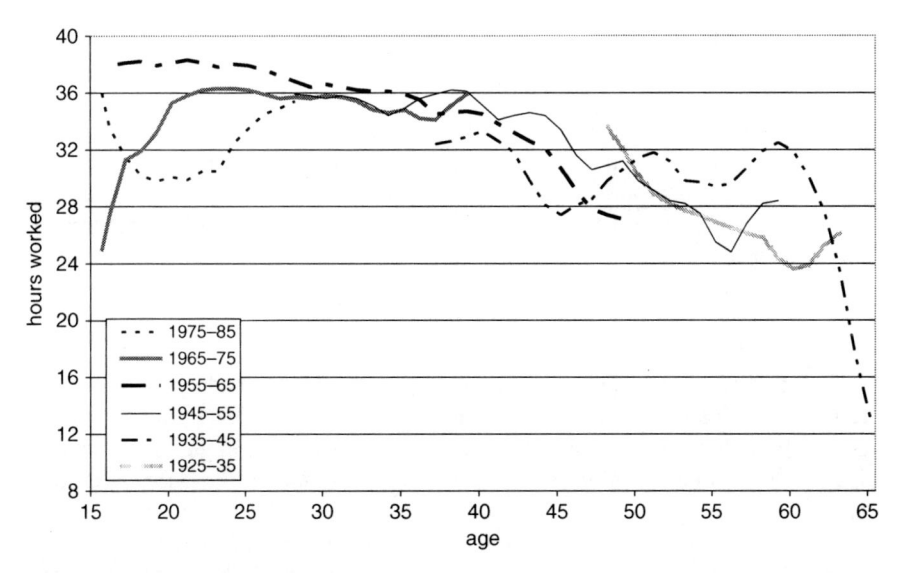

Fig. 7.4 Weekly hours by age and cohort, women without children measured between 1980 and 2004. Source: Román & Schippers (2007)

1 day a week – does by no means correspond to the weekly hours women spend on the care for children, as measured by the Dutch *Emancipatiemonitor* (SCP/CBS, 2006). If it was for this difference women without children could supply substantially more hours. Another remarkable fact with respect to mothers' work hours is that the average numbers per cohort hardly rise even after women of a cohort have

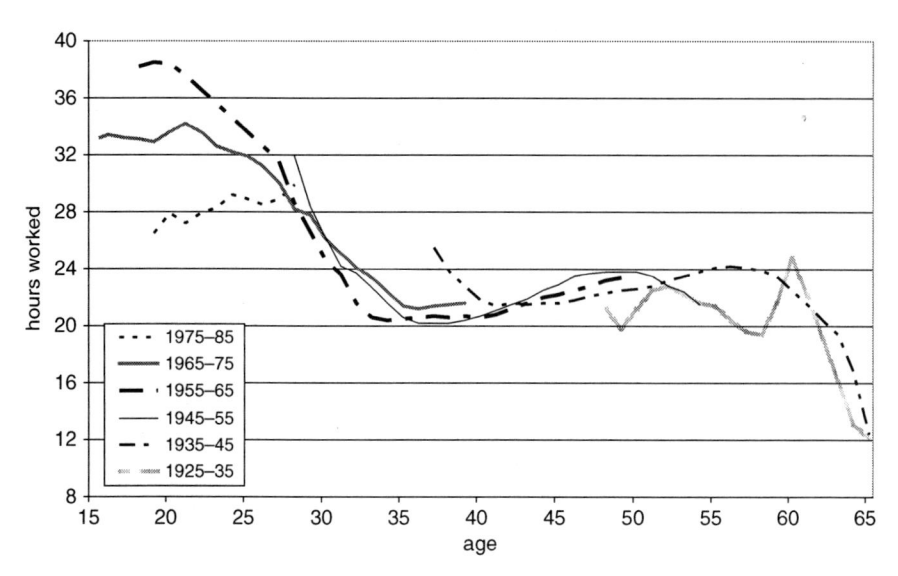

Fig. 7.5 Weekly hours by age and cohort, women with children measured between 1980 and 2004.
Source: Román & Schippers (2007)

reached the stage in their life course at which children cannot be expected to call upon mother's presence continuously. Framed in the language of rational choice theory: after a certain age children are no longer a restriction on their mother's labour market participation. But all the same those mothers do not opt for working more hours. Women of consecutive cohorts show hardly any differences at this point. It looks like for many women a parttime job serves like "a warm, comfortable coat" that is not taken off easily or only reluctantly. Not only do women lack the desire to change their parttime job for a fulltime job (again); so far within the Dutch welfare state there was no necessity to do so either: breadwinners' incomes sufficed to pay for all necessary family expenditures. In many families women's incomes can be used for additional expenditures: the cream on the cake.

With respect to parttime work the situation in the Netherlands is quite different from the situation in most European countries (see Fig. 7.6). There is no other country where mothers on average work so little hours as in the Netherlands. However, also women without children work about 1 day a week less than their European "sisters".

In some European countries having a parttime job is a kind of second best solution for those who cannot find a "proper", fulltime job. This is, however not the case in the Netherlands. Parttime work in the Netherlands is the "first best" choice that highly corresponds to women's preferences. This is illustrated by the answers to the question with respect to the preferred number of weekly work hours. Only a small minority of women aspires to a fulltime job (see Table 7.1). Many women work parttime and are satisfied with that (apart from the fact that some of them would prefer to work half a day more or half a day less). Men show much more unfulfilled preferences for a parttime job. A large group of male fulltime workers would actually prefer a parttime job. Research also shows, however that only a small share of men with

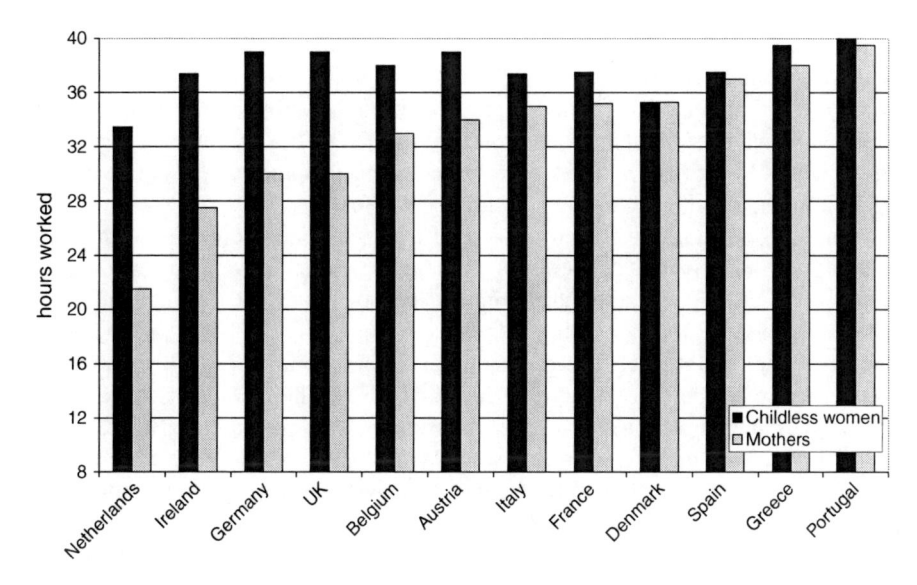

Fig. 7.6 Average weekly working hours of mothers and childless women between 25 and 54 years old (2001, for some countries the figures refer to earlier years). Source: Van Nimwegen & Beets (2006, p. 120)

Table 7.1 Preferred weekly work hours (% by age group)

	25–34 yr	35–44 yr	45–54 yr	55–64 yr
Men				
25–34 h	15	16	18	28
35+	83	81	78	61
Women				
13–24 h	34	54	50	50
25–34	31	24	32	27
35+	33	13	13	13

Source: OSA-Labour supply panel 2006.

a stated preference for a parttime job practically realises this preference (Baaijens, 2005). And so most men continue to work fulltime, also when they become a father. As a consequence – as we can learn again from the *Emancipatiemonitor 2006* (SCP/CBS, 2006; see for example Fig. 5.9 at p. 135) – also in the year 2006 a skew distribution of care tasks between partners continues to exist.

When we compare Dutch women's weekly work hours with those of women from other EU Member States the conclusion seems obvious that the extent to which women in the Netherlands are actively participating in the labour market should hardly be considered an obstacle for the opportunities to become a mother and raise a family. Dutch women work massively in parttime jobs and they adapt their labour market career to their family career. Culturally the ideology of mother-hood is the dominating force. The idea is still firmly rooted in society, including in many women's head, that a woman's life is incomplete without children. And if – as a woman; for men it is a completely different thing – you have a child in the first place you have to be a good mother. As a consequence many women like to keep a large share of the care for and the raising of their children in their own hands. Of course, growing numbers of women cherish the aspiration to be a good and successful professional in the labour market too. But when the activities and obligations in the two domains of life, labour and care, are in each other's way most women still give priority to their caring tasks. So, if already Dutch women would not be able to opt for motherhood, which women in Europe would?

One may conclude that even at the end of the first decade of the twenty-first century children in the Netherlands put a firm restriction on women's labour market activities. Especially the crumbled school hours and opening hours of daycare facilities that show a big lack of uniformity (SCP, 2006a) appear to be a major obstacle. Moreover, daycare and after school facilities suffer from a rather unfavourable image: parents have their doubts about the quality of daycare and many of them complain about the lack of flexibility (see for example SCP, 2006b). The decline over the life course of work hours for women *without* children and the fact that the number of work hours of mothers does not increase after their children have entered their teens reveals that children are not the only factors that can (for a limited period in life) explain Dutch women's relatively low number of work hours. There are also other determinants involved, like a strong commitment to motherhood and the family.

Economics of the Family

This way of reasoning is completely in line with the ideas of Nobel Prize winning economist Gary Becker (1981). He argues that rational individuals balance costs and benefits of their decisions, be it in the supermarket, be it on educational choices or be it on raising a family. Children present benefits as they give you love, as young children they may be cute, as grown ups they may support you (with care or financially) and they offer you an opportunity to pass on your genes and ideas. Undoubtedly there are also costs involved: raising children takes time and money.

Looking at what has happened over the years with these costs and benefits one can notice several trends. A first one is that the potential benefits have fallen. The role of grown up children in parents' late life has declined. Contrary to the situation in pre-welfare state society old parents do not have to depend on their children for their physical survival any more. Or – as an old Dutch grandmother put it in the 1960s – "since the introduction of the old age state pension in 1956 I can choose to live where I want in stead of being passed on from one child to another every 4 weeks. Now I can pay for my own living and housing." Of course, children may be important from a social and psychological point of view, but in well developed welfare states of the social democratic type (Esping-Andersen, 1990) there is a growing number of arrangements that may replace family members in this area too.

As better health care has resulted in higher survival rates for new born babies there is no need any longer to have large numbers of children to secure the survival of at least a few of them. This also implies that as a woman you do not have to spend your complete fertile period in life on being pregnant and having babies, but that there is room for other activities during this period.

Next to these trends on the benefit side of the balance there is one major trend on the costs side and that is the increase of women's wage levels. Due to increasing education or (as economists like to put it) human capital investments women's opportunities to earn an income in the labour market have increased dramatically. Their time has become so costly that they will spend only a small part of it on housework and raising a family. For the rest of their time they have "more rewarding" things to do. This argument could, when we still follow the path set out by Becker, also explain why high educated women more often choose to have only one child or no children at all and low educated women more often have more children.

Of course, this typically economic way of arguing – and some even consider it a typically male way – has been criticised in several ways. Some criticise the way "human values" are reduced to simple costs and benefits, others doubt the concept of rational economic (wo)man and still others think there is much more involved in terms of feelings, hormones and values than Becker (and his adherents) are inclined to incorporate in their models. Still, the fact remains that the relatively simple economic model performs rather well in explaining the major long term trends regarding demographic behaviour.

The Rationality of "Late" Parenthood

From the perspective of individual women or couples who desire to have children there seem to exist mainly considerations (be they implicit or explicit) not to start the process of family formation too early in life. To start with, the length of the period of young adulthood has increased over the years (see also SZW, 2002). In many cases there is no need to take up "the responsibilities of adulthood": when one is young, the world offers a variety of things and places to be discovered and a lot of things to be experienced. Why exclude options in life when this is not necessary (yet)? An important drive behind this development is the ever increasing educational level of consecutive cohorts of young people, which as such has resulted in the postponement in the average age at which they leave the educational system and enter "the grown up" world. On average today's school leavers enter the labour market at a later age than those of a quarter or half a century ago. Besides, most recent cohorts know the way of the world: having grown up with television and the internet they are well aware of all options in life (concerning places to go, films to be seen, books to be read, goods to be bought, parties to go to, etc.). Moreover, they have grown up in an era in which they have learned that opportunities are there to be taken and chances to be seized. Personal development has become a major maxim for those who have completed initial education. Growing welfare offers many young people the opportunities to realise part of these personal ambitions while they are still participating in education. For many of them the theme of the first part of their labour market career is to earn money to realise the rest of these ambitions. But of course, all these things not only take money, but also time. As a consequence other "things to be done" and other choices – especially difficult ones like those with respect to entering a lasting bond with a partner and creating and taking the responsibility for new life – are pushed away into the future.

In many cases women in their (late) 20s report that they do not have a well-established relationship (yet) and/or do not confide in entering the process of family formation with their current partner (Esveldt et al., 2001). Earlier we mentioned the limited role many men (do and want to) play when it comes to care. Many women, and especially high educated women, are fervent adherents of equally, i.e. on a 50/50-base, sharing care tasks with their male partners (Schippers, 2006). Moreover at an individual level twenty-first century babies in Western societies are no longer a necessary guarantee for parents' survival in later life (see also the box on "Economics of the family"); it is not *your* kids that are responsible to provide for *you* when you are old and can no longer earn a living by yourself. This respon-sibility has been "outsourced" to the welfare state. Getting/raising a child – and this is closely connected with the "personal development argument" presented before – seems to have become more and more of an experience (if not an event) on the list that should be completed to reap the fruits of modern life as much as possible. In that case, however, one single child suffices and the timing of this "experience" is of less concern. Economists might say that in stead of an "investment good" children have developed more and more into a "consumer good". This last development is also reflected in the fact that many parents are no longer satisfied with a child or children as such, but that it matters very much to them that the children are "nice" and "attractive", i.e. that they are "high-quality" kids[1] – like you are talking about a car or a tv-set!

Also from the perspective of having a career for many women getting your chil-dren at a later age seems more attractive than having your children during an earlier stage of the life course. A woman who has her first child when she is in her early 20s starts the process of family formation during a career stage when the career dies have not been cast yet. Reducing work hours or interrupting the career at that stage might easily give way to the employer's perception of the woman as being less committed and less career oriented than when she postpones the process of family formation for a while. As a – also theoretically well-founded – consequence organisations may conclude that it will not be very rewarding to invest in these rel-atively young mothers (for instance in terms of training, management development

---

[1] From the perspective that "high-quality" children cost extra money this might constitute an argument by itself to enter the process of family formation only after one has settled financially.

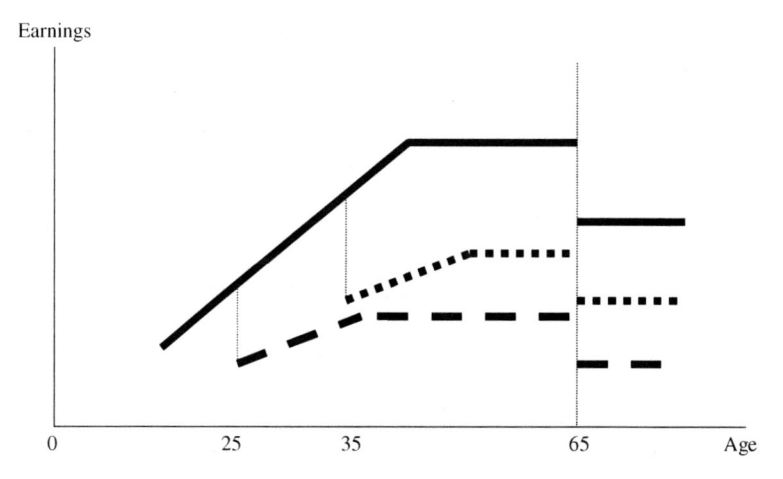

Fig. 7.7 Lifetime earnings and the "timing" of the first child

etc.). Women who actively show commitment during the early stages of their job career and put their heart and soul into their work build up a strong position within the organisation. When in time they eventually decide in favour of motherhood, the employer has invested so much in them and they have become important enough for the organisation that it is in the employer's interest to have them back at work after the period of pregnancy and maternity leave. So, it is not by coincidence that employers are particularly willing to invest in arrangements and facilities for high educated professional women to help them reconcile work and family life (Remery et al., 2002). Staff members that are difficult to replace are one up in this respect compared to those who come ten a penny. However, this one up has to be earned first.

Figure 7.7 presents a stylized image of these different career paths. The continuous line belongs to a career without children or a career that is at least not influenced by the presence of children (like we usually find for men). The large-dotted line represents early motherhood and the small-dotted line represents relatively late motherhood. In both cases we hypothesize that women will continue to work part-time after the birth of their first child. A woman who has established a firm bridgehead with her employer experiences far less "damage" in terms of lifetime earnings (i.e. the total amount of earnings throughout the life course) of a (partial) career interruption than those women who do not hold such a bridgehead yet. So, for women who want to combine a career in paid employment with a career in motherhood it pays not to start the process of family formation too early.

It has to be noticed that this argument leans heavily on the prevailing career system in most organisations. Main characteristics of this system are that you make your way up in the organisation between the age of 25 and the age of 40 or 45, at the age of 45 your career has to be home and dry, because afterwards you are not likely to make major career steps. During this crucial part of the work life – often also crucial from the perspective of family formation – the sheep will be separated from the goats. He or – often – she who has not got ahead before the age of 40 will – notwithstanding the favourable exceptions – hardly be able to do so anymore. The (economic) argument brought forward by organisations is simple: the closer employees get to their (actual) retirement age the shorter the pay-off period of and thereby the lower the return on any investment in the employee's career. So, decisions to invest in workers will usually be in favour of those who are in their 20s or 30s and at a disadvantage of those who are already in their 40s or even older. A similar line of reasoning is often brought forward to explain why it is much less likely for part-timers to get ahead than for full-time workers.

Empirical studies by Mertens (1998) and Bloemen and Kalwij (2001) show that the higher women's educational level the more likely that they choose a later moment in life to be a mother for the first time. According to Bloemen and Kalwij this postponement does not affect women's total fertility rate; in the end they realise their desired number of children and achieve – at least from their own individual perspective – "the best of both worlds": a successful professional career and a successful career in motherhood.[2]

Opposed to this triplet of arguments – more opportunities for individual development, a bigger chance of having found "Mister Right" and a better chance of having your career going and achieving a higher lifetime income – that point into the direction of "let's wait a while with having kids", there is usually just one single argument against postponement of motherhood and that concerns the risk that postponement might increase the risk of not getting pregnant, not getting pregnant right away or of any complications around pregnancy and birth. First, not all women may be aware of these risks and if they are aware it is not unlikely that these risks are widely underestimated when it comes to translating them into *personal risks*. "Of course, these things happen, but how big are in the end the odds that it will happen to me?" is a natural reaction of many women. Besides, many women (and men) of consecutive generations have – stimulated by a strong media focus on new "inventions" on the frontier of medical science – developed a rock-solid confidence in possible solutions offered by medical technology in case of any future problems.

So, if the benefits are legion and the perceived costs only limited, from an individual perspective the choice for late motherhood or parenthood can be considered a rational one.

The Government: Mother's Little Helper?

As mentioned in the introduction European governments are heavily committed to stimulate women's labour market participation and increase women's labour supply.

---

[2]Bloemen and Kalwij (2001) underline the importance of taking account of the (large) variation in women's preferences in the analyses. Disregarding this variation results in an overestimation of the effect of the restrictions and of the possibilities to change individual behaviour by way of the price mechanism.

Increased labour supply is a remedy against future labour market shortages resulting from the ageing and dejuvenation of the labour force. It also contributes to a firm financial base and the affordibility of the welfare state (all women engaged in paid work contribute to the nation's tax base). It safeguards the returns to investments in women's education (which these days in many EU-Member States tend to be equally high for women and for men) and it contributes to equal opportunities for women and for men in society. Ever since the establishment of the EU and its predecessors the latter goal has been a key one in European cooperation.

From this perspective promoting (early) motherhood does not sound as the logical thing to do for the Dutch government; doing so it would only make things difficult for itself. Earlier born or more children do not contribute to the increase in labour supply that is necessary to counter the outflow of older workers during the next 2 decades. On the contrary, as mothers reduce their participation or at least their work hours an increase in birth rates would *reduce* labour supply during the next decades. When this new "green wave" would enter the labour market from about 2025 these "new recruits" would be too late from the perspective of ageing labour markets. In stead, they would again challenge the equilibrium that is expected for the period after the baby boom generation has left the labour market. In the meantime they would add to and complicate labour market and welfare state problems with additional claims on the work force and government budgets for childcare and education. Finally, even those who fear a decline of the original European population (whatever that may be!) do not have to worry: total fertility rates for the post war birth cohorts of women amount to 1.6 or 1.9 in many countries, which is not dramatically below the replacement level. So, also from this perspective there is no justification for a government to call upon women to increase their "reproductive activity rate".

But even if a national government would like to, it can hardly change individual women's or couples' cost-benefit analysis as described earlier in this chapter. Of course, by way of media campaigns the government may expressly point to the possible risks of the postponement of motherhood, just like the government frequently warns against smoking, against not wearing one's seat belts, against the combination of drinking and driving. Usually these campaigns have only limited and temporary success and often they drown in the everyday stream of news, commercials and the "noise of daily life". And of course, the government might – and should – start a discussion with social partners about the (de)merits of the prevailing career system and point to the fact that due to the extension of the life course more people reach the age of 65 in good health. As a consequence employees of 40 years old still have a quarter of a century ahead in their paid career. So, investing in training and management development of individuals who are in their 40s may be rewarding after all (see e.g. Sap & Schippers, 2005). If this form of "social innovation" finds any response, its effects will only become manifest in the long run. Even though it may take a while before changes in this field may in the end result in behavioural changes of individual women and men. Thus, even though the government should not leave aside these opportunities, it would be a mistake to expect too much from this type of intervention.

A similar warning is in order when it comes to "dealing with" problematic school hours, which currently are a major obstacle for many Dutch women to take any more than just a small part-time job. Of course, these problems should be solved and examples from other EU-Member States show that they can be solved successfully, i.e. to the advantage of both the children and the parents *and* the national economy that may benefit from higher activity rates. There is even evidence that better facilities could boost birth rates, but this does not seem to be a lasting effect as it effects mainly the timing of children and not the number.

Even if the government would set all signals at clear and even if it would invest heavily in arrangements to facilitate the combination of care for children and paid work – which is absolute necessary, looking from the perspective of emancipation and equal opportunities for women and men – there is no ground for the assumption that women would spontaneously get their children earlier or that women would have more children. A government that is to play this card, is likely to be disappointed. In this respect modern citizens, including modern, emancipated women do not want the law to be laid down on them – and the government rightfully supports this independent attitude – nor do they fall automatically for financial incentives. The maximum the government seems to be able to achieve is to facilitate the reconciliation of work and family life to such an extent that a further increase in the age at which women get their first child will be prevented. Even though this can not be empirically founded (yet) it seems that the (potential) father may be one of the spearheads of policy, even though many women do not have very high hopes of men when it comes to realising better opportunities to combine work and family life. Many women – we have mentioned it before (see also SCP/CBS, 2006, p. 135) – are in favour of equally sharing care tasks. The more men are prepared to share these tasks, the less women will feel to be the only one responsible for the combination of paid work and unpaid care. "Attachment leave" for fathers, at the end of the mother's maternity leave (which itself has to last at least as long as the mother feels healthy and capable to go back to work again), may be a first step as it helps her to resume her professional activities with an easy mind ("the father is watching our little one"). Reconsidering and developing "smart" variations of the so-called combination scenario that has been developed in the Netherlands during the 1990s (SZW, 1995) and the "two times three quarters model" of the National Committee on Equal Opportunities (Emancipatieraad, 1996) seem to be necessary and logical sequel steps.

References

Baaijens, C. (2005). *Arbeidstijden: tussen wens en werkelijkheid*. Utrecht: Dissertatie Universiteit Utrecht.

Becker, G.S. (1981). *A Treatise on the Family*. Cambridge, MA: Harvard University Press.

Bloemen, H.G., & Kalwij, A. (2001). Female labor market transitions and the timing of births: a simultaneous analysis of the effects of schooling. *Labour Economics*, 8, 593–620.

CPB (2006). *Reinventing the Welfare State*. Den Haag: Centraal Planbureau.

Den Dulk, L. (2001). *Work-Family Arrangerments in Organisations. A Cross-National Study in the Netherlands, Italy, the United Kingdom and Sweden.* Amsterdam: Rozenberg Publishers.

Emancipatieraad. (1996). *Met zorg naar nieuwe zekerheid.* Den Haag: Emancipatieraad.

Esping-Andersen, G. (1990). *The Three Worlds of Welfare Capitalism.* Cambridge: Polity Press.

Esveldt, I., Beets, G., Henkens, A.K., Liefbroer, A.C., & Moors, H. (2001). Meningen en opvattingen van de bevolking over aspecten van het bevolkingsvraagstuk 1983–2000. Rapport no. 62. Den Haag: Nederlands Interdisciplinair Demografisch Instituut.

Mertens, E.H.M. (1998). *Loopbaanonderbrekingen en kinderen: gevolgen voor de beloning van vrouwen.* Utrecht: Dissertatie Universiteit Utrecht.

Remery, C., Doorne-Huiskes, A.van, & Schippers, J.J. (2002). *Zorg als arbeidsmarktgegeven: werkgevers aan zet.* Publicatie A188. Tilburg: Organisatie voor Strategisch Arbeidsmarktonderzoek.

Román, A.A., & Schippers, J.J. (2007). *Vrouwen, gezinnen en werk: een cohortbenadering van de arbeidsparticipatie in Nederland.* Tilburg: Organisatie voor Strategisch Arbeidsmarktonderzoek.

Sap, J., & Schippers, J.J. (2005). Moderne levenslopen bieden kans voor doorbreken van m/v-beroepensegregatie. In H. Galesloot (Red.), *De glazen muur* (25–32). Den Haag: Ministerie van Sociale Zaken en Werkgelegenheid.

Schippers, J.J. (2006). We willen werk en zorgtaken gelijk delen. SiS, 2 (3), maart 2006, 52.

SCP (2006a). *Tijd voor de basisschool. Factsheet ten behoeve van de* invitational conference 'Tijd voor school 2006' *op 31 mei 2006.* Den Haag: Sociaal en Cultureel Planbureau.

SCP (2006b). *Hoe werkt het met kinderen?* Den Haag: Sociaal en Cultureel Planbureau.

SCP/CBS (2006). *Emancipatiemonitor 2006.* Den Haag: SCP/CBS.

SZW (1995). *Onbetaalde zorg gelijk verdeeld. Toekomstscenario's voor herverdeling van onbetaalde zorgarbeid.* Den Haag: Commissie Toekomstscenario's Herverdeling Onbetaalde Arbeid.

SZW (2002). *Verkenning Levensloop. Beleidsopties voor leren, werken, zorgen en wonen.* Den Haag: Ministerie van Sociale Zaken en Werkgelegenheid.

Van Nimwegen, N., & Beets, G. (Eds.). (2006). *Social Situation Observatory Demographic Monitor 2005, Demographic Trends and Policy Implications in the European Union* (355 pp). NIDI Report #72. The Hague, Netherlands Interdisciplinary Demographic Institute.

Chapter 8
The Complexity of Parenthood
in Modern Societies

Anneke van Doorne-Huiskes and Ingrid Doorten

Introduction

This chapter describes the complexity of parenthood in modern societies, with a special focus on motherhood. The question is raised whether the institutional structure of welfare states can help to simplify modern parenthood, specifically from the perspective of reconciliation between work and family life. Is it true that institutions and social policies matter in the way young couples shape and experience their parenthood in combination with their paid work? And if so, what does that mean for the social conditions and for the cultural meaning and significance of parenthood and motherhood in the near future?

Main focus of this chapter is the question how young couples design and experience motherhood and fatherhood within the context of their societies. Countries included in this chapter are: United Kingdom (UK), France, Norway, Sweden, Netherlands, Portugal, Slovenia and Bulgaria.[1]

In order to clarify the national contexts in which these young parents live, Section 2 of this chapter describes briefly the basic ideas of social policies that support the reconciliation of work and family life in the different countries to a more or lesser degree. This will be done in view of five types of welfare state regimes: the social democratic regime, the conservative corporatist regime, the Mediterranean regime, the liberal regime and the post-communist regime. To get an idea how much room there is, so to speak, for having children in the various countries, Section 3 explores whether and to what extent these models of social policies at the national level are related with fertility rates. As the division of paid and domestic work between parents could also be considered as an indicator – specifically for women – to what degree motherhood is possible in a country, more general figures on this division will be presented.

A. van Doorne-Huiskes (✉)
Emeritus Professor of Sociology, Utrecht University, Utrecht, The Netherlands
e-mail: doorne.huiskes@wxs.nl

[1] This chapter is partly based on the research project TRANSITIONS: Gender, Parenthood and the Changing European Workplace, funded by the European Union carried out in 8 European countries between 2003 and 2006.

G. Beets et al. (eds.), *The Future of Motherhood in Western Societies*,
DOI 10.1007/978-90-481-8969-4_8, © Springer Science+Business Media B.V. 2011

Section 4 attempts to answer the question whether there are differences in the cultural meaning of motherhood in the European countries. How is motherhood culturally framed in the various countries? Have cultural ideas with respect to motherhood changed? How does the cultural meaning of motherhood relate to the demands on women telling them that they need to be economically independent? In Section 5 we focus on young couples. What are their most important concerns in designing parenthood? How do they manage the different and often contradictory demands in relation to economic and caring responsibilities? Is there space for parenthood and – more in particular – for motherhood in modern societies and what price has to be paid for that? Section 6, finally summarises what has been said so far and elaborates on possible consequences of this analysis for the conditions of satisfying motherhood and parenthood in modern societies.

Various Types of European Welfare Regimes

Welfare state regimes offer a general framework and a starting point for analysing the differences and similarities in institutional contexts that affect the work/family strategies of working parents. The term "regime" refers to the typical ways in which the provision of welfare is allocated between the state, the market and the family (Esping-Andersen, 1990, 1999). It acknowledges that one should consider the broader country-specific packages of work/family policies rather than the impact of one specific policy (Blossfeld & Drobnič, 2001). In addition, a broader framework takes into account that it is not only policy measures that matter, but also the dominant political ideology, preferences and labour market conditions. Based on the typology proposed by Esping-Andersen (1990, 1999), and following Blossfeld & Drobnič (2001), five welfare state regimes are distinguished: the social democratic welfare state regime, the liberal regime, the conservative corporatist regime, the Mediterranean regime and the post-communist regime.

The Social Democratic Welfare State Regime

The social democratic regime is characterised by an elaborate system of public work/family policies that makes the combination of work and family life less difficult to manage. The Nordic countries represent this type of welfare state. Public work/family policies have a long tradition in these countries. One of the objectives of Swedish family policies since the 1930s has been to create equality between men and women. However, up to the 1960s, family policy was dominated by a family ideal based on complementary gender roles of equal value rather than equal roles (Näsman, 1999). Women were supposed to be responsible for looking after the home and children, whereas men's primary responsibility was to support the family. In the 1960s, these ideas and cultural prescriptions changed. Men and women got equal rights as citizens, employees, partners and parents (Näsman, 1999). As a result of these cultural changes from the 1970s onwards, universal services, for example a substantial public day care system, support the employment of working parents. In Sweden the tax system is individualized since 1971. The state is seen as the main provider of welfare; private welfare provision is almost non-existent. Women in particular tend to work in public services. Within Europe, Sweden, Denmark, Norway and Finland come nearest to this particular welfare state regime. All have a high level of publicly funded child care services. In addition, parents pay relatively little for child care in these countries (e.g. Den Dulk & Van Doorne-Huiskes, 2007) and professional care is seen as beneficial for children (Kremer, 2005). Substantial public child care provisions are combined with relatively long paid leaves. Sweden was the first country in Europe to introduce parental leave for both mothers and fathers.

The Conservative Corporatist Welfare State Regime

Compulsory social insurance and fragmented occupational schemes, which means only available for specific categories of workers, for instance with permanent contracts – used to be important features of the conservative welfare state regime. In contrast to the social democratic regime, social policy is less individualized. Germany, Austria, the Netherlands, France and Belgium represent this type of welfare state regime. The Netherlands has long been characterised by the family as norm and the principle of maintenance (Sainsbury, 1996). Up until far in the 1980s, men were supposed to maintain their families, women's first – and for long time only – responsibility was to take care of the home and children. All social policies, as developed in the 1950s and 1960s, were based on this traditional division of men's and women's roles in society. Times are changing, however. Recent research on social exclusion in Europe (Soede & Vrooman, 2008) classifies the Netherlands as a hybrid type of welfare state, in between the social democrat and corporatist welfare state regime. In Germany also, views on traditional gender roles slowly changed. It was in the 1980s that the whole issue of work and family life as a subject of public and political debate came on the agenda. A late response to the challenges of the traditional woman's role, brought into focus by the women's movement of the 1970s, as Erler (1999) concludes.

France and Belgium are ambiguous cases in this cluster of conservative welfare states. Both countries have extensive child care and pre-school facilities. Germany and the Netherlands place much more emphasis on the role of parental care (Anttonen & Sipilä, 1996; Kremer, 2005). Here, large numbers of women work part-time in order to combine work and child care. In Germany, 85% of all eligible households take up their parental leave, mainly the women (only 5% of fathers take up leave). In the Netherlands, take-up of parental leave is much lower: 27% of parents (42% of mothers and 16% of fathers) (Plantenga & Remery, 2005).

Mediterranean Regime

Southern European countries have fewer public provisions, but they also do not support the breadwinner family model with tax disincentives to women's paid employment, as is the case in countries like Austria, Germany and the Netherlands (in the latter case until 2001) (Esping-Andersen, 1999). An interesting point regarding policy attention for families is brought up by Trifiletti (1999). Italy, she argues, has a certain cultural inertia that creates a great unwillingness to make the family subject of a political debate and policy decisions. Memories of family policies of the totalitarian regime during the Second World War have long been uncomfortable close. It was preferable, so to speak, to consider families as private affairs, whose problems could and should be solved privately. Interventions in "normal" families were considered as not desirable. Civil law imposed heavy responsibilities on families to solve problems of maintaining and caring of all family members (Trifiletti, 1999). This ideology went long together with a traditional pattern of gender roles and with a relatively high number of children per family. The decline in fertility rates in the Southern European countries only started at the 1980s.

The Liberal Welfare State Regime

Compared to the social democratic and post-communist regimes, both liberal and conservative regimes take a minimalist approach to public work/family policies, but for different reasons. In a liberal welfare state regime, government involvement and national regulations are limited and the development of work/family arrangements is left to market forces.

Caring for children is still primarily seen as a private responsibility of the parents. State intervention is focussed on children with special needs. Lack of public child care facilities forces women to organise private child care via the market – specifically the higher educated women – or all sorts of informal care provided by family members, which was and is often the way lower educated women cope with the challenge of combining work and domestic responsibilities.

Post-communist Welfare State Regime

Like the social democratic regime, the post-communist regime is typified by a broad range of public policies that support the combination of paid work and care for children. Under state socialism, women's labour market participation rate was high and the common employment pattern was based on a family model of two full-time earners (Blossfeld & Drobnič, 2001). However, the issue of gender equality at home – that is, the equal division of housework and care tasks – was not acknowledged or debated as in the social democratic regime (Kocourková, 2002). Diefenbach (2003) analysed gender role orientation in various OECD countries (using 1994 ISSP data) based on the respondents' agreement or disagreement with the statement "a man's job is to earn money; a woman's job is to look after the home and family". An egalitarian gender role orientation (i.e. strong disagreement with the statement) was found in countries such as Sweden, Norway, East Germany and the Netherlands. In Eastern Europe, in contrast, the response was highly traditional.

After the transition to the market economy, state provisions declined but are still substantial compared, for instance, to the liberal or conservative regimes. Generally, post-communist countries such as Poland, Slovenia, Czech Republic, Bulgaria and

Hungary witnessed a decline in child care services and wage compensation for leave arrangements. However, parental leave provisions are still considerable and vary from 1 year in Slovenia to 3 years in, for instance, Hungary and the Czech Republic.

To Conclude

One of the most remarkable findings so far, is the – in comparison to other European countries – early start of the principle of equality in gender relations in the Nordic countries. Already in the 1970s, it became common knowledge that men as well as women were badly needed to maintain and extent the welfare state. The implications of this fact were politically accepted and considered as taken-for-granted: the state is highly responsible for creating opportunities to combine work and family life. This is particularly so, because having children was considered to be very desirable as well, if only for having people who could help to maintain the welfare state in the future. The legacy of this culture of gender equality is well known. One could conclude, that the Nordic countries offer the most favourable conditions for modern parenthood in Europe.

Not everybody, however, does agree with that view (see also the Chapter 12 by Hakim elsewhere in this book). In the Netherlands, for instance, many politicians and policy makers point out the disadvantages of expansive welfare state arrangements that require full-time labour market participation of both men and women to survive. A culture of part-time working women, as is very common in the Netherlands, growing in Belgium and to a lesser degree in Germany, would give more space to those parents who prefer to take care of their children – primarily – themselves. Working part-time by one of the parents might be advantageous for caring children. Parents, mostly the mothers, are at home at a regular base and children can – at least for part of the week – grow up in a familiar environment. Of course, this arrangement has disadvantages as well, specifically for women. Women give up parts of their income and with their incomes often also a perspective on an interesting career. Not all women are willing to pay those high opportunity costs for having children. We will return to this point below.

In the Eastern European countries, public provisions for child care were a common part of the institutional structure. Almost all women had full-time jobs under the communist regimes. As said before, after the transition to the market economy, state provisions declined but are still substantial compared, for instance, to the liberal or conservative regimes. But because domestic work was and still is so unevenly divided between women and men, women seem to be overburdened with full-time jobs and a great share of the work at home. This situation undoubtedly will have consequences for the space and timing of motherhood.

It seems most likely that institutional arrangements at the level of society have an impact on what men and women consider to be personal decisions: the decision of having children or not, at what moment in their life course and how many children they wish. Is it true that this impact is expressed in the fertility rates of the European countries and in the way paid and domestic work between men and women are divided? We turn to this question in the next section.

Fertility Rates and the Division of Paid and Domestic Work between Women and Men in European Countries

In the European Union, the average total fertility rate is currently around 1.5 children per woman. Rather significant differences are observed in total fertility rates between European countries and the clusters of countries that represent the above-mentioned welfare state regimes. In the Nordic countries, the total fertility rate is relatively high: about 1.8. In Finland the total fertility rate of 1.8 (in 2005) has remained more or less at the same level for the past 15 years. The average age of first mothers has risen to 28 years (Taipale & Hirvonen, 2006).

The picture of the conservative welfare states is rather inconsistent. Germany and Austria show the lowest birth rates. In Germany, this fertility rate has declined rapidly over the last five decades. Since 1975, the fertility fluctuates within a range of 1.2 and 1.4, with – as everywhere in Europe – a rising mean age of women at the birth of their first child to currently 29 years (Beham et al., 2006). Interestingly in this respect is the measure implemented by the German government in 2007 to financially compensate women or men who stay at home during the first year of their child. This compensation is linked with the level of earnings and could reach a maximum of 1,800 euros per month. In Germany, it is often higher educated women who decide not to have children because of too high opportunity costs in terms of career. This new policy could be seen as specifically targeted at this group, to seduce them – so to speak – taking time for getting children.

France, as part of the conservative welfare state regime, shows a relatively high fertility rate. This is probably due to a long tradition of pronatalist policies in France, including financial compensations and good and comprehensive facilities for child care.

In the UK and Ireland, as representatives of liberal welfare state regimes, the fertility rates are rather high in comparison to a number of other European countries. The Irish figures could be interpreted as a legacy from a still recent Roman-Catholic past. It appears that the UK total fertility rate is relatively high, with currently an average number of 1.8 children per woman in England and Wales (Lewis & Purcell, 2006). These researchers suggest the possibility that government policy to promote gender equality and retain human capital by facilitating combining work with parenthood, may be encouraging more births (Lewis & Purcell, 2006). And, likely, also the continuous economic growth in the UK during recent years encouraged people to have (more) children.

Southern European countries show more or less consistent patterns in their total (period) fertility rates: a rather recent but unmistakably low number of children per woman. Looking in more detail at Portugal, Das Dores Guerreiro & Rodrigues (2006) suggest this low fertility rate being an indicator of changes in family relations, changes in cultural values, a rapid rise in the level of education of Portuguese women and their increasing entrance into the labour force.

Also in the post-communist societies, the pictures are clear and consistent: low total fertility rates, but different from other European countries still a relatively low, although rising average age of the mother when having her first child. In Bulgaria for instance, this average age is 24.8 years in 2005 (Kovacheva et al., 2006). The researchers speculate whether the decrease of birth rates in Bulgaria may have to do with avoiding the birth of a second or subsequent child and thus showing a transition to a one-child family model. However, the decrease of birth rates is most likely also related to the rising age at first birth, which causes a bust in the number of first births during the period of postponement, and consequently also in the number of higher order births (see the Chapter 6 by Beets elsewhere in this book).

Summarising these findings, a relation – but not a very consistent one however – could be assumed between family friendly policies in countries and the average number of children women have. Having said this, the most striking conclusion so far is perhaps the general low fertility rate in whole Europe, well below replacement level as noticed before. It is likely that this social phenomenon of declining birth rates during the last decades is caused by general changes in economy and culture: growing economies, more prosperity, rising educational levels and an increasing labour force participation of women, processes of individualisation and a growing wish to enjoy life and personal freedom. But countries differ and family friendly policies could make a difference when deciding about (when) having children or not. In its *Five ways to defuse the demographic time bomb*, the European Commission (2006) sets out five areas for concrete actions to help Member States adapt to demographic change in their own national context. One of these action areas is helping people to balance work, family and private life, so that potential parents can have the number of children they desire.

Observing the different fertility rates in European countries and linking them to different systems of family policies, it seems possible to extend the room for parenthood and more specifically for motherhood, in most countries. It is rather unlikely, however, that this will lead us to a fertility rate above the replacement level of 2.1 children per woman. With regard to this, it is interesting to note, in a Swedish National Report on Socio-Economic Trends and Welfare Policies (Lane et al., 2006), the two decisive variables for making a decision about starting a family: having a stable job on the labour market, and finding a suitable partner. Specifically the partner is an important condition (see also RVZ, 2007; E-Quality, 2008). A suitable partner to start a family with, is not simply a man (or a woman) who is able to pay for the kids and maintain them, but increasingly so a man (or a woman) who is willing to share all the costs of raising a child. Not just economic costs, to be clear, but all social costs associated with caring duties and households. Specifying these costs in gainful and domestic work and raising the question who does what, it seems that these costs are still rather unevenly divided between women and men in Europe. Table 8.1 shows some – rough – figures.

As it is a well-known fact that gender inequality in the division of paid and domestic work increase when people have children, it is worthwhile having a closer

Table 8.1 Gainful and domestic work of parents living as a couple with youngest child aged up to 6, in hours and minutes per day and in percentages of total time (1998–2002)

	Women		Men	
	Gainful work	Domestic work	Gainful work	Domestic work
Social democratic regime				
Finland	2.14 (27)	6.05 (73)	5.15 (65)	2.48 (35)
Norway	2.15 (29)	5.26 (71)	4.47 (60)	3.12 (40)
Sweden	2.17 (29)	5.29 (71)	4.53 (59)	3.21 (41)
Conservative regime				
France	2.13 (28)	5.49 (72)	4.55 (66)	2.30 (34)
Belgium	2.38 (33)	5.27 (67)	4.47 (62)	2.57 (38)
Germany	1.12 (16)	6.11 (84)	4.32 (60)	3.00 (40)
Liberal regime				
United Kingdom	2.00 (25)	6.09 (75)	5.33 (67)	2.46 (33)
Post-communist regime				
Hungary	1.31 (17)	7.33 (83)	4.47 (60)	3.11 (40)
Estonia	2.03 (23)	6.51 (77)	3.32 (63)	2.41 (37)
Slovenia	3.01 (33)	6.15 (67)	5.38 (66)	2.54 (34)

Source: European Commission, Eurostat (2004).

look at data on paid and domestic work by the parents of young children. The presence of small children in families seems to intensify the traditional division of labour (see Table 8.1).

Parents with young children work longer hours. Their total working time per day is between 1 and 2 hours longer than the average for persons aged 20–74. The fact that mothers with young children spend between 70 and 85% of their total working hours on domestic work is particularly relevant. Young mothers see an increase in their total working time, but their share in paid work decreases significantly compared with women in general and compared with men. There is no similar correlation between gainful and domestic work for the fathers. Men maintain their share of paid work, so to speak, even when they have young children. In terms of economics, then, gender inequality increases significantly when children are born. This is true for all the welfare state regimes, although less so in the social democratic model, where women manage to spend almost 30% of their total time on gainful work. The lowest percentages of gainful work for women are in Germany (16%), Hungary (17%) and Estonia (23%).

So, generally speaking, the costs of children – in terms of loss of human capital for paid work and careers – are higher for women than for men. In twenty-first century Europe, with a still rising level of education for many women, the impact of this fact should not be underestimated, when it comes to couples deciding to start a family or not (see the Chapter 7 by Schippers elsewhere in this book). It seems to be a real challenge for European countries, to set up effective conditions that equate the social and economic burden of having children for women and for men and/or to minimize the costs of children for young parents by taking over some of the practicalities.

Cultural Meanings of Motherhood

It is not just the economic perspective which is relevant when it comes to the current ambivalences of motherhood. Motherhood has also a significant cultural meaning. We attempt to answer the question whether there are differences and changes in the cultural meaning of motherhood in various European countries. Motherhood is a multi-layered concept. Motherhood consists of at least a biological dimension, a social dimension, and a symbolic dimension (Knijn & Verheijen, 1991). These dimensions are culturally coloured and have changed over time. Here we focus on the biological and social dimension.

In the 1960s, the biological dimension of motherhood changed significantly with the introduction of the pill in the various European countries. Contraception then became common use and common knowledge in the Western world. The broad practice of contraception has had and continues to have major implications for women (and men) personally and for society as a whole. One implication is that the timing of starting a family has become a clear choice, a choice that – within limits – could be made in an earlier or later stage of life.[2] Another more general social implication of "the pill" might be the idea that the process of fertility could be controlled entirely. Postponement of the choice for starting a family seems to be most common these days throughout Europe, as we have seen in the previous section. Postponement for various reasons, but all reasons have to do with the wish and the necessity for men and women to build up a – more or less – independent economic life before starting to get children. Although this trend was firstly seen among higher educated couples, it has nowadays become more general also among the middle and lower educated women.

Not just the biological dimension of motherhood changed, also the social dimension has been changing during the past century. Within this social dimension, Knijn & Verheijen (1991) distinguish two significant norms, which could and can not easily be ignored. Firstly, in the Western world the ideal mother is seen as the main caretaker of her children: motherhood is *exclusive* motherhood. Although mothers are having paid jobs and for this reason share the care for children with others, exclusive motherhood is the basic assumption for the way in which for instance school times and professional day care are organised, or in some cases were organised recently. And although we might have expected differently, also in Eastern Europe the exclusive norm of motherhood seems to be the leading principle, according to the strong support for the statement "a man's job is to earn money; a woman's job is to look after the home and family" of the Eastern European population (ISSP 1994 data).

Secondly there is a norm of *sensitivity*: we expect a mother to develop a warm and deep relationship with her child. This is also a rather unique development starting in the twentieth century. It is not that mothers in former centuries did not care about their children, but families usually needed to survive all kinds of day to day, often

---

[2] Recent research by Rijken (2009) however shows that the decision making process between partners about the timing of having a child is rather implicit.

poverty related circumstances. In England and France of the seventeenth century for instance, poor mothers in the cities brought their small children to a wet nurse in the countryside in order to go to work. In those days the cultural meaning of children differed much from the meaning we assign to children nowadays. Children were not regarded as being a separate group that needed special attention. As soon as children were able to participate in daily life of adults they were treated like adults. The fact that there were no separate words for the different phases of childhood (Ariès, 1962) is significant in this respect.

De-standardization and the Notion of Individualistic Motherhood

Poverty was for a long time the main reason for women to work outside the home, even in the beginning of the twentieth century. Only rich and bourgeois families could afford mothers who stayed at home. At the same time these women were also *expected* to stay at home. This, nevertheless, was not always what they wanted, leading to the first women's movement by the end of the nineteenth century. During the twentieth century this ideal of women staying at home became the norm for all classes in society. Roughly speaking two phases can be distinguished in the way people shaped their family lifes: one of increasing standardization (1900–1960) and one of *de-standardization* (1960–2000) (Liefbroer & Dykstra, 2001). The model of the traditional breadwinner family dominated only in the 1950s and early 1960s. Since the 1960s, more emphasis has been given to individual freedom and autonomy for mothers, and also to personal development and equality between partners. This ongoing process of emancipation and individualization created increasing room for individual decisions (Liefbroer & Dykstra, 2001; see also Blumstein & Schwartz, 1983; Beck & Beck-Gernsheim, 1995; Lewis, 2001; Jansen, 2002; Raley et al., 2006). Motherhood transformed from "sacrifice" in the 1950s and 1960s and before, to motherhood as "personal development" in the 1980s and beyond (Knijn & Verheijen, 1991). Since the 1980s women are expected to consciously and independently choose whether they want to become mothers or not, and if they are mothers, how they shape their own "motherhood". Not just one form of motherhood is natural or normal, and working outside the home is increasingly accepted for a mother. She however remains the primary responsible person for the children. In this light Knijn & Verheijen distinguish two kinds of mothers: *traditional* mothers and *individualistic* mothers, of which the latter fit the "new motherhood" concept, characterized by personal development and fulfilment. These types of motherhood are related to the social-economic class of women: the higher the educational level and occupational status of the couple, the more likely that women represent an individualistic type of motherhood. This concept of individualistic motherhood may open the way to a new model of fatherhood: fatherhood as personal expression. An interesting model indeed, probably a rather new phenomenon in the history of mankind.

It is plausible that these different models of motherhood are apparent to a more or lesser extent all over European countries, depending on the processes of emancipation and individualization in the specific countries and the level of social-economic development of the population. Hakim (2001) distinguishes five stages in the recent history of emancipation, which might be helpful to clarify the notion and the appearance of the individualistic mother in European societies. These stages are: the contraceptive revolution, from about 1965 onwards; the equal opportunities revolution; the expansion of white collar occupations; the creation of jobs for secondary earners, and finally the increasing importance of personal preferences in the lifestyle choices of affluent modern societies. This fifth stage, the increasing importance of personal preferences seems to be connected with the development of *de-standardisation* or *individualization* of family life, as mentioned above. Hakim states that women are heterogeneous in their preferences and that countries differ to the extent in which women are home-centred (10–30%), adaptive (in combining work and family; 40–80%) or work-centred (10–30%).

Motherhood as a More or Less Joint Collaboration with the Partner

An interesting study on the construction of motherhood comes from the United States. Cowdery & Knudson-Martin (2005) identified, by 50 qualitative interviews among couples with young children, the importance of "motherhood" in the way these couples dealt with care for their children. The 50 interviewed couples were distinguished in so-called *postgender* couples, *gender legacy* couples and *traditional* couples. Postgender couples assume all tasks are shared, gender legacy couples do not cite gender as the basis for their division of responsibilities but operate with so-called hidden gender-base. Traditional couples maintain and advocate a gendered division of labour and consider both gender roles as equal. In their role as parents, these couples seem to create two different models of mothering young children: mothering as a gendered talent and mothering as a conscious collaboration. It is interesting to see how specific processes – in terms of definition of the situation and behaviour based on these definitions – set in motion mechanisms of self fulfilling prophecies that create and continuously confirm two models of motherhood. As the authors observed, some couples believe that mothers have a natural connection with their children and a natural knowledge of how to take care of their children. As a consequence, fathers stepped back and (thus) mothers organised the time around their children and – inevitable – took continual responsibility. The opposite model is interesting as well. When partners assume responsibility for children is shared, they compensate for biological differences, fathers take on tasks without mothers' instructions, fathers are open to learning and mothers do not intervene.

A more or less analogous classification to the Cowdery & Knudson-Martin study has been found on the basis of a large scale quantitative study conducted in the Netherlands (Doorten et al., 2008). These authors distinguish different patterns of dependency in couples with children by comparing the relative share of paid work, the relative share of housework, perceived support on both work decisions and practical matters and the amount of personal friends of both partners. These are

Table 8.2 Logistic regression of outsourcing household work and outsourcing child care on dependency class (unstandardized coefficients)

	Outsourcing household work	Outsourcing child care
Dependency class[a]:		
Peer couples (reference)	−0.722****	−0.983****
Traditional tight couples		
Traditional loose couples	−0.234	−0.888****
Unbalanced couples	−0.557*	−0.918***

[a]Reference category consists of the peer couples.

$* <0.10; **p <0.05; ***p <0.01; ****p <0.001$.

traditional tight couples (54.4%), traditional loose couples (16.5%), unbalanced couples (5.3%) and *peers (23.7%)*. Although the Doorten study focuses on the division of housework and paid work a similarity with the Cowdery & Knudson-Martin study can be found. The cultural importance of motherhood might be closely related to the division of housework. Within this framework the traditional tight couples seem to be very similar to the traditional couples of the Cowdery & Knudson-Martin study and the peers to the so-called post-gender couples. The traditional loose couples and unbalanced couples can be compared to the gender legacy couples. The peer couples in the Doorten study have a much less skewed division of housework than the other couples, the likelihood that men and women share housework tasks is much higher. The peer partners as well as the traditional tight partners are both feeling very supported on both decisions about work and practical matters and are equally happy in their relationships, whereas the women in the traditional loose couples and the men in the unbalanced couples are feeling less support from their partners and are feeling less happy compared to the peer couples. Whether the less skewed division of housework of the peer couples is the result of conscious negotiations is doubted. The more equal division of housework of peer couples is very likely the result of outsourcing housework and child care (significantly more than the other couples, see Table 8.2).

Table 8.2 contains information on outsourcing household work and child care. As can be seen in this table, peer couples (reference category) outsource household work and child care more often than the other couples. Interestingly, the difference between peer couples and traditional loose couples is not significant for household outsourcing. This may indicate that in the traditional loose couples, the man does so little that even though the couple outsources a great deal of the household work, the woman still does considerably more than her partner.

The Context of Childbearing Choices

Fertility behaviour can not be seen outside a context, as we argue in this chapter. Rijken (2009) finds that the quality of family and partner relationships is important for understanding fertility behaviour. People who experienced little conflict between their parents and who had frequent contacts within the larger kinship network when growing up have more children and have them earlier. "Happy families" have a larger number of children. Couples are most likely to have children when their relationship is at least "good enough". However, lots of positive interaction or great satisfaction about one's partner relationship does not form an extra stimulus for having (more) children. Rijken also concludes that couple's decision making resulting in either early or postponed parenthood might generally be characterized as rather implicit, although both partners' consent seems to be very important. Consequently, not only work and care issues and financial incentives are important in childbearing choices. Nevertheless, care and especially work arrangements might improve the quality of relationships in families and couples and thus facilitate the decision to have (more) children.

A study about childlessness (Keizer, 2010) considers employment issues to be a factor in fertility behaviour. It states that ensuring that new mothers can easily return to the labour market is preferable in the light of enhancing fertility rates, and also for mothers' own wellbeing. Unemployment hampers men's transition into parenthood. Longer security of job tenure and the elimination of very short-term contracts might help to increase feelings of security among men and therefore stimulate men to procreate. Thus, providing more occupational security may result in a larger share of personal choice in the decision to have children.

Designing Motherhood and Parenthood in Modern Europe

It is not easy to design parenthood and motherhood in a modern European world. This is shown in the so-called TRANSITIONS project "Gender, Parenthood and the Changing European Workplace" (2003–2006) that aimed to examine how young European working men and women negotiate motherhood and fatherhood and work-family boundaries in the context of different national welfare state regimes, family and employer support (Lewis & Smithson, 2006). Part of this study was a series of biographical interviews conducted with parents who were employees of public and private organisations in seven European countries. We present some illustrations.

Designing parenthood is dependent on where people live and in which country the newborn baby is welcomed. Look at Gro, a Norwegian 36 years old female engineer. Working in a male-dominated profession, earning a high salary, committed to her job. When talking about the decision to have children, she says:

> When you get to my age you have to make a choice. Will we ever? And then I thought "of course I still have many years" but then again, you have to start thinking about it by the age of 35. It was unthinkable that I would never ever want one, had I been 25 I would probably have postponed it. It was actually my husband who brought it up and asked if we'd give it a think. And when I'd thought it for a couple of months . . . we decided.

Gro's husband turns out to be a very committed father. Gro demands equal sharing of child care and domestic work. They are both in higher paid jobs on permanent work contracts, and in spite of it being unusual at her husband's workplace to take extended leave, he nevertheless was supported by his colleagues and managers in his decision (Nilsen & Brannen, 2005).

Alexandra from Portugal, 32 years old and mother of two children, has a degree in business studies. She lived with her parents until she got married, which she and her husband did when both were 25. Her first child was born a year after the wedding. The pregnancy was not planned, but she is happy with this since she would not have liked to have a child late in life. Alexandra had a lot of help and support from her parents when the first child was born, as her mother looked after him during the day. Alexandra's and her husband's income were high enough to have paid help in the house. Her husband does not take much part in either childminding or housework (Nilsen & Brannen, 2005).

Janez, a Slovenian father of 25 years old, does not feel overburdened by fatherhood. He sets a very clear boundary between work and family life. Janez' wife, with the help of her parents, is the main carer. Janez is not a very active father, even though he thinks that family roles are in general becoming more equal. He says:

> Well it is a fact, no matter how much you are trying, the children are still more attached to the mother, at least as far as their needs are concerned. You may jump in it, if you want to. But you have to make an effort. It is true, the majority of men do take the easiest way.

Interesting to see how different models of motherhood and fatherhood are presented in this internationally-comparative study on parenthood. Interesting also to see how societal contexts influence the way parents shape their family life in combination with paid work. For Norwegian couples this seems less complicated than for couples from the UK, from Slovenia or from Portugal. In Slovenia and Portugal however, the help of grandparents is still more or less taken for granted, at least when the grandparents live close by. Parents of young children in UK face complicated situations, as it seems. This also depends on the socio-economic situation of the parents. Diane, a manager in a private company, 34 years old when she became a mother, is far better off than Uche, a 37 years old unqualified social worker of African origin, living in London. Her Social Services office is situated in an expensive part of London. Impossible for Uche to live in that part, which means commuting on a daily basis – a journey that may take up to 4 hours in all. The two small children need child care, which Uche found difficult to obtain, being used to an extended family network in her own family of origin. Uche found it difficult to leave the children in the care of strangers. Finally, an elderly aunt moved in with her and her children, to help with child care. Not an ideal situation, but better than nothing at the moment in Uche's stressful life (Nilsen & Brannen, 2005).

Welfare states and their arrangements do matter when it comes to the question how complicated it is for modern parents to combine parenthood with the demands of work. Practically speaking, this means that some welfare states offer their citizens more opportunities for having (more) children than others do. Let us assume that paid work is a fact of – economic – life in modern Western societies. Not just for men, but also and increasingly so, for women. Women work for economic reasons, for social reasons, and possibly for reasons of intrinsic motivation. The view that women have paid jobs because socio-economic policies push them into the labour market, seems rather unrealistic. And not just unrealistic, but superseded as well. Women – more or less – wish to work and, in order to be economically independent from husbands or state, need to work. Sufficient economic resources of mothers are an important buffer for the negative effects of divorce on children (Fischer, 2004). Since one out of three marriages (in the Netherlands) end in a divorce, this factor can not be overlooked. On top of this, societies need the economic contributions of women.

If this sounds reasonable, one can convincingly argue that institutional support for parenthood is badly needed in modern societies. Children, after all, are the promise and "materials" of the future. Politicians and policy makers should be aware of this important fact. To put it strongly, policies of equal opportunities for women and men make no real sense when societies offer too little room for raising children. Evidence from the TRANSITIONS project however shows, that for none of the parents it is an easy job to raise children and to meet the continuously increasing demands of modern working life. The costs of parenthood are still gendered, even in the most modern welfare states of Europe. Again, this fact deserves a high place on the priority lists of social policies in Europe. Specifically so, because the decision to become a mother is framed by these costs of motherhood.

Some Concluding Remarks

Modern societies differ in the space they provide couples to shape parenthood, motherhood and fatherhood. It seems that the Nordic countries offer the most favourable conditions for modern parenthood in Europe. This conclusion might be contested by politicians from the Netherlands for instance, who praise the opportunities for having decent part-time jobs for mothers – and for fathers. Decent part-time jobs, however, give hardly entrance to more interesting, challenging high-level positions and – more basically – to economic independence. This fact prevents – some – women in the Netherlands from having children.

Fertility rates are influenced by the demands of modern life. The most striking conclusion so far might be the general low fertility rate in whole Europe, well below replacement level. Moreover the first child arrives much later in the mother's life than before. A return to the 1960s and before, when fertility in almost all European countries laid (far) above the replacement level of 2.1 children per couple and the first child was born much earlier, is not very likely. This does not say, however, that governments and employers could not help to make parenthood in its combination with modern life, less complicated. Specifically the socio-economic price of having children for women should decrease. Men and women who would like to start a family should not be confronted with all sorts of practicalities that make parenthood such a complex enterprise in modern days. In this context, the ideas of Esping-Andersen (2002) on a new gender contract deserve attention. Interesting is Esping-Andersen's view that – as he writes – only the genuinely thick-headed will have failed to realise that the employment of women is fundamental for household welfare as well as for the collective good. This might be true for the progressive

Nordic welfare states, but is not always the general and politically supported opinion in the more liberal and conservative welfare states. At least not in the sense that implications of this statement, in terms of sufficient institutional support, are taken seriously.

With a still increasing level of education, careers and perspectives in their work will gain in significance for many women in the years to come. Not just for economic reasons, though very important, but even so for reasons of self-development and fulfilment. Parenthood will not loose its attraction for most modern young couples, one could – rather – safely assume. But the price of parenthood, and more specifically of motherhood, is and certainly will stay an issue when considering having children or not. Too high costs of motherhood are no longer acceptable, so to speak, given the indeed highly economically relevance of the employment of women.

So, the challenges for the European societies are entirely clear: organise institutional support for parents of young children, do take seriously the social and economic necessity of using all talents of women and men, do avoid an unilateral burden of parenthood imposed on women, create practical, affordable and accessible opportunities for young couples to have children at a decent moment in their lives and to keep good perspectives in work and career. Europe has to face many challenges those days. In terms of sustainability, the challenge of creating modern conditions for parenthood and motherhood is certainly not the least important.

References

Anttonen, A., & Sipilä, J. (1996). European social care services: is it possible to identify models? *Journal of European Social Policy*, 6(2), 82–100.
Ariès, P. (1962). *Centuries of Childhood*. New York, NY: Random House Inc.
Beck, U., & Beck-Gernsheim, E. (1995). *The Normal Chaos of Love*. Cambridge: Polity Press.
Beham, B., Drobnič, S., & Verwiebe, R. (2006). Germany: national report on socio-economic trends and welfare policies. In *Quality of Life in a Changing Europe: National Reports on Socio-Economic Trends and Welfare Policies*. Deliverable 3.1. The Netherlands: Utrecht University.
Blossfeld, H.P., & Drobnič, S. (Eds.) (2001). *Careers of Couples in Contemporary Societies. From Male Breadwinner to Dual Earner Families*. Oxford University Press: Oxford.
Blumstein, Ph., & Schwartz, P. (1983). *American Couples: Money, Work, and Sex*. New York, NY: Morrow.
Cowdery, R.S., & Knudson-Martin, C. (2005). The construction of motherhood: tasks, relational connection and gender equality. *Family Relations*, 54(3), 335–345.
Das Dores, G., & Rodrigues, E. (2006). Portugal: national report on socio-economic trends and welfare policies. In *Quality of Life in a Changing Europe: National Reports on Socio-Economic Trends and Welfare Policies*. Deliverable 3.1. The Netherlands: Utrecht University.
Den Dulk, L., & Doorne-Huiskes van, A. (2007). Social policies in Europe: its impact on families and work. In R. Crompton, S. Lewis, & C. Lyonette (Eds.), *Women, Work and Family in Europe*. Houndmills, Sasingstoke: Palgrave Macmillan.
Diefenbach, H. (2003). Gender ideologies, relative resources, and the division of housework in intimate relationships: a test of Hyman Rodman's Theory of resources in cultural context. *International Journal of Sociology*, 43(1), 45–64.
Doorten, I., Lindenberg, S.M., Dykstra, P.A., & Knijn, T. (2008). Dependency within couples with children living at home: comparing portable and relation-specific investments. In I. Doorten

(Eds.), *The Division of Unpaid Work in the Household: A Stubborn Pattern?* Dissertation, Utrecht University.

E-Quality. (2008). *Gezinnen van de toekomst. Cijfers en trends*. Den Haag: E-Quality.

Erler, W. (1999). Work-family reconciliation in Germany: trends in public and corporate policies. In L. den Dulk, A. van Doorne-Huiskes, & J. Schippers (Eds.), *Work-Family Arrangements in Europe*. Thela Thesis: Amsterdam.

Esping-Andersen, G. (1990). *The Three Worlds of Welfare Capitalism*. Cambridge: Polity Press.

Esping-Andersen, G. (1999). *Social Foundations of Postindustrial Economics*. New York, NY: Oxford University Press.

Esping-Andersen, G., Gallie, D., Hemerijck, A., & Myles, J. (2002). *Why We Need a New Welfare State*. Oxford: Oxford University Press.

European Commission, Eurostat (2004). How Europeans spend their time, everyday life of women and men. Labour Force Survey. Luxembourg: Eurostat.

Fischer, T. (2004). *Parental Divorce, Conflict, and Resources. The Effects on Children's Behaviour Problems, Socio-Economic Attainment, and Transitions in the Demographic Career*. ICS-Dissertation, Nijmegen.

Hakim, C. (2001). *Work-Lifestyle Choices in the 21st Century. Preference Theory*. Oxford: Oxford University Press.

Jansen, M. (2002). *Waardenoriëntaties en partnerrelaties. Een panelstudie naar wederzijdse invloeden*. Utrecht: ICS.

Keizer, R. (2010). *Remaining Childless. Causes and Consequences from a Life Course Perspective*. Dissertation, Utrecht University.

Keuzenkamp, S. (2006). Arbeid en zorg in internationaal perspectief. In SCP, *Emancipatiemonitor 2006*. Den Haag: Sociaal en Cultureel Planbureau & Centraal Bureau voor de Statistiek.

Knijn, T., & Verheijen, C. (1991). *Kiezen of delen. Veranderingen in de beleving van het moederschap*. Amsterdam: Uitgeverij An Dekker.

Kocourková, J. (2002). Leave arrangements and childcare services in Central Europe: policies and practices before and after the transition. *Community, Work & Family*, 5(3), 301–318.

Kovacheva, S., Peeva, R., & Andreev, T. (2006). Bulgaria: national report on socio-economic trends and welfare policies. In *Quality of Life in a Changing Europe: National Reports on Socio-Economic Trends and Welfare Policies*. Deliverable 3.1. The Netherlands: Utrecht University.

Kremer, M. (2005). How welfare states care: Culture, gender and citizenship in Europe. *Downloadable at:* http://www.igitur.nl/igiturarchief/searchresults.php?language=nl&author=Kremer&title=

Lane, L., Bäck-Wiklund, M., & Szücs, S. (2006). Sweden: national report on socio-economic trends and welfare policies. In *Quality of Life in a Changing Europe: National Reports on Socio-Economic Trends and Welfare Policies*. Deliverable 3.1. The Netherlands: Utrecht University.

Lewis, J. (2001). The End of Marriage? Individualism and Intimate Relations. Cheltenham: Edward Elgar.

Lewis, S., & Purcell, C. (2006). United Kingdom: national report on socio-economic trends and welfare policies. In *Quality of Life in a Changing Europe: National Reports on Socio-Economic Trends and Welfare Policies*. Deliverable 3.1. The Netherlands: Utrecht University.

Lewis, S., & Smithson, J. (2006). Final report. A framework 6 EU Project. Manchester: MMU.

Liefbroer, A., & Dykstra, P. (2001). Een breder perspectief. In *Samenleven. Nieuwe feiten over relaties en gezinnen*. Voorburg/Heerlen: CBS.

Nilsen, A., & Brannen, J. (2005). *Transitions. Interview Study. Consolidated Report*. Manchester: MMU.

Näsman, P. (1999). Sweden and the reconciliation of work and family life. In L. den Dulk, & A. van Doorne-Huiskes, & J. Schippers (Eds.), *Work-Family Arrangements in Europe*. Amsterdam: Thela Thesis.

Plantenga, J., & Remery, C. (2005) (with assistance of Helming, P.). Reconciliation of work and private life: A comparative review of thirty European countries. Downloadable at: http://europa.eu.int/comm/employment_social/gender_equality/docs/2005/reconciliation_report_en.pdf

RVZ – Raad voor de Volksgezondheid en Zorg. (2007). *Uitstel van ouderschap: medisch of maatschappelijk probleem?* Den Haag: RVZ.

Raley, S.B., Mattingly, M.J., & Bianchi, S.M. (2006). How dual are dual-income couples? Documenting change from 1971 to 2001. *Journal of Marriage and Family*, 68, 11–28.

Rijken, A.J. (2009). *Happy Families, High Fertility? Childbearing Choices in the Context of Family and Partner Relationships.* Dissertation, Utrecht University.

Sainsbury, D. (1996). *Gender, Equality and Welfare States.* Cambridge: Cambridge University Press.

Soede, A., & Vrooman, C. (2008). *A comparative typology of pension regimes.* Brussels: CEPS (Enepri Research Report nr. 54; www.enepri.org en www.ceps.eu).

Taipale, S., & Hirvonen, H. (2006). Finland: national report on socio-economic trends and welfare policies. In *Quality of Life in a Changing Europe: National Reports on Socio-Economic Trends and Welfare Policies.* Deliverable 3.1. The Netherlands: Utrecht University.

Trifiletti, R. (1999). Women's labour market participation and the reconciliation of work and family life in Italy. In L. den Dulk, A. van Doorne-Huiskes, & J. Schippers (Eds.), *Work-Family Arrangements in Europe.* Amsterdam: Thela Thesis.

Chapter 9
The Importance of Children and Families in Welfare States

Gøsta Esping-Andersen

Introduction

Do we invest sufficiently in our children? Does the welfare state provide adequate support to families? Most parents would probably say no. European welfare states are generally slow to adapt to new circumstances and family policy is no exception. The reluctance to shed the traditional familialistic paradigm is perhaps most evident in the Mediteranean basin, but core attributes of familialism remain very present in all but a handfull countries.

Familialism reflects a traditionalist view of what pro-family policy means. Its roots lie in the subsidiarity principle that was enshrined in the Papal encyclical, *Rerum Novarum* (1891). In post-industrial society, familialism becomes counter-productive because women have redefined their life course, families are more fragile, "a-typical" households become the norm, and the male bread-winner is no longer a credible guarantee of adequate living standards. The greatest irony of all is that familialism is now anathema to fertility and family formation.

We need to redefine what family-friendly policy implies. Families face new and often more intense social risks while they increasingly lack the means to cope with them. This results in welfare lacunae unless market or government provision steps in. Market failure is to be expected, in part because the price of commercial services exceeds most families' ability to pay. People that most need services are often those, like the poor and young child families, that least can afford them. For another, private welfare incurs serious information assymetries. If families and markets fail in tandem, public support is, by definition, the last alternative.

Failure to support families may affect both the quantity and quality of children. If motherhood remains incompatible with work, fertility will suffer. And if parents fail to invest adequately in their children, Europe can definitely say goodbye to its dream of becoming the World's most competitive knowledge economy. Skill requirements

G. Esping-Andersen (✉)
Professor of Sociology, Department of Political and Social Sciences, Universitat Pompeu Fabra, Barcelona, Spain
e-mail: gosta.esping@upf.edu

G. Beets et al. (eds.), *The Future of Motherhood in Western Societies*,
DOI 10.1007/978-90-481-8969-4_9, © Springer Science+Business Media B.V. 2011

Table 9.1 Public support in favour of families

	Public spending as percent of GDP (2005)	
	Cash transfers	Services
Belgium	1.7	0.9
Denmark	1.6	1.7
France	1.4	1.6
Germany	1.4	0.7
Italy	0.6	0.7
Netherlands	0.6	1.0
Spain	0.5	0.7
United Kingdom	2.2	1.0
United States of America	0.1	0.5

Spending as a share of GDP is from OECD's SOCX data files.

are rising rapidly and those with a poor start are likely to see their life chances severely impaired.

Government spending in favour of families varies tremendously across the EU, ranging from over 3% of Gross Domestic Product (GDP) in Denmark to half of 1% in the US (Table 9.1). Measured on a per capita basis, Danish outlays are exactly 10 times the Spanish and 3 times the Dutch. Neither is there any coherent trend. Some, like Germany and the UK, have increased their efforts over the past decade while others, notably the Netherlands, are retreating. Dutch per capita spending has stagnated which implies that it lags behind GDP growth. To be sure, this has been partially offset by more (tax-subsidized) private spending. And tax allowances do not figure on expenditure accounts. Were we to focus on total GDP use rather than solely *public* accounts, the EU nations would look far more convergent.

The simple reason why a new *social contract* is called for is that fertility and child quality combine both private utility and societal gains. And like no other epoch in the past, the societal gains are mounting while families' ability to produce these social gains is weakening.

In the following I first examine the twin challenges of fertility and child development. In the second part I turn to the role of welfare reform, posing one basic question: can we identify an optimal policy mix that will ensure both the socially desired level of fertility and investment in our children? The task is to identify a Paretian optimum that will maximize efficiency gains and social equity simultaneously.

Fertility

Contemporary fertility falls short of citizens' preferences. Citizens in advanced countries generally express a desire for 2.2–2.4 children (Van de Kaa, 2001; Sleebos, 2003). The preferred number declines with age, but it is unclear whether this mirrors peoples' resignation to a *fait accompli* or, alternatively, a more mature and reasoned assessment of what is optimal (McDonald, 2002).

Table 9.2 Childlessness and the probability of having a second child within 5 years of the first (Kaplan Mayer Hazard rate estimation)

	Percent women childless at age 40	Probability of having a second child within 5 years
Denmark	12	38
France	9	42
Germany	15	26
Italy	17	25
Netherlands	20	51
Spain	17	24
United Kingdom	17	43

Estimated from ECHP.

Most advanced nations boasted total fertility rates (TFR) well above the replacement level 30 years ago and then experienced a sharp drop that, in most cases, bottomed out in the mid-1980s. The Nordic countries, France, and the US managed a recovery, while others moved to levels below 1.3 (Italy and Spain in particular).

The period TFR will of course not tell us whether women will eventually end up with a number of children that corresponds to preferences (Sobotka & Lutz, 2009). The completed cohort fertility depends on the incidence of childlessness, postponement of fertility, and on the likelihood of catching-up even when starting late. The contemporary child gap correlates to a degree with rising childlessness, especially among highly educated career women (Gonzalez & Jurado, 2005). But much more important is the postponement of first births, a trend quite similar across all advanced societies (Gustafsson, 2001; see also the Chapter 6 by Beets elsewhere in this book).

If delayed fertility were simply period-specific, we would expect a return to "normalcy". But data suggest otherwise. Delaying first births is part-and-parcel of the new female life course in which education and career-consolidation are *sine qua non*. The question, then, is whether a late start will inevitably thwart citizens' quest for children. The answer is no, since in some countries women do manage to catch-up despite a late start. The Danish (period) TFR is 50% higher than the Italian even though the average age at first birth is virtually identical. And Sweden's spectacular fertility boom prior to the 1990s was mainly due to an acceleration of second births (Jensen, 2002). As Table 9.2 shows, women in Denmark, France, and the Netherlands are twice as likely to catch up as are German, Italian and Spanish women.

Generally speaking, immigrants boast far greater fertility than natives, although not so for second generation immigrants. There are often large differences between rural and urban women, and female education is usually associated with fewer children. Urbanization, the disappearance of the housewife, and women's huge gains in education go a long way in explaining the fall in births. As the gender wage gap narrows, fertility may also decline.

Still, there are counter-tendencies. One, the "new" woman is generally not a careerist but rather one who prefers the "dual-role" model of motherhood and lifelong employment (Hakim, 1996). Both labour supply and child-preferences confirm this. Two, in some countries – notably in Scandinavia – the traditional education-fertility profile is being revolutionized. We now register the highest fertility rates among women with tertiary education, and the lowest among women with only compulsory schooling (Esping-Andersen et al., 2005). Hence, more female education and employment do not necessarily imply fewer children.

Explaining the Child Gap

There is certainly no dearth of theories. One school of thought emphasizes the historical shift towards "post-materialist" values (Van de Kaa, 2001). In this view, children stand in the way of individual fulfilment and liberty. There is no doubt something to this story, at least in terms of portraying a general trend. Public policy would appear irrelevant if this were the *main* explanation.

The values-theory confronts too many empirical inconsistencies, not least the fact that actual fertility falls far short of peoples' preferences. It is also difficult to reconcile the theory with observed variation. Values aside, most theories are policy relevant. A common core premise is that low and late fertility mirrors the tensions that mount when gender roles and family behaviour fail to adapt to the changing preferences of women (McDonald, 2002). Low fertility occurs when women embrace a new life course in a world of traditional familialism. The tensions are related to rising costs of children and to the barriers to family-work reconciliation.

There are direct monetary costs related to children. Standard research estimates these to be roughly one-third of the cost of an adult. They are almost certainly higher, especially if parents are committed to their children's welfare. Family benefits may help offset the cost but since even the most generous benefits, like the Danish, are equal to only 4% of average earnings, the effect is at the margin. In any case, research shows that family cash transfers have no real effect on fertility (Gauthier & Hatzius, 1997; Sleebos, 2003).

The really important cost of children lies in the opportunity cost (or child penalty) of motherhood in terms of lost potential lifetime income. Considering women's rising earnings power, work interruptions can result in substantial income penalties (Polacheck, 2003).

Women respond by shortening interruptions and delaying births.[1] Sigle-Rushton & Waldvogel (2004) show a general decline in the lifetime income loss – but only for some countries. For medium-educated mothers with two children, the gross income loss up to age 45 ranges from 23 to 25% in Scandinavia and the US to 40% in Germany and the Netherlands. Extending the estimate up to age 60 suggests

---

[1] This is the case for the Netherlands and the UK, but in Germany interruptions have actually become longer (Gustafsson et al., 2002). In the 1990s, the average number of interrupted months ranges from 32 in Germany to 10–13 in Scandinavia. The UK has undergone a dramatic change in just one decade since the average declined from 25 in the 1980s to 14 in the 1990s (Gustafsson et al., 2002).

that an important part of the child-penalty is eventually recuperated *if* women remain in uninterrupted employment until retirement. The great difference between Scandinavia and elsewhere lies in the duration of interruptions and in subsequent work histories. Whereas British, Dutch and German women have long interruptions and then resume with reduced working hours, Scandinavian women return relatively quickly and usually opt for full-time work. In a British study, Rake (2000) identifies a polarizing trend because higher educated women now emulate the Nordic pattern while low educated women reduce even further their post-birth labour supply.

This is where childcare matters. If access is limited to commercial care parents must dish out up to 10,000 euros for a full-time, full-year place in a quality centre in countries like Germany, Britain or the Netherlands.[2] This implies, in essence, a *regressive tax* on mothers' labour supply and is in any case prohibitively expensive for most young families, not to mention low income and lone parents. If no cheaper alternatives are available families must choose between one of two evils: either forego children in the interest of the woman's career, or sacrifice the mother's career in the interest of family formation.

Not surprisingly, fertility correlates with childcare (Kravdal, 1996; Esping-Andersen, 2002; Del Boca, 2002; Aaberge et al., 2005).[3] There are three possible ways to make care more affordable: via familial support (the grandmother), via de-regulated product markets (the American way), or via generous government subsidies (the Nordic approach). Grandmothers have been the main solution in Southern Europe, but the reservoir of available carers is diminishing (Gonzalez & Jurado, 2005). The highly differentiated price structure in the US, coupled to tax deductions to parents, may meet demand but at the price of extremely uneven quality. In the Nordic model, public subsidies defray the lion's share of costs. Considering that attendance is now de facto universal, net parental costs are evidently affordable to all families. Some countries, notably the UK and the Netherlands, pursue a hybrid model that combines commercial provision with some public subsidies.

Childcare policies, however generous, will not solve all problems alone. Their impact depends, firstly, on the length of paid maternity leave; if the latter is too brief, mothers are compelled to make a radical choice between returning to work or interrupting their careers. Low educated women are more likely to curtail their careers, while higher educated women will respond with reduced fertility.

Secondly, we know that much of the reconciliation problem lies buried in the labour market. Flexible time schedules and access to part-time work are essential. Job security matters because women now insist on economic autonomy.

---

[2] As the OECD (2002: Table 3.5) shows, the cost of one child in private, unsubsidized Dutch daycare is equivalent to 91% of the wives' average wage.

[3] There is even stronger evidence that mothers' employment is very sensitive to the price and/or availability of childcare. For the US, Anderson & Levine (2000) show that a 10% reduction in the cost of daycare would raise employment by more than 3%. For Europe, Gustafsson & Stafford (1992), Kreyenfeld & Hank (1999), and Del Boca (2002) show that availability is decisive for participation.

Table 9.3 Employment insecurity and fertility. Logistic odds ratios. The regressions include controls for education level and full-time/part-time status

	Denmark	Netherlands	Germany	Spain	UK
Unemployed	2.5***	0.64*	0.22**	0.54***	0.33**
Permanent contract	1.4	2.6**	0.30*	2.5***	1.9
Public sector job	1.0	1.1	1.6**	2.2**	3.4

Estimated from ECHP (1995 wave).
* <0.10; **p <0.05; ***p <0.01.

Unemployment, unstable and precarious jobs all affect fertility negatively. The fact that (young) women are hugely over-represented among the unemployed and those with temporary contracts – in particular in Southern Europe – helps explain pervasive lowest-low fertility (Bernardi, 2005; Esping-Andersen, 2002; Gonzalez & Jurado, 2005; McDonald, 2002). Seen from a different angle, Scandinavian research shows that high fertility among educated women is mainly found among public sector employees (Jensen, 2002; Datta Gupta et al., 2003). Table 9.3 illustrates the importance of job status for women's decision to have children.

Except in Denmark, unemployment is everywhere an obstacle to fertility. In Germany and the Netherlands it lowers the likelihood of a birth to almost half. Job insecurity is an impediment as well. In the Netherlands and Spain, permanent contracts raise the odds of fertility by a factor of 2.5. The coefficient for public sector employment, which undoubtedly offers more cushioned working conditions, is everywhere positive but only statistically significant in Germany and Spain.

As noted, low fertility reflects a disjuncture between the changed life course of women and the persistence of traditional gender roles. The first part of the disjuncture, women's changing roles, is evident in the importance of employment conditions and career status: women hesitate to give birth until their careers are adequately assured.

The second part of the disjuncture has to do with gender roles. Duvander & Andersson (2005) show that the decision to have a second child in Sweden depends very much on whether the father took parental leave around the first birth. Esping-Andersen et al. (2005) show that Danish fathers' involvement in caring for the first child also correlates strongly with the decision to have a second child. In other words, a more egalitarian division of paid *and* unpaid work may emerge as a bottom-line condition for future fertility.

Time use data show that men typically increase their share of domestic work when mothers work full-time, but perfect substitution occurs nowhere.[4] Scandinavian and American males in full-time double earner couples are more prone to pitch in. For example, the ratio of unpaid hours between women and men is now 1.4 in Denmark, and 1.7 in Sweden and the US. In Britain the ratio rises to 2.4, and

---

[4] In fact, in the UK the male's share is smaller than when the spouse works part-time (OECD, 2002: Table 4.5).

in Italy to an embarrassing 3.6 ratio.[5] The male contribution to childcare activities is also positively related to the level of education. Increasing women's autonomy and educational attainment may lead to further improvements in gender equality within couples.

The Quality of Children

The evolving knowledge economy raises the human capital "ante" that is needed to ensure good job prospects. There is no clear consensus as to what skills, precisely, matter most (Bowles et al., 2001). Formal education is obviously a *sine qua non*, especially for early career moves. Today's early school dropouts are likely to end up being the low wage and precarious workers of tomorrow. Remedial policy, such as "activation" and adult training is generally an ineffective corrective (Heckman & Lochner, 2000). The non-completion of upper-secondary level education provides one very good benchmark of our social exclusion problem in the decades to come.

Other human capital dimensions are gaining in importance. Modern companies put a premium on social skills and "emotional intelligence", and social capital can be very important for getting ahead. Regardless, the reigning consensus is that strong cognitive skills are the first and foremost precondition; in part because cognitive abilities are decisive for learning and hence for school completion and, in part, because – almost by definition – knowledge-intensive production assumes that people have the skills to understand, interpret and productively apply information. Cognitive skills, like the motivation to learn, are developed very early in life, but their importance continues throughout life.

The continuous and powerful impact of social origins on children's life chances that inter-generational stratification studies identify is very much due to the fact that children's basic cognitive stimulus is concentrated in the early years (0–6), i.e. when they are mostly "privatized". Inequalities in parental stimulus are subsequently transmitted to the schools that, in turn, are generally poorly equipped to rectify differentials in learning abilities.

Post-war reformers believed that social inheritance could be effectively diminished through free access to education. The guiding idea was that this would eliminate liquidity constraints and thus equalize chances across the social classes. Since the path-breaking Coleman report to the US Government we know that the design of education systems has only a very limited impact on inequalities of opportunity. Early tracking, under-staffing, and segregated schools no doubt worsen social inequalities, but the core mechanisms lie in the family of origin (Shavit & Blossfeld, 1993; Erikson & Jonsson, 1996). This view has received powerful confirmation in the PISA studies (OECD, 2003).

---

[5]The ratio in the Netherlands is 2.3 but refers to wives in part-time employment (OECD, 2002: Table 2.13). Scandinavian and American men's contribution has more or less doubled over the past 10–15 years. The Danish female:male ratio of household work fell from 1.7 (1987) to 1.4 (2001) (Deding & Lausten, 2004).

Explaining Inequalities in Child Outcomes

Parental investments in their children take two principal forms. One is monetary, the other is crudely speaking "cultural". Although free education diminishes the role of income inequalities, money continues to crucially influence child outcomes. In most countries, enrolment in quality pre-school learning depends on household income. Well-off parents are far better positioned to invest in additional extra-curricular learning activities and child health is generally also related to family income.

Far worse is poverty and income insecurity. US research shows that a poor child will, on average, have 2 years less of schooling and, subsequently, earn roughly 30% less when adult (Mayer, 1997; Haveman & Wolfe, 1995). Most troublesome, the poor child is far more likely to end up as a poor parent, thus reproducing the syndrome from generation to generation. European research identifies similar poverty effects (Maurin, 2002; CERC, 2004).

Since economic insecurity harms child outcomes, ongoing trends in income distribution must be of serious concern since young households and, in particular, child families are losing ground in a major way. With the sole exception of Scandinavia, child poverty has risen over the past two decades in Germany by 4% points, in the Netherlands and the UK by 5. The child poverty level is now around 9–10% in France, Germany and the Netherlands, 15% in the UK, and a whopping 22% in the US.

Put differently, as far as the income effect is concerned, most advanced nations are swimming upstream at the very same moment that the need to secure strong child outcomes is intensifying. It follows that any measure that effectively combats child poverty amounts to a key investment in children's life chances and in our collective future. This point is emphasized in Erikson & Jonsson's (1996) analyses of why the Nordic countries boast far more egalitarian educational attainment than elsewhere. They stress, in particular, the effectiveness of public income support to families with children and, indeed, as the data show, there has been no increase in Scandinavian child poverty notwithstanding that these nations, too, have witnessed rising income inequalities.[6]

The "cultural" dimension is substantially more difficult to identify with any precision. To be sure, it is very multifaceted. One effect is represented by the ability of parents to inculcate their children with the kinds of middle class cultural norms, styles and expressions that prevail in most schools. A second effect, arguably far more important, has to do with the kinds of parental cultural and educational resources that ensure a strong cognitive stimulation and learning environment. One way to capture this dimension is through information about families' reading habits and possession of books (De Graaf, 1998; OECD, 2002). This cultural dimension is of far greater importance than is parental socio-economic status in explaining children's cognitive abilities (Esping-Andersen, 2004).

---

[6]The effectiveness of the Scandinavian model is evident in comparative child poverty levels: in 2000, less than 3% in Denmark and Finland; 4% in Sweden.

And, finally, "culture" includes a third dimension, namely the intensity and quality of parent-child interaction and nurturing. Here we confront a rather controversial issue, namely whether mothers' employment outside the home has adverse consequences for child development. If so, we may again be swimming upstream considering that the majority of modern women insist on career continuity.

There is some evidence that the reduced intensity of parent-child interaction that results from motherly employment can be harmful (Ermisch & Francesconi, 2002; Ruhm, 2004). Maternal employment can be harmful in the child's first 9–12 months (Waldvogel et al., 2002; Ruhm, 2004; Gregg et al., 2005). But the effect thereafter depends very much on the quality of mothers' jobs and of outside care. Job-related stress and fatigue are demonstrably problematic. And there is ample evidence that high-quality childcare more than offsets any potential negative effects (Currie, 2001; Waldvogel, 2002). Indeed, evaluation studies of early intervention programmes uniformly conclude that children from problem families who participate in sponsored quality pre-school centres do far better in terms of school completion and a host of other variables, such as crime and teenage pregnancy (Haveman & Wolfe, 1995; Waldvogel, 2002). In countries where access to quality childcare is scarce, as in Spain, Germany and the US, full-time employment does appear to have adverse effects (albeit not very strong) on children's cognitive development while in Scandinavia, where attendance is essentially universal, the impact of motherly employment appears in fact to be positive.

There are two important riders to this conclusion. Reduced interaction with mothers may be offset by more paternal dedication to children. In fact, the total number of parental hours with children in the US and Scandinavia has actually risen since the 1960s; in part because of reduced working hours; in part due to fathers' greater involvement (Bianchi, 2000).

The second rider is that mothers' employment has distinct effects on boys and girls. I find that the effect is, surprisingly, completely orthogonal: always positive for girls but often rather negative for boys (especially if the mother works full-time). The positive effect for girls has surely something to do with the role model of mothers (Esping-Andersen, 2005). If fathers increase their time with children, the negative effect on boys may diminish to the extent that boys are more influenced by the paternal role model.

When we put together these different strands of evidence, we also have a ready-made explanation for why the Scandinavian countries are the only clear cases where the impact of social origins on educational attainment (and cognitive development) has declined significantly over the past decades (Esping-Andersen, 2005). On one hand, the income effect has been almost de facto eliminated via the eradication of child poverty. On the other hand, the "culture" effect weakened because all children, irrespective of parental resources and social origin, benefit from identical quality care. The net effect is bound to be redistributive in the sense that children from the weakest families gain the most. It is telling that the combined effect of the socioeconomic status and parental cultural capital variables on child literacy performance is half as strong in Sweden as it is in most other OECD countries (Esping-Andersen,

2005).[7] It is equally telling that the Nordic countries exhibit unusually little variation in children's cognitive abilities.

Redesigning the Welfare State: A Social Investment Approach

The foremost objective of social policy is to secure citizens against risks. We live in a society in which rapid population ageing tends to monopolize policy debates. Ageing implies substantial future spending commitments. Many fear that the welfare state may prove financially unsustainable and such fears will undoubtedly mount if it is also called upon to invest seriously in children.

A myopic *categorical* focus on the elderly versus the young leads to poor policy because it fails to connect old age with peoples' life course. Today's retirees do well not solely because pensions are generous but in large part because they enjoyed good lives with stable employment and steadily rising wages. The magnitude of the demographic crunch that will climax at mid-century will depend very much on the quality of our children's life course, on the quantity of young workers, and on their productivity.

Contemporary youth cohorts are historically speaking tiny and must shoulder an unparalleled demographic burden. They also confront a far more intense set of risks since life chances are more and more contingent on strong skills. Investing well in our children does not come at bargain basement prices but will yield a double bonus by delivering individual and societal welfare gains at once.

It may be difficult to pinpoint the exact *net social value* of children. For one, the heterogeneity of children in terms of their potential skills, productivity and lifetime contribution is huge. The precise amount is not very important, but the fact itself alerts us to several core principles that a recast social policy must adhere to.

Firstly, if the social benefit of children is substantial while the parental cost of having children is rising, there is a ready-made case for redistribution in favour of child families. Besides the direct monetary outlays related to having children, the time investment that parents make on behalf of their children is of substantial monetary value. Klevemarken (1998), using rather conservative assumptions, has cashed out the equivalent value at around US$22,000–29,000 for an average Swedish family. This implies that Swedish parents' collective care for their children would add an equivalent of 20% to GDP. When we consider that social spending on families is nowhere greater than 4% of GDP, society is undoubtedly getting a good deal, and the childless in particular.[8]

Hence, there is a ready-made case for redistribution in favour of children and, logically, the level of taxation required should correspond to the collective returns. This leads me to the second principle. If it can be demonstrated that expenditures

---

[7] The two variables, jointly, explain 11% of the variance in Sweden compared to an OECD average of 20%.

[8] Including also public spending on education would add another 4 or 5% of GDP.

on children yield an increase in their lifetime net social value, the public outlays involved will have a clear investment character.

Public Policy and Fertility

As discussed above, raising fertility requires that we help reconcile women's altered life course preferences with family formation. Even if our main goal must be to help citizens to have their desired number of children the social gains from raising fertility will be substantial.

The question is whether the welfare state can be made to produce such quantity and quality improvements. Policy makers in the past were often pronatalist and in France, especially, generous income inducements were thought to raise fertility. We now know that such incentives bear little fruit.[9] Within the EU at large there now exists broad support for a basic package of "family friendly" policy: a combination of paid maternity-parental leave, affordable quality childcare, and mother-friendly employment provisions such as flex-time.

If having children is now mainly related to the opportunity costs of mother-hood, any measure that effectively diminishes the child penalty should help families towards social preference levels. Family allowances may not have much of an effect, but family-work reconciliation policies – and childcare in particular – do appear to matter. Since nations' reconciliation policies tend to evolve in synchrony it is very difficult to statistically separate the distinct effects of the main components (i.e. day-care, leave schemes and workplace measures). For Norway, Kravdal (1996) finds that doubling childcare raises the TFR by more than 0.1 point. Knudsen (1999), analyzing Danish data, estimates that fertility rose by 0.3 points (from a TFR of 1.5 to 1.8) as a result of the expansion of daycare plus child leaves since the early 1980s. Del Boca (2002) also finds strong effects in Italy and, for the US, Blau and Robins (1989) show that both the cost and the availability of care reduce fertility.

It is especially provision for the under-3s that yields positive fertility responses (Esping-Andersen, 2002). Aaberge et al. (2005) conclude that mother-friendly job measures, such as flextime, positively influence fertility. And, as mentioned, more gender equality in the division of household labour will raise the birth rate, at least among educated women. Policy considerations must include stronger childcare and leave incentives for men.

Overall, the *direct* fertility dividend of a family-friendly policy package is not likely to be of overwhelming proportions, but insofar as it also helps reconcile work

---

[9]The best – but still not very robust – econometric estimates suggest that a 25% increase in family cash benefits may raise the TFR by 0.07 per woman (Gauthier & Hatzius, 1997; for an overview, see also Sleebos, 2003). If, say, the Netherlands wishes to narrow the child deficit to a 1.9 TFR via cash inducements, the value of family cash benefits would have to be more than 9 times their present value. And since these estimates are quite shaky it is far from certain that the fertility response would be as expected. Ermisch (1988) argues that cash benefits affect the timing but not the volume of births.

with motherhood there is undoubtedly a positive *indirect* effect. Its impact is no doubt uneven across the population: arguably most effective among women who face the steepest opportunity costs of motherhood. And even if the fertility gains appear quite miniscule we must remember that even a small rise in the (period) TFR amounts to a substantial individual and societal welfare gain. It means that parents come closer to their preferred family size.

Public Policy and Children's Life Chances

There is no simple ready-made formula that will guarantee good child outcomes. Since we know that cognitive abilities correlate with social origins, it comes as no surprise that the level of cognitive inequality among children depends on the over-all degree of inequality between families. In highly inegalitarian societies, such as the UK and US, the share that falls in the lowest (essentially dis-functional) cog-nitive quintile is far larger than in egalitarian nations, such as Sweden, Norway or the Netherlands (approximately 20% compared to 8% in Norway and 11% in the Netherlands). Computing Gini coefficients for cognitive test scores provides a telling indicator: The Danish Gini is 0.08 compared to 0.16 for the US. In Fig. 9.1, I regress nations' cognitive score Ginis on a social inheritance variable (the strength of the association between children's and parents' educational attainment). The cor-relation would be even higher if we regressed cognitive Ginis on nations' income distribution Ginis. In fact, there is a very strong correlation also between inequalities of income distribution and inter-generational inheritance.

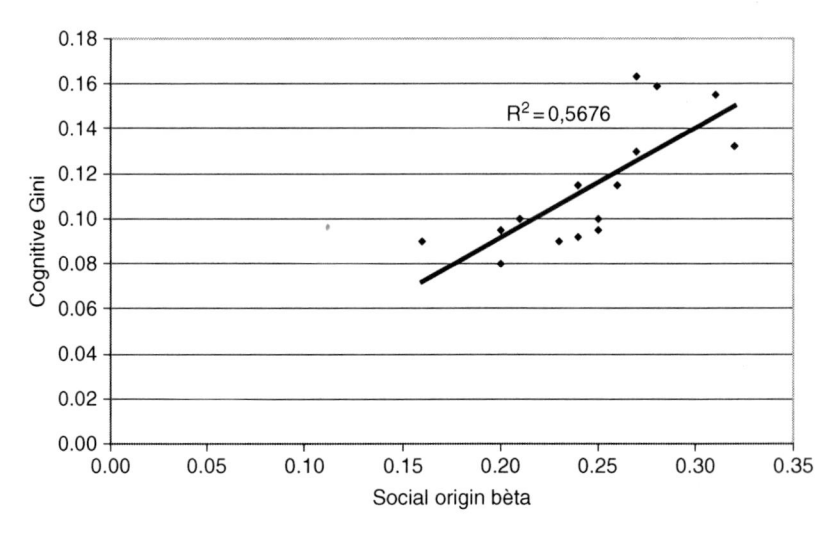

Fig. 9.1 The Relationship between cognitive inequalities and the strength of inter-generational social inheritance. Source: Esping-Andersen (2004, p. 123). The regression is based on 15 OECD countries

All told, this indicates that policy must focus primarily on those monetary and cultural mechanisms that link social origins to child outcomes. There can be substantial gains from minimizing the effect of low income. A policy that effectively eliminates child poverty would yield positive results in terms of equalizing children's educational chances.

It is more difficult to see how policy might affect the "cultural" mechanisms. How, for example, might we compel parents to read for their children, or to help them with their homework? Weak parental "cultural" resources may translate into less cognitive stimulation which, in turn, may impair children's schooling. There is also a possible indirect effect since weak parents are disadvantaged in terms of navigating the school system on behalf of their children. Information assymetries are likely to be especially accentuated among low educated parents and within immigrant communities.

Educational reformers have sought to introduce numerous policies aimed at remedying such inequalities and deficiencies. On this front Sweden may very well represent the vanguard, in particular with its emphasis on an anxiety-free and individualized learning environment. It is telling that between-school effects on children's cognitive skills are very small compared to other countries. But still, remedial programmes within schools, no matter how well designed and financed, have not proven very effective in eradicating the impact of social origins. This is primarily because the first 6 years in children's lives are decisive – and these years are, in most societies, shaped almost exclusively within the parental home.

A major clue as to how social policy can effectively address socio-cultural handicaps comes from early intervention programmes in the US. The gist of these is to intervene in problem families where children's development is at special risk. They are highly targeted and reach only a small minority of US children. The menu of interventions is large but the most successful has been to place at-risk children in high quality childcare centres. These programmes have been shown to yield very positive results in terms of school completion, staying off crime, and later adult earnings and job attainment (Currie, 2001; Duncan & Brooks-Gunn, 1997; Haveman & Wolfe, 1995; Karoly et al., 1998). It is tempting to speculate that if early intervention were expanded to, say, 20% of American families the percentage youth with a dysfunctional cognitive performance would decline to North European levels.

The magnitude of the "cultural" problem is related to the size of the parental generation that lacks the resources to adequately stimulate their children's learning abilities. In Spain and Italy there remain large numbers of adults with only minimal education. Within the typical parenthood age bracket (35–44), 54% of Spanish mothers only have compulsory education, compared to 12% in Sweden (OECD, 2003). The rapid growth in educational attainment will diminish this problem in the decades to come. But we also face counter-tendencies that emanate from large waves of generally low educated immigrants that, in addition, face multiple cultural and educational disadvantages that can seriously jeopardize their children's chances. Even in Sweden, where the school system has most ambitiously sought to rectify immigrant children's learning disadvantages, the cognitive score gap between native and non-native children is one of the largest in the OECD, and the probability of school failure is roughly 5 times higher for immigrants than for natives.[10]

Many analyses of US early intervention policy trace its success to the fact that it redistributes cognitive stimulation in favour of the most needy. A very similar phenomenon has, by *fiat* rather than by intention, unfolded in the Nordic countries as they expanded early childcare in response to women's rising employment rates. The policy deliberately emphasized uniform "middle class" quality standards, perhaps more for electoral than other reasons.

The Nordic model has undoubtedly had a non-trivial impact on equalizing children's school preparedness.[11] Denmark, Norway and Sweden are the only advanced countries that show a substantial reduction in the effect of parental education, income, and also "cultural capital" on children's educational attainment. To illustrate, the impact of parents' education on the likelihood of attaining upper secondary and tertiary education has been cut in half for those born in the 1970s for whom childcare attendance became the norm. In countries like the US, UK or Germany, the parental impact remains as strong as it was. The equalizing potential of universal early care is also evident when we focus specifically on children of parents with very low education (obligatory or less). In Denmark, their chance of completing upper secondary education has doubled for the youngest cohorts and in Norway even tripled. Again, this stands in sharp contrast to other countries where by and large there has been no relative improvement in the fortunes of similar youth.[12]

There are two potential downsides to the childcare strategy. One, as discussed above, children may suffer from less intensive child-parent interaction, especially when mothers work full-time and return quickly to work after birth. Evidence suggests that such adverse effects disappear if (a) children remain with the mother during most of their first year, if (b) mothers have quality jobs, and if (c) childcare quality is high. Secondly, the cognitive homogenization process built into pre-school – and by extension also into comprehensive school models like the Swedish – implies a lowering of standards, a move towards a low common denominator of learning. Analyses of the Swedish education system suggest that this cannot be the case.

The key question is how social policy can be designed to address negative family effects. A first principle must be to uphold family incomes. Few countries boast an income maintenance policy that de facto guarantees against child poverty, although the Nordic countries come close when we add together the impact of family benefits, housing allowances and social assistance.

The good news is that the additional public cost of eliminating child poverty is a bargain, financially speaking. Adopting the 50% of median poverty benchmark, it would absorb 0.26% of GDP in the UK – the EU country with the highest poverty

---

[10]This evidence derives from the author's participation in an OECD mission to Sweden in February 2005.

[11]For an overview of research on the impact of childcare on child outcomes, see Waldvogel (2002).

[12]For detailed analyses, see Esping-Andersen (2005).

rates (Esping-Andersen & Sarasa, 2002). In any case, the rise in mothers' employ-ment provides a far more effective anti-poverty guarantee. When mothers work – in single parent and couple families alike – the probability of poverty falls by a fac-tor of 3 or 4. Improving the compatibility of motherhood and employment yields a major pay-off in terms of child poverty risks.

In other words, we return once again to reconciliation policies. If, as research concludes, maternal employment is problematic for child welfare during the first year there exists a clear case in favour of extending the mix of maternity and parental leave.

The EU has recently issued a directive that calls for a minimum of 3 months parental leave in addition to maternity leave. Still, the combined entitlement avail-able to mothers (plus fathers) varies enormously across the EU, from a miserly 4 months in Spain to 12+ months in the more generous countries. Leaves that are either too brief or too extended can produce adverse effects in terms of reconciliation.

To minimize the career effects of short leaves, mothers will attempt to place their children with others. This, we know, can have adverse "quality" effects. Very early childcare attendance is often the option among career-committed women, especially in the US where paid leave does not exist and where the career penalty of interrup-tions can be especially high (Waldvogel et al., 1999). A combination of paid leave arrangements that cover *at least* the child's first 9 months would accordingly appear optimal. We know from Scandinavian experience that (a) the standard paid leave period – now a minimum of 48 weeks – does not produce any appreciable lifetime income penalty, that (b) the majority of mothers soon return to full-time employ-ment, and that (c) women come fairly close to having the number of children they actually desire.

Most EU countries have leave provisions that appear consistent with these mul-tiple objectives but appearances are deceptive since optional parental leaves often imply sharply reduced benefits. It is doubtful that women committed to employ-ment will opt for extended periods of uncompensated leave and they are, hence, driven back to work.

Most EU countries pay lip service to gender equity in parental leave schemes, and Sweden is the only country where the father-share is seriously used. Feminists, unsurprisingly, lobby fiercely for more parity in the take-up of leaves. Their case is strengthened when we consider that fathers' contribution may make the choice for parenthood easier and, turning to the "quality" dimension, the sex of the parent that cares for the child must be of minor importance (Ermisch & Francesconi, 2002).

Designing a Childcare System

Early child programmes may yield very positive results but they are often narrowly targeted towards exceptionally needy children. The problem is that the size of the "at-risk" population is usually far larger than the realistic scope of such policies. The British Labour government's Sure Start, very much inspired by Head Start, seeks to widen its reach by intervening in deprived neighbourhoods rather than in specific families. The shortcoming here is that problem families do not necessarily live in such communities. There is a lot to be said in favour of special measures that address the really needy children. Still there is even more ammunition in favour of a global high-quality universal childcare approach since this simultaneously addresses reconciling motherhood and work: childcare kills two birds in one throw.

If childcare emerges as centre piece of any child welfare strategy, we need to examine its policy ramifications carefully. Obviously universal and affordable quality childcare does not come cheap. Worse, the inherent cost-disease problem of care services (due to lagging productivity) implies constantly rising financial pressures. Insuring quality implies pedagogically qualified personnel and small staff-child ratios.

National norms governing quality aspects for the under-3s range from a staff-child ratio of 1:12 in Spain to Denmark's exceptionally low 1:3 ratio. Affordability boils down to the size of the subsidy and the parental co-payment. In turn, the level of childcare supply will depend directly on effective demand – again largely a question of subsidies and affordability.

Nowhere is early childcare predominantly public. The Nordic countries pursue a mix of municipally run centres (about 70% in Denmark) and co-operatives, often established by parent associations. Commercial centres have no claim to public subsidies and, hence, basically do not exist. The model evidently succeeds in delivering broad access since 85% of 2 year olds attend – virtually all on a full-day basis (OECD, 2002). At the other extreme, the US manages also to achieve ample coverage with an almost exclusively commercially run system. Yet, only a minority of all centres are of certified quality standard. In most EU countries public childcare for the under-3s is extremely scarce, largely income tested and targeted to families with special needs. Usually the only alternative is expensive for-profit care. Two countries, the UK and the Netherlands, pursue ample coverage by subsidizing commercial centres.

If quality standards are assured across-the-board, there is no particular reason why one might prefer either public or private unless there are associated equity or efficiency costs involved. In the Netherlands, the market strategy was preferred as a way to limit public spending and also to promote parental choice.

A private system will probably produce greater competition, innovation, and variety. Of course, a Nordic-style mixed model that does not discriminate against private non-profit initiatives may, in principle, reap similar benefits. A major problem with commercial welfare markets is that they easily provoke serious inequities due to information asymmetries and client creaming: choosing the best solution for one's children may require substantial resources (such as knowledge). Thus, less educated and, specifically, immigrant families may find themselves handicapped – especially in an environment where demand exceeds supply.

Many EU countries boast high enrolment rates for children aged 3+. For the under-3s most countries fall short of the EU's benchmark of 33% coverage. We can distinguish three sets of countries. The Nordic group has now achieved near-universal coverage, which is not surprising since access is legally guaranteed to all families and since municipalities are compelled to uphold the guarantee. In a second group that includes Belgium and France, coverage hovers around 30%. Most EU countries fall in the third group, with coverage below 10%.

The key to equity and adequacy lies, of course, in affordability. Undoubtedly, the failure to produce anything near full childcare coverage lies on the financial side. Despite public subsidies (via tax credits), British parents' co-payment is almost half of the total cost, and there exist no exemptions for low-income families. This may explain why the ambitious plan to create new places is faltering (Evers et al., 2005: 202). The Dutch strategy has been to stimulate expansion by subsidizing parents and by inducing firms to defray part of the cost. The latter's share of total costs is 25%. Employer participation appears limited to two-thirds of all. Since their financial contribution implies added fixed labour costs, small firms are undoubtedly loath to participate. The consequence is easily a double hazard: on one hand, the employer quota may lead to discrimination against women in hiring decisions; on the other hand, uneven employer participation provokes social dualisms.

A second reason why the Dutch model may falter is that the net parental cost of childcare is quite steep. A full-time place for one child amounts to 60% of the average wife's net earnings, and for 2 children it rises to 77% (special deductions for low income parents reduce the payment substantially). This is a de facto very steep "tax" on mothers' employment and may be one reason (together with shortages) why a sizable number of mothers either abandon the workforce or only have 1 child. The Dutch model, of course, is designed to cater to a part-time environment. But we may here have double causality since the cost (and scarcity) of full-time care may induce mothers to opt for part-time employment.

Comparatively speaking, Sweden probably offers the most generous conditions with a parental co-payment equal to 10–15% of total cost. Neighbouring Denmark has a graduated pay scale. Families with less than 60% of median income go free and a full fee (equal to 30% of total cost) kicks in at median household income. Considering that participation is now de facto universal, one would conclude that this is an affordable system for all. The cost is bound to increase as the educational credentials of personnel are raised – unless matched by higher staff-child ratios. Are childcare expenditures a good social investment? Would low spenders like Britain or the Netherlands reap additional benefits that can be justified if they were to emulate Danish or Swedish expenditure levels?

To answer such questions we must first of all do the right kind of financial accounting. To begin with we must remember that the effective overall cost of childcare remains pretty much identical whether it is financed through one pocket or another. If the political objective is to furnish quality care for all children, the total slice of GDP that we must dedicate will not change much however costs are allocated. If we accept that Denmark comes close to both objectives, then we should expect that total spending will end up around 2.7–2.8% of GDP. A Dutch public spending of 0.2% of GDP gives the deceptive appearance of cost-effectiveness. If the Netherlands were to pursue universal coverage on a full-day schedule, total GDP use would end up like in Denmark. The choice of whose pocket must be emptied

Table 9.4 Dynamic accounting of the costs and returns from daycare provision during 5 years (in Euros)

Assumptions:	
• Mother, aged 30 years, with two children	
• She does not interrupt employment, except 1 year maternity	
• Her wage is 67% of APW, and	
• She continues working until age 60	
• We apply 1.5% p.a. "Mincer estimate" of cumulative loss for 5 year interruption	
Cost to government:	
2 years in crèche (×2)	24,000
And 3 years in pre-school (×2)	48,850
Total	72,850
Gains to mother:	
(a) 5 years with full earnings	114,300
And (b) life-time wage gain from no interruption	200,100
Total	314,400
Gains to exchequer:	
Additional revenue from (a)	40,000
And additional revenue from (b)	70,000
Total	110,000
Net return to exchequer	
On original outlay (110,000–72,850)	37,150

Note: The price and income data derive from the Danish government.

may have efficiency or equity repercussions, but hardly any consequences for how much we really spend.

Rosen (1996), in a controversial analysis, argues that the public expenditures destined to help reconcile motherhood and work in Sweden are inefficient, yielding a high *negative return* – which he estimates to be about half of the total. The calculations that underpin this conclusion compare total public expenditures against total earnings of mothers of small children. This is, however, a fallacious analysis because it completely ignores how lifetime earnings (and thus also lifetime tax payments) are affected by mother-friendly programmes. A dynamic life-cycle method produces different results.

In Table 9.4, I present estimates for Denmark on lifetime income effects. To be on the conservative side, my model mother is a full-time low wage earner – 2/3rds average wage – who, at age 30, has 2 children. I assume she interrupts for 5 years if she does not have access to childcare, whereas if she does make use of daycare, she will return to employment immediately after her standard maternity leave entitlement terminates. I also assume that she remains employed until age 60.[13]

---

[13] A study conducted by Price-Waterhouse on behalf of the Blair government arrives at similar estimates.

Table 9.4 shows that (in 1995) the cost to government of providing pre-school care for a mother of two (over a 5 year period) amounts to roughly 73,000 euros. Since this allows the mother to return to employment she receives full earnings during the period plus she avoids substantial experience and human capital loss. Hence over her lifetime she will earn about 314,000 euros more than if she has interrupted. This, in turn, implies that she will pay more taxes on a lifetime basis: an additional 110,000 euros. Comparing the additional revenue dividend to the exchequer with the original government outlay on daycare yields a net return to government of 37,000 euros – a respectable 50% return on the initial investment! The net return would have been far greater had we examined the case of a median wage earner.[14]

The Danish model is arguably optimal for reconciliation in an environment where the vast majority of mothers insist on returning to full-time employment.[15] And the initial high outlays will eventually be recuperated – but primarily because Danish women do indeed work full-time for most of their lives.

In the Dutch context where mothers' employment rates are 10% points lower, and where part-time employment prevails, both the expenditure and revenue side of the equation changes. The reconciliation policies – child leaves as well as daycare – are designed with a part-time economy in mind (and probably create difficulties for women pursuing full-time employment). Does it make a difference in terms of facilitating "equilibrium fertility rates"?

It is impossible to forecast future employment behaviour but if women will follow the Nordic pattern, we expect to see a gradual shift from part-time to full-time job preferences, because female educational attainment and earnings prospects are rising. The 10% participation gap between the Netherlands and Denmark is likely to narrow with more childcare and longer maternal leaves. If so, public expenditure on affordable childcare plus adequate child leaves will, as in Denmark, constitute a social investment that is quite profitable and indisputably optimal (in the Paretian sense).

The impact of family-friendly policy on child welfare cannot be easily monitorized. Nevertheless, if maternity leaves are inadequate or if coverage of childcare is incomplete there will inevitably emerge inequalities in child development. Infants whose parents are compelled to work will suffer, as will those whose parents have insufficient income because they must remain home with their children. If there exist large lacuna in childcare coverage, those children that are enrolled will be given a major head start in life while those that remain excluded will not.

The core problem is not only that such dualisms are undesirable but, worse, that they are inevitably socially skewed. It is likely, indeed almost certain, that the children that would benefit the most from childcare are the ones most likely to be

---

[14]Only in the case of high income families might the net return be negative since we can assume that such families would purchase private care in the absence of subsidized public provision.

[15]The main weakness of the model is that it does not provide serious incentives for fathers to take up their share of parental leave and, as argued, this may have a negative impact on births.

excluded. This is particularly the case if unaffordability is the chief reason behind non-participation. The largest marginal gain of early childhood stimulation will by definition go to children from socially, culturally and economically disadvantaged homes.

During the decades of childcare expansion the Nordic countries learned these lessons the hard way. Subsidized childcare was, in the past, denied to unemployed mothers and to mothers on maternity or parental leave. Since unemployment correlates with low education, low incomes, and with multiple family problems it is evident that these children and mothers will benefit disproportionally from enrolment (caring for small children is counterproductive for escaping unemployment). Similarly, extended child leaves turn out to be very concentrated in immigrant families – again a group for whom early childhood enrolment is urgent. Also, our societies now include very large – and recent – immigrant communities that, for a host of reasons, have difficulties in integrating. For these reasons there is a strong case, indeed, in favour of special "affirmative action" measures that will give children from underprivileged milieus an extra boost *as early as possible*. To exemplify, some municipalities in Denmark are experimenting with a bussing system for pre-school children to combat heavy ethnic or class segregation in childcare and kindergartens. Similarly one might favour the most at-risk children by placing them in top-quality care centres. And one may even contemplate a more elaborate "carrot and stick" policy. In many immigrant communities husbands are loath to allow their wives to work and this indirectly also means that their children do not attend pre-school institutions. If social assistance and other public transfers were made conditional on childcare attendance, one may help eradicate yet another source of social inequality.

Conclusions

Any discussion of welfare reform in the twenty-first century must accept a number of givens, novel circumstances that no rational policy maker can pretend will disappear in future. The first is that women's embrace of lifelong employment is here to stay. The second is that success in life depends more and more on possessing adequate skills. The third is that the family is increasingly fragile and less equipped to shoulder conventional welfare responsibilities. And the fourth is that population ageing cannot be halted over the next four decades.

If our goal is to build a welfare architecture that better responds to the new realities there are compelling reasons to give first priority to children. First, and foremost, most women and men want to become parents and it is the obligation of social policy to ensure equal opportunities for society's children. Secondly, and virtually by definition, the task of social policy is to insure its future citizens against social risks. Today's children will face different and more intense risks than previous generations. And thirdly, for any nation that is genuinely committed to a future with minimal social exclusion and maximum economic competitiveness, investing in children must come first.

As we contemplate welfare reform we also need yardsticks of equity and justice, in particular because the kinds of policies that will help establish a positive equilibrium do not come cheap. A child-centred welfare strategy combines two elements that must dictate our equity fundamentals. It represents, on one hand, a substantial investment component. Expenditures that benefit child welfare today yield a positive return over many years. On the other hand, it represents also a unique combination of individual private gains and positive social externalities. At the core of the new welfare edifice lays therefore a strong social investment component that logically requires redistributive financing.

If we desire to improve upon both the quantity and quality of children, my treatment suggests that – on either front – there exists no single ready-made policy remedy. The reasons why citizens do not have the desired number of children are multifaceted: problems of reconciling motherhood and careers. It is not difficult to demonstrate that a well-designed package of leave entitlements and affordable childcare is a first and necessary precondition. But evidence suggests that such a package needs to be accompanied by factors that are usually ignored, such as the characteristics of female employment. It is very likely that a new optimal fertility equilibrium will necessitate a fundamental change of the male life course.

When we examine contemporary life course change it is immediately evident that women have been doing the lion's share of the changing. Put crudely, women are adopting a life course pattern that is ever more masculine. In contrast, men have – except at the margin – hardly altered their life course behaviour. In the past, women's primary concern when contemplating maternity was their husbands' earnings power. This male role is losing relevance since women's concerns centre increasingly on their personal opportunity costs. Hence, the relevance of the male in the fertility equation will increasingly hover around his contribution to childcare and domestic chores. It may require that men embark on a "feminization" of their life course. A major obstacle to this lies in the intensifying competitive nature of economic life. As Sweden exemplifies, policy cannot be effective if the incentives are not strong enough. Since the Swedish earnings structure is unusually compressed, adapting the Swedish approach may be difficult or costly in other countries.

The pursuit of child quality is similarly multifaceted, but it is clear that our attention must focus on the family milieu. A first and necessary step is to minimize economic insecurity within families and, hence, some kind of public guarantee against child poverty would appear an urgent priority. But "money" matters perhaps less than "culture", something that would appear to paralyze policy making. And, yet, we have evidence that investments in children's early development via quality care and other intervention programmes yield very positive results. The key, in a way, lies in minimizing the parental impact among those children that are unluckily born. Targeted intervention can produce excellent results, but then the beneficiary group ends up being far smaller than the truly needy population. Scandinavian experience suggests that we may reap a much greater benefit via universal and quality-invariant childcare.

Finance ministers are likely to oppose such reforms, pointing to the very high costs involved. Were we simply to take Danish practice then we would have to convince the finance ministry to come up with something equivalent to 4% of GDP. Any cost estimate must, nevertheless, take two key considerations into account. Firstly, the kinds of expenditures that will foster births are pretty much the same that will promote child quality and, hence, the same spending commitment kills two birds – indeed three – with one stone. Secondly, the initial public spending on childcare – the heaviest item – will yield a net positive return to government in the long haul – at least if *mothers embrace a full-time, full-life employment preference.* And thirdly, we will probably end up spending similarly, be it through the public purse or from peoples' own pockets. When we debate costs we should always remember that what is cheap for the government ends up more expensive for the citizen.

To end, I emphasize the importance of the long haul for two reasons. One, there is in my opinion only one way to conduct good welfare policy analysis and that is to think in terms of the dynamics of peoples' life course. Two, policy making is myopically timed to the electoral cycle and will, accordingly, easily under-prioritize reforms – however urgently needed – that mainly produce rewards in the long run, i.e. when we are all dead. Realizing how different phases of the life cycle are interconnected goes a long way in improving our ability to pursue the right kinds of welfare reform.

References

Aaberge, R., Columbino, U., & Del Boca, D. (2005). Women's participation in the labour market and fertility. In T. Boeri, D. Del Boca, & C. Pissaridis (Eds.), *Women at Work. An Economic Perspective* (121–239). Oxford: Oxford University Press.

Anderson, P., & Levine, P. (2000). Childcare and mothers' employment decisions. In D. Card & R. Blank (Eds.), *Finding Jobs*. New York, NY: Russell Sage.

Bernardi, F. (2005). Public policies and low fertility. *Journal of European Social Policy*, 15, 123–138.

Bianchi, S. (2000). Maternal employment and time with children. *Demography*, 37, 401–414.

Blau, D., & Robins, P. (1989). Fertility, employment and childcare costs. *Demography*, 26(2), 287–299.

Bowles, S., Gintis, H., & Osborne, M. (2001). The determinants of earnings: a behavioural approach. *Journal of Economic Literature*, XXXIX, 1137–1176.

CERC (2004). *Child Poverty in France*. Paris: Conseil de L'emploi, des Revenues et de la Cohesion Sociale (Report number 4).

Currie, J. (2001). Early childhood intervention programs. *Journal of Economic Perspectives*, 15, 213–238.

Datta Gupta, N. Oaxaca, R., & Smith, N. (2003). Swimming upstream. Floating downstream. *CLS Working Paper,* 01–06. Aarhus University: Department of Economics.

De Graaf, P. (1998). Parents' financial and cultural resources, grades, and transitions to secondary school. *European Sociological Review*, 4, 209–221.

Deding, M., & Lausten, M. (2004). 'Choosing between his time and her time?' Working Paper 4:2004. *Danish Institute for Social Research*, 22 pp.

Del Boca, D. (2002). The effect of childcare and part time in participation and fertility of Italian women. *Journal of Population Economics*, 15, 549–573.

Duncan, G., & Brooks-Gunn, J. (1997). *Consequences of Growing Up Poor*. New York, NY: Russell Sage.

Duvander, A., & Andersson, G. (2005). Gender equality and fertility in Sweden. MPIDR Working Paper 2005-013. Rostock: Max Planck Institute for Demographic Research.

Erikson, R., & Jonsson, J. (1996). *Can Education be Equalized? The Swedish Case in Comparative Perspective*. Boulder, CO: Westview Press.

Ermisch, J. (1988). The econometric analysis of bith rate dynamics in Britain. *Journal of Human Resources*, 23(4).

Ermisch, J., & Francesconi, M. (2002). The effect of parents' employment on children's educational attainment. *ISER Working Paper*, 21, University of Essex.

Esping-Andersen, G. (2004). Education and equal life chances. Investing in children. In O. Kangas & J. Palme (Eds.), *Social Policy and Economic Development in the Nordic Countries*. London: Palgrave Macmillan.

Esping-Andersen, G. (2005). Inequality of incomes and opportunities. In A. Giddens & P. Diamond (Eds.), *The New Egalitarianism*. Cambridge: Polity Press.

Esping-Andersen, G., Gallie, D., Hemerijck, A., & Myles, J. (2002). *Why We Need a New Welfare State*. Oxford: Oxford University Press.

Esping-Andersen, G., Guell, M., & Brodmann, S. (2005). When mothers work and fathers care. Joint household fertility decision making. *DEMOSOC* Working Paper, no. 4. Universitat Pompeu Fabra.

Esping-Andersen, G., & Sarasa, S. (2002). The generational conflict revisisted. *Journal of European Social Policy*, 12, 5–22.

Evers, A., Lewis, J., & Riedel, B. (2005). Developing childcare provision in England and Germany. *Journal of European Social Policy*, 15, 195–210.

Gauthier, A., & Hatzius, J. (1997). Family benefits and fertility: an econometric analysis. *Population Studies*, 38(3), 295–306.

Gonzalez, M., & Jurado, T. (2005). Is there a minimal set of conditions before having a baby? *DEMOSOC Working Paper*, Universitat Pompeu Fabra (June).

Gregg, P., Washbrook, E., Propper, C., & Burgess, S. (2005). The effects of mother's return to work decision on child development in the UK. *The Economic Journal*, 115, 48–80.

Gustafsson, S. (2001). Optimal age at motherhood: theoretical and empirical considerations on postponement of maternity in Europe. *Journal of Population Economics*, 14(2), 225–247.

Gustafsson, S., & Stafford, F. (1992). Childcare subsidies and labor supply in Sweden. *Journal of Human Resources*, 27, 204–230.

Hakim, C. (1996). *Key Issues in Women's Work*. London: Athlone.

Haveman, R., & Wolfe, B. (1995). *Succeeding Generations. On the Effects of Investments in Children*. New York, NY: Russell Sage Foundation.

Heckman, J., & Lochner, L. (2000). Rethinking education and training policy: understanding the sources of skill formation in a modern economy. In S. Danziger & J. Waldvogel (Eds.), *Securing the Future* (47–86). New York, NY: Russell Sage.

Jensen, P. (2002). The postponement of child birth: does it lead to a decline in completed fertility or is there a catch-up effect? Unpublished paper. Aarhus University: Department of Economics (November).

Karoly, L. et al. (1998). *Investing in Our Children. What We Know and Don't Know About the Benefits of Early Childhood Investment*. Santa Monica, CA: Rand Corporation.

Klevemarken, A. (1998). Microeconomic analyses of time use data. Did we reach the promised land? Unpublished paper. Uppsala University: Department of Economics (May 15).

Knudsen, L. (1999). Recent fertility trends in Denmark. The impact of family policy in a period of increasing fertility. Odense: *Danish Centre for Demographic Research,* Research Report, 11.

Kravdal, O. (1996). How the local supply of daycare influences fertility in Norway. *Population Research and Policy Review*, 15(3).

Kreyenfeld, M., & Hank, K. (1999). The availability of childcare and mothers' employment in West Germany. *DIW Discussion Paper,* 191.

Maurin, E. (2002). The impact of parental income on early schooling transitions. *Journal of Public Economics*, 85, 301–332.

Mayer, S. (1997). *What Money Can't Buy*. Cambridge: Harvard University Press.

McDonald, P. (2002). Low fertility: unifying the theory and the demography. Paper presented at the *Population Association of America,* Atlanta, 9–11 May.

OECD (2002). *Babies and Bosses. Reconciling Work and Family Life*. Volume 1. Paris: OECD.

OECD (2003). *Knowledge and Skills for Life*. Paris: OECD.

Polacheck, S. (2003). How the human capital model explains why the gender wage gap narrowed. *Maxwell School Working Paper,* no. 375, Syracuse University.

Rake, K. (2000). *Women's Incomes over the Lifetime*. London: HMSO.

Rosen, S. (1996). Public employment and the welfare state in Sweden. *Journal of Economic Literature*, 34, 729–740.

Ruhm, C. (2004). Parental employment and child cognitive development. *Journal of Human Resources*, 34, 155–192.

Shavit, Y., & Blossfeld, H.P. (1993). *Persistent Inequality*. Boulder, CO: Westview Press.

Sigle-Rushton, W., & Waldvogel, J. (2004). Family gaps in income: a cross national comparison. *Maxwell School of Citizenship and Public Affairs Working Paper,* no. 382.

Sleebos, J. (2003). Low fertility rates in OECD countries. *OECD Social, Employment and Migration Working Paper,* 15.

Sobotka, T., & Lutz, W. (2009). Misleading policy messages from the period TFR. Unpublished paper, Vienna Institute of Demography.

Van de Kaa, D. (2001). Postmodern fertility preferences: from changing value orientation to new behavior. *Population and Development Review*, 27(supplement), 290–331.

Waldvogel, J. (2002). Child care, women's employment and child outcomes. *Journal of Population Economics*, 15, 527–548.

Waldvogel, J., Han, W., & Brooks-Gunn, J. (2002). The effects of early maternal employment on child cognitive development. *Demography*, 39, 369–392.

Waldvogel, J., Higuchi, Y., & Abe, M. (1999). Family leave policies and women's retention after childbirth. *Journal of Population Economics*, 12, 523–546.

Chapter 10
The Post-career Mom: Reproductive Technology and the Promise of Reproductive Choice

Elisabeth Beck-Gernsheim

Introduction

Prologue: From Baby Boom to Fertility Decline

In the social sciences the 1950s and early 1960s are considered the "Golden Age" of marriage and the family. At that time, family behaviour in most Western countries followed clear-cut and definite rules. In fact, there was a standard model of family life. Most men and women started family building early, and the move from one stage to the next did not take long. In a nutshell, it was "love – marriage – baby carriage": First Cupido and the rose colours of young love; followed by a public commitment, the young couple sealing their union in an official ceremony; and soon after pregnancy and, with birth and the first baby, the transition form couple to family.

Tempi passati, fundamental changes have taken place meanwhile. While some people still follow the so-called traditional model, in increasing numbers men and women choose other options, from staying single to cohabiting to same-sex unions to forgoing parenthood. Notwithstanding some national and regional differences, the basic pattern is similar throughout most of Europe. Compared to the mid-1960s, by far fewer people marry and have children; and of those who do so, most do so later and later in life (Allan et al., 2001; Beck-Gernsheim, 2006, 2010).

An Anniversary: The Pill Turns 50

1960 marked a crucial moment in the social history of reproduction. In that year, the contraceptive pill was launched. At first its availability was strictly limited in most countries, tied to narrowly defined clauses (for married women only, for medical

E. Beck-Gernsheim (✉)
Professor of Sociology, Universität Erlangen-Nürnberg, Erlangen, Germany
e-mail: beck-gernsheim@soziol.phil.uni-erlangen.de

G. Beets et al. (eds.), *The Future of Motherhood in Western Societies,*
DOI 10.1007/978-90-481-8969-4_10, © Springer Science+Business Media B.V. 2011

conditions only etc.). But notwithstanding such restrictions it made the headlines, became the subject of heated debates and public controversies, political comment and religious doctrine. To some, it meant the break-down of Christian morality, a sin against the laws of God and nature. Others praised it for freeing women and men from the tyranny of nature, a gift to mankind and a symbol of progress. Yet throughout the debate there was one basic agreement: separating sexuality from reproduction meant no less than a social revolution. Of course, in everyday life the Pros and Cons of the pill were also broadly discussed. Within a few years, the subject of talk here was no more the contraceptive pill – but, symbol of its spreading fame, simply "the pill".

In the 1970s and 1980s, with the rise of the women's movement, the pill gained further momentum. It joined in with the growing unrest and discontent of women, their uprise against strictly defined gender roles, a polarized gender division of labour and "compulsory motherhood". In this context the pill became a symbol of "women's right to choose" (Cisler, 1970; The Boston Women's Health Book Collective, 1971). Gradually and over the span of some time a new era for women began.

Methods of birth control had of course been known for a long time, but the pill was a fundamental breakthrough. For the first time there was a means of contraception which was both simple to use and highly reliable. For the first time women who had sexual intercourse, or wished to have it, could do so without the pressing fear of becoming pregnant. Now, so the promise, women had the freedom of choice: Now they would be able to choose whether or not they wanted children, how many they wanted to have, and when they wanted to have them. Now they could wait until motherhood would fit into their lives and whatever else their plans, hopes, and ambitions. And if for some reason they decided against having children, this option would also be open to them.

Reproductive Freedom Revisited

In the following I take the 50th anniversary as an opportunity to reassess the pill and how it contributed to a transformation of reproductive behaviour. My paper falls into two parts. First I will look into the recent social history of women, motherhood and the family, roughly outline some major trends, and then go on to discuss the following questions: What impact did the pill have? Did it affect the patterns of family building? And more specifically, did it fulfil its promise and bring reproductive freedom for women?

In the second part I will turn from recent social history to scenarios of the future. Building on the trends outlined in the first part, I will suggest and compare two basic options for tomorrow. This will take us to the following questions: Will postponement of motherhood continue and even gain in importance? Will increasing numbers of women have their first child in their 50s, 60s or even 70s? In short, will we witness the rise of new patterns of reproduction, maybe even a reversal of the life cycle, a turn in the timing of crucial events?

Trends in Medical Technology: From the Pill to Reproductive Medicine and Prenatal Diagnosis

From the 1960s onwards, increasing numbers of women gained access to higher education, went to university and entered the labour market. Because these demands stood in stark contrast to the demands of motherhood, many women were caught in a dilemma. They did not want to give up their newly won options, yet they did not want to miss out motherhood either. Hence the appeal of the pill promising women: You can have both.

Postponement

In the wake of the students' movement and women's movement, gender roles became less rigidly and narrowly defined. In many and often subtle ways, the role model for young women began to change. To hurry towards marriage and baby carriage gradually lost its appeal. Instead, some teachers, parents, sisters began to warn girls against settling down too early in marriage and motherhood and thus close down their further options in life. Some media, and in particular some of the women's magazines, started to present glamorous new life-styles and featured the "Top Girl" (Angela McRobbie): young, dynamic and active, single and care-free, endowed with unlimited energy and unlimited ambitions, and making fast progress on the way to success. Last but not least feminist authors joined into the debate. In broadly selling books they took up issues of women's rights, women's bodies, women's lives, and in this context discussed the pill at great lengths (Häussler, 1983; The Boston Women's Health Book Collective, 1971).

Within a few years, marked changes in reproductive patterns began to show. In growing numbers, women took the pill and began to postpone motherhood. Mostly, they did not mean to decide against ever having children. Rather, women wanted them later in life. Now that they had the chance to do so they wanted some time to themselves, whether travelling or more education or just having fun, before starting on the joys and duties of motherhood and family building.

And gradually, expectations began to rise. In growing numbers, women wanted to prepare for motherhood and find the best timing (Rerrich, 1988). They began to wait for the "right moment" to arrive, a time when everything would fit together: finished education, settled in the labour market, gaining a decent income and obtained a nice flat, and last but not least, when they had found Mr. Right. When all seemed fine (or when their longing for a baby overcame their rational planning) they decided for motherhood and stopped taking the pill.

For some women, however, that magic moment never arrived. There was always one piece of the puzzle that would not fit. For example, when they had at last established themselves in their job and could afford a baby-break, their relationship came to an end and they were single again. Or they had at last found their man, but then suddenly their job was being outsourced and their salary gone. So the years passed, yet the moment for having children would not come. In the end, their careful planning and timing produced a paradoxical effect: The better these women wanted to prepare for motherhood, the more likely they would miss out on motherhood.

The Pill as First Step in Reproductive Technology

Postponement also turned out to be problematic in other ways. After a period of postponing, some women decided for motherhood and stopped taking the pill. But then: disappointment. As a pregnancy failed to come, time and again, they came to learn a basic biological fact. Fecundity decreases with advancing age. For this reason, there were more effects to the pill than they had anticipated or wished for. The pill not only made contraception easier, it also made conception more difficult when contraception had ended. Hence once again, a paradox constellation, a full turn of hopes. Women who before had taken great pains to avoid getting pregnant now despaired at *not* being able to get pregnant.

In due course, the demography of childbearing took a new turn. In increasing numbers, women looked for medical help. In increasing numbers, they went for assisted reproductive technology. Here was hope, or at least the promise of hope. Since the 1970s and 1980s, since biotechnology had advanced rapidly, an ever wider range of new infertility treatments were being launched, from hormone stimulation and in vitro fertilization (IVF) to egg cell donation.

Yet again, these options did not come free but with a price-tag attached. To begin with, the financial costs (depending on country and provision the patient has to pay a greater or smaller proportion of the cost of treatment). Furthermore, a range of physical, social and emotional risks, from sexual intercourse according to schedule (more duty than fun) to the emotional strain, the monthly highs and lows while waiting for the results of yet another treatment. Not least the physical strain resulting from extensive interventions into the woman's body (e.g. hormone stimulation). If the woman was lucky, she got pregnant after some time and finally had a child. If not (the success rate of many fertility treatments is as yet limited), the woman was left with a deep sense of disappointment and loss.

Here again, the freedom of choice promised by the pill has turned into its opposite. It has made women clients of reproductive technology and subject to major interventions and risks.

The Risks of Late Motherhood

Yet another group of women got caught in the web of side-effects. After having postponed for years, they opted for motherhood, stopped taking the pill, and got pregnant soon after. Yet now they were in their 30s or even 40s, labelled "late mothers", hence inside a group which, with recent advancements in prenatal and genetic diagnostics, has become the subject of medical statistics, doctors' warnings and public attention (the risks of a genetic deficiency of the embryo increasing with advancing age of the mother). As these statistics made their way into newspaper stories, women's magazines and TV shows, within a few years they became part of public knowledge – and a common fear among pregnant women.

Here again, biotechnology has offered ways for addressing such fears. In prenatal and genetic diagnostics, ever more tests for checking the embryo; and among them various methods to test for Down syndrome, the genetic deficiency most broadly known because closely correlated with the age of the mother. Confronted with medical information and statistical probabilities, confronted with by risks and seeking reassurance from risks, many of today's late mothers-to-be opt for testing. Fluctuating between hope and fear, many hold back their emotions, feel like being in an interim stage, somewhere between being pregnant and not yet being pregnant: a condition of "tentative pregnancy" sets in (Rothman, 1986). Time and again, they have to fight an unsettling question, each starting the same way: What if . . .? What if the amniocentesis should result in a miscarriage (I am now 38, I've waited so long for a baby, perhaps this pregnancy is my last chance)? What if the test shows a serious deficiency (and what does "serious" mean in this context, and how much will the child be affected, or our relationship, or my own life)?

In the end, most women receive good news and feel relieved. Yet if otherwise, they are confronted with more questions and more data, caught between conflicting values and troubling dilemmas, urgently pressed for decisions. To continue and have the baby, wilfully ignoring the negative prospects indicated by the medical data? To decide against having this child, and wilfully end this growing life? Knowing that they are near the end of their reproductive years, they are torn between different risks and pathways. They are into a nightmare of questions (Beck-Gernsheim, 2009; Lemke, 2009), on a "moral odyssey" (Anthony Giddens). And mostly, they are not prepared.

Summing Up

On the one hand, the pill has given women an almost perfect means of contraception and, by way of postponing, a chance for individual timing of motherhood. On the other hand, by offering such options, the pill has contributed to reduce the chances of conception. In this way it has produced a growing demand for more reproductive technology and contributed to the rapid increase in the number of fertility treatments, fertility doctors, fertility clinics. While women in earlier times often were desperate not to get pregnant, many women today desperately *hope* to get pregnant, after years on the pill.

Prospects for the Future: Late, Later, Latest?

Given this constellation, we may now ask: What prospects for the future? Is the trend towards fewer and later births here to stay, will it continue or even increase, or can we expect it to come to a stop sooner or later?

In the following, I will certainly not be able to fully answer such questions. This would imply discussing a broad range of issues (from future advancements in biotechnology to future trends in gender relations, the labour market, economic stability or instability etc.). Instead, I will address such questions in part. Building on the above analysis, I will outline two scenarios for the future: first, a political one; second, a technological one.

First Scenario: The Political Option

In this scenario, first priority is given to the "Why"-question: why do women feel the wish – or need, or pressure – to postpone? Here we will have to take a closer look at the major institutions of modern society (from education to law to social policy and the labour market), in respect to their rules and regulations. Because of its crucial importance, special attention will be given to the labour market. Then, the rapidly increasing pressures in times of a globalizing labour market will come into sight, as shown by recent studies (Blossfeld et al., 2006; Franks, 1999). Today such pressures will be felt by anyone looking for a job; and even more so if he/she should be striving for a moderately attractive position. And for those who set out for the high-ranking positions the pressures will be most urgent. Whether in academia or in other professional fields: young candidates for the road to success have to be prepared for maximum demands in respect to on-the-job availability and on-the-job mobility, or else they needn't apply (Hochschild, 1975; Metz-Göckel et al., 2009).

Given such rules, it is easy to see why early mothers will rarely be able to cope. Unless they are endowed with unlimited energy and optimal health, they will never make it to the top, and rarely to one of the middle-ranking positions. The odds are that early mothers will be stuck in the lower strata of the job hierarchy, with less income, less job stability, and poor prospects for the future. This will barely seem attractive to women who in growing numbers have acquired certificates of higher education or even academic degrees. Hence, they postpone motherhood (Metz-Göckel et al., 2009).

Following this analysis, if we want to address the "Why"-question of postponing, the crucial question is: how to change, adapt, or else banish such rules; how to get rid of rules that implicitly discriminate against motherhood, and even more so against early motherhood.

To some, this may seem an utopian vision. But it isn't, or only to some degree. In recent decades, the Scandinavian countries and France have done much to address such questions and act accordingly, with strategies ranging from political measures and social regulations to economic incentives and subsidies. In Germany, with the country's birth rates still levelling far below replacement, politicians and social scientists have recently started to move in this direction. A prominent example is the Seventh Family Report (published in 2006 by the Ministry of Family, Seniors, Women and Youth). Its authors have focused their analysis on the "rush hours in life", the dead-lock between the care tasks coming with starting a family and the career tasks of getting established in the labour market, both stress-producing and requiring strong personal commitment; in short, two major tasks both squeezed into a short time span, the early years of adulthood. To address the resulting dilemmas, the authors advise against prevailing regulations in education and the labour market which imply a strict and rigid time regime for personal life. Instead, the authors suggest implementing more flexible regulations which allow for individually tailored commitment to family needs; for instance specific regulations which allow young fathers and mothers to interrupt their educational careers during early parenthood, or to reduce working hours temporarily and then go back to their previous schedules.

Second Scenario: The Technological Option

If political efforts of this kind should fail to come, then young women will continue to confront regulations heavily discriminating against early motherhood. To answer this problem, many will continue postponing. Probably quite a few will be willing to experiment with the "How to"-question: how to find better ways of postponing. They go for what I call the "technology option", simply put: bringing in even more reproductive technology.

For instance, some will go for egg freezing, a method as yet in its beginnings but offered already by various foreign clinics, from California to Eastern Europe.[1] On the websites of these clinics, egg freezing is explicitly linked with women's career aims. No more worries that, by the time they are at last ready for motherhood, their ovaries might produce too few or deficient eggs. With egg freezing, so the promise, they can by-pass the biological clock and concentrate on building and pursuing their careers.

According to this vision, "Late, later, latest" will be the model for the future of motherhood, allowing women to have their cake and eat it, make fast progress on the road to success *and* enjoy the joys of motherhood. In a nutshell: From Top Girl to Post-Career Mom. At first sight, this may seem the feminist dream come true, or maybe the post-feminist version of the feminist dream. But again, this option comes with a series of side-effects:

First the physical toll on women's bodies, produced by hormone stimulation. Second, low success rates, at least for the time being. Third, the physical and mental strain on the mother: serving the needs of an infant is a round-the-clock job, its demands are easier to cope with at age 28 than three decades later. Fourth, the consequences with respect to the child: The odds are that his/her mother will (relatively speaking, in comparison to young mothers) sooner feel exhausted, sooner suffer from minor or major physical impairments or some chronic illness, sooner be

---

[1] To analyse trends of an emerging international fertility tourism, I have in the past months visited the web-sites of as yet 30 fertility clinics, situated in various countries, for instance Austria, California, the Czech Republic, Denmark, Israel, Russia, Spain, Turkey, Ukraine, and studied their offers. The results of my analysis will be published.

reduced in her caring capabilities; or, if it comes to the worst, she might even die as a result of some medical condition, leaving behind a young child in need of care.

Fifth, the costs in terms of money: Neither egg freezing nor any of the other options offered by reproductive technology come free. On the contrary, they require medication, tests, laboratory apparatus, and medical staff (in varying degrees, depending on the nature of treatments). While in some cases the costs will be moderate, in others they may rise to staggering heights, especially so in case of repeated IVF attempts, multiple births (often a result of IVF) or surrogacy. Obviously, someone has to pay for all this, whether public health institutions, insurance companies, or the clients themselves, out of their own individual pockets. In any case, the bill will be high.

Conclusions

Does reproductive technology bring reproductive choice? The answer depends on how we define "choice". It is obvious that reproductive technology presents new options to women. Yet, as I have argued in this paper, these new options come not free but at the cost of major interventions and with a high potential of side-effects and risks.

Seen like this, the technological option is no answer. Instead, there are definite (physical, emotional, social, economic) limits to "Late, later, latest", to ever more postponing, combined with ever more reproductive technology to compensate for side-effects.

As shown by numerous studies, the so-called Golden Age of marriage and the family was no Golden Age for women. And "love – marriage – baby carriage", the pattern dominant then, did not leave much room for women and any individual hopes and ambitions they might have. Yet the Post-Career Mom promised by today's reproductive technology is neither a model for a sustainable future. In a nutshell: The technological option, addressing the "How to" of postponing, will not do. Priority must be given to the political option, to address the "Why" of postponing. Otherwise, existing regulations – for instance in the labour market – will continue to stand in the way of gender equality and women's rights. If we fail to invest in the political option, reproductive freedom will continue to be: unfinished business.

References

Allan, G., Hawker, S., & Crow, G. (2001). Family diversity and change in Britain and Western Europe. *Journal of Family Issues*, 22(7), 819–837.

Beck-Gernsheim, E. (2006). *Die Kinderfrage heute. Über Frauenleben, Kinderwunsch und Geburtenrückgang*. Munich: Beck.

Beck-Gernsheim, E. (2009). Der kontrollierte Embryo. Pränataldiagnostik zwischen Wahlmöglichkeiten und Erwartungsdruck. *Die Hebamme*, 22(2), 76–80.

Beck-Gernsheim, E. (2010). Was kommt nach der Familie? Alte Leitbilder und neue Lebensformen. Munich: Beck.

Blossfeld, H.-P. et al. (Eds.) (2006). *Globalization, Uncertainty and Youth in Society*. London and New York, NY: Routledge.

Cisler, L. (1970). Unfinished business: birth control and women's liberation. In R. Morgan (Ed.), *Sisterhood is Powerful. An Anthology of Writings from the Women's Liberation Movement* (274–323). Vintage Books: New York, NY.

Franks, S. (1999). *Having None of It. Women, Men and the Future of Work*. London: Granta.

Häussler, M. (1983). Von der Enthaltsamkeit zur verantwortungsbewußten Fortpflanzung. Über den unaufhaltsamen Aufstieg der Empfängnisverhütung und seine Folgen. In M. Häussler, et al. (Eds.) *Bauchlandungen. Abtreibung – Sexualität – Kinderwunsch* (58–73). Munich: Frauenbuchverlag.

Hochschild, A.R. (1975). Inside the Clockwork of Male Careers. In F. Howe (Ed.), *Women and the Power to Change*, (47–80). New York: McGraw Hill.

Lemke, T. (2009). Kinderwunsch im Spannungsfeld zwischen von Risikodiagnosen und Verantwortungserwartungen. *Die Hebamme*, 22(2), 81–84.

Metz-Göckel, S., Möller, C., & Auferkorte-Michaelis, N. (2009). Wissenschaft als Lebensform – Eltern unerwünscht? Kinderlosigkeit und Beschäftigungsverhältnisse des wissenschaftlichen Personals aller nordrhein-westfälischen Universitäten. Opladen: Verlag Barbara Budrich.

Rerrich, M.S. (1988). Kinder ja, aber... Was es Frauen schwer macht, sich über ihre Kinderwünsche klar zu warden. In D. Jugendinstitut (Ed.), *Wie geht's der Familie?* (59–66). Munich: Kösel.

Rothman, B.K. (1986). *The Tentative Pregnancy. Prenatal Diagnosis and the Future of Motherhood*. New York, NY: Penguin Books.

Seventh Family Report (Siebter Familienbericht) (2006). Familie zwischen Flexibilität und Verläßlichkeit. Perspektiven für eine lebenslaufbezogene Familienpolitik. Bundestagsdrucksache 16/1360, April 26.

The Boston Women's Health Book Collective. (1971). *Our Bodies, Ourselves*. New York, NY: Simon and Schuster.

Chapter 11
On Delayed Fatherhood: The Social and Subjective "Logics" at Work in Men's Lives (a UK Study)

Karen Henwood, Fiona Shirani, and Joanne Kellett nee Procter

As in much of Europe more widely, UK demographic statistics display a striking trend; that the number of men delaying fatherhood has dramatically increased in recent years. For example, in Britain in 2004 more than 75,000 babies were born to fathers aged 40 and over – accounting for more than one in ten children born. This indicates an increase of almost a third from 1999 when only just over 57,000 children were born to a father of the same age group (This is London, 2006). It appears that the average age of both parents is increasing. As birth statistics from the Office for National Statistics (ONS; the UK statistics authority) show, the mean age of the mother at first birth increased from 26.5 in 1994 to 27.5 in 2004, and the majority of births within marriage occurred among women aged 30–34 (ONS, 2005). However, as men are likely to be slightly older than their partners, men are becoming fathers later than women become mothers. There also appears to be a difference in age depending on the relationship status; statistics for fathers show that the modal age of fathers for paternities within marriage was 33 in 2004 compared to 29 for births outside marriage. Whilst births inside marriage have shown an overall 18% decrease between 1994 and 2004, there have been dramatic changes within age groups. For example, there has been a 50% decrease in births inside marriage for men aged 20–24 and 25–29, but a dramatic 40% increase for men aged 40–44. There have also been increases for the 35–39 and 45–49 age groups at 22 and 21% respectively. The dramatic increase in age of fathers at first births is indicative of a growing trend towards delayed fatherhood. ONS statistics (2001) also indicate a striking increase in the number of births outside marriage; 1/3 births were extra-marital in 1999 compared to 1/25 in 1974.

Perpetual Postponers?

Delaying parenthood to this extent has caused concern amongst professional practitioners involved in couples' fertility decision making (Te Velde and Beets, personal

K. Henwood (✉)
Professor of Psychology, School of Social Sciences, Cardiff University, Cardiff, UK
e-mail: HenwoodK@cardiff.ac.uk

G. Beets et al. (eds.), *The Future of Motherhood in Western Societies*,
DOI 10.1007/978-90-481-8969-4_11, © Springer Science+Business Media B.V. 2011

communication), and prompted interest in the phenomenon of "perpetual postponers" among fertility researchers (Berrington, 2004) and the media (Observer, 2009).

Many questions that have been put on the agenda concern men's particular contribution to decision-making about conceiving and raising children. Why do some men wish to remain childless, even when their partners have decided in favour of having a child? Do men who have doubts about becoming fathers nonetheless simply follow their wife/partner's wishes? Or do they further delay the arrival of a first child at the moment when their wives are trying to conceive? Do men generally have a greater reluctance to become fathers than women have to becoming mothers? A further, rather different type of question has been asked querying the lack of interest too often shown in men's involvement in fertility issues. Why is it that some national surveys do not see it as important to collect data on men's contribution to fertility decision making, and assume that money is better spent on surveying only women, as in this way everything about a couple's fertility plans would be known (Beets, 1983)?

While these questions are not, in themselves, the focus of this chapter, they nonetheless provided an essential part of the backdrop to writing it. In discussions with the editors, we realised that we had a rich resource for writing a rather different chapter on delayed fatherhood, in the form of interview data with men who had just become fathers for the first time.[1] Accordingly, the stimulus for the arguments and observations presented in the chapter is a specific analysis of 30 in-depth interviews conducted between December 1999 and March 2000 with first time fathers from a study by Henwood & Procter (2003), showing that there is, potentially and in reality, a multitude of subjectively and socially pertinent reasons for men delaying fatherhood. Of course, we were aware at the stage of preparing our chapter that we were not going to be producing representative claims at population level about men's impact on the timing of parenthood. Nor would we be speaking about our topic using data generated from interviews with men who intended to remain childless or who had not yet taken the step of becoming a father themselves. However, our investigation of men who had just taken the step of making the transition to fatherhood had the advantage of engaging men at a time when the prospects and challenges of fatherhood were very real to them, and when they had to give them serious consideration because they had become part of the very fabric of their existence and lives.

We found it of interest that quantitative studies of perpetual postponers conducted in the UK did not indicate a discrepancy between men and women's fertility intentions and decisions. Berrington's (2004) report showed men's fertility intentions to be remarkably consistent with women's in terms of their patterning by age, intended completed family size (there is no evidence that men intend to have smaller families), and number of children. Such studies suggest the possibility of differences

---

[1] All but three of the men's wives/partners were also first time mothers; two had a young, dependent child, and another had two teenage children, by a previous relationship.

between prospective parents' intentions and ideal and desired family size, and the operation of constraints undermining people making rational choices about if and when to have children. But how far should researchers rely on the idea that people will make rational choices linking their intentions and actual reproductive decisions, all other things being equal? An alternative strategy is to ask "what are the various social and subjective 'logics' at play as people make choices and decisions about such individually and socially complex issues as conception and childbearing?" This is the strategy we followed, as we wished to investigate whether people find such choices and decisions routine and natural, challenging and difficult, and/or whether they approach them in a more or less planned, volitional or "rational" way.

Previous research (Brannen & Nilsen, 2006; Liefbroer, 2005; Heath, 1994) has suggested that men attempt to delay fatherhood, either unconsciously or intentionally, for various reasons. One suggestion is that whilst these "perpetual postponers" accept that women's biological clocks restrict fertility, they do not acknowledge that they also have a reproductive time limit, yet significant risks are associated with older fathers. For example, conception is much less likely with an older man, whilst the risk for conditions such as Down's syndrome and autism is dramatically increased. However, Beckett (2006) suggests that although women who have children at an older age are often regarded as selfish or freakish, older fathers are seen as physically heroic, thus emphasising their masculinity. This implies that many men may intend to have children at some stage but do not believe there is a time limit in which to do so.

Statistics also indicate that socioeconomic status has an impact on the timing of parenthood. Using data from the British household panel survey, Berrington (2004) examines men and women's fertility intentions. Findings indicate that being in the upper earning quartile is positively associated with starting a family at older ages, possibly because the opportunity cost for having a child is highest for women in this group. Alternatively, this group may delay having children because of longer periods in education and time spent establishing careers. Pears et al. (2005, p. 432) state:

> Families with higher socioeconomic status levels, particularly professional families and their offspring, may choose careers involving prolonged higher education and are likely to put off the transition to parenthood.

Other suggestions for delayed parenthood include Tanfer & Mott's (1999) contention that trends of declining marriage, increasing divorce and increasing numbers of children being born out of wedlock signal a weaker commitment of men and women towards one another, making them less inclined to undertake the commitment of having children. In a similar vein, Dennis & Erdos (2000) argue that with the increasing pace of liberation from the family as an institution, men are free to follow their own interests and are becoming less attached to their partners and children. However, these arguments offer a simplistic explanation for delayed parenthood; that in a society characterised by individualism, men are disinclined to embark on parenthood as it involves too much commitment and responsibility.

Our Analytical Approach

In this chapter, our analytical approach involves moving beyond statistics-based speculation, and explanations of delayed fatherhood based on an individualistic account of men's decisions, relationships and lives. As already mentioned above, we also depart from making over-rationalist (and materialist) assumptions about how people come to make reproductive choices and decisions.

A number of assumptions underpin our approach to our research. Becoming a father is a major life transition for men, as is motherhood for women. Yet what it means to men themselves is not simply obvious and transparent to them as they encounter the prospect of becoming a father for the first time (Daly, 1996). Accordingly, it is necessary to investigate men as they talk about, and reflect upon, their thoughts, beliefs, expectations and experiences of becoming a father. This can bring to light the meanings and significance attached to fatherhood as men live out their lives, and how they are connecting with some of the major controversies and issues of the day – in terms, for example, of the links between fatherhood and masculinity.

By investigating men's talk, their perceptions, and how they account for life transitions and social change, in a qualitative, in depth, and nuanced way, it is possible for researchers to listen closely to men's thoughts and ideas, and by so doing attend to more than clear and coherent meanings. At times, what may be important in the men's talk may be more tacit, psychologically invested and emotion-laden (Hollway & Jefferson, 2000). Listening to these moments makes it possible for researchers to consider more than the most non-conflictual, conscious thoughts and acceptable feelings at play in men's lives. This means that, through careful listening, a researcher is less likely to take at face value any simple assertions of interviewees' beliefs and opinions; since the men's accounts will offer more depth and substance than is provided by simple propositions and isolated statements of the kind found in surveys. We believe that such close listening increases the "validity" of our interpretations of the interview data (Henwood, 2004). In turn, we are able to make careful connections with, offer support for, or make arguments against specific prior claims, observations and propositions in the theoretical and substantive literature.

We attach a lot of importance to grounding claims about how best to interpret men's words, and their contributions to delayed parenthood, in the rigors of conducting original, qualitative, empirical research (Charmaz, 2006; Mason, 2002; Pidgeon & Henwood, 2004; Henwood & Pidgeon, 2003; Coffey & Atkinson, 1999). We also recognise the possible limits imposed on some of our conclusions, by relying upon our particular interview sample. As part of this, we do need to make clear the socio-demographic composition of our group of men. The 30 fathers interviewed included a mix of mainly married and cohabiting men, with just one non-resident father. Fathers were aged 20 to late 30s, with a majority in their early to mid 30s. There was a good range of different socio-economic/class backgrounds and types of occupational position, including some lowest paid casual workers and unemployed men, through to higher managerial, administrative and service professionals. Mostly interviewees were in full time paid employment before and after birth, with just two working part time; there was one houseparent, and one man remained by choice without work, with his wife as sole economic provider, after the birth.

Of particular concern was the relative lack of young fathers in our sample. Young fathers have often been neglected in comparison with teenage mothers in efforts to understand parenting transitions, experiences and contributions to child welfare and family life (Quinton et al., 2002; Sigle-Rushton, 2005). Frequently they are not included in studies aiming to appreciate the range of ways in which men and fathers subjectively view their fatherhood ideals and their practices (see e.g. Dermott, 2003). In research aiming to generate knowledge and assist in the development of professional practice, finding any possible ways to remedy this gap is considered important (Bunting & McAuley, 2004; Fisher, 2004; Reeves, 2006). Consequently, we take the unusual step in the concluding section of this chapter of supplementing our core arguments and observations with a commentary that takes into account the rather different circumstances of younger fathers, and considers the meanings and experiences of fatherhood from their life perspectives. We believe that so doing adds an important point of reflexive analysis (Adkins, 2002; Henwood, 2008; May, 2002) of the contingencies impacting upon our investigation, and that it promotes understanding of the implications and significance of the main body of presented findings.

Our aim, in conducting and reporting the research, is to begin to tease out some of the personal and wider, social implications of longstanding, continuing and changing familial arrangements, social expectations, and cultural ideals pertaining to men's positions and roles as fathers. How such arrangements and changes are being interpreted, how they are being responded to, negotiated and/or contested by fathers themselves is a critical form of "data" to be acknowledged, sifted and discussed, as one part of informed commentary on the present realities and future prospects of parenthood and family life. The social and moral "imperatives" of caring and earning in family life, as they are sometimes called, need to be interrogated, through careful consideration of competing social, political and evidence based claims (see e.g. Neale & Smart, 2002). In this chapter, we use an interpretive, qualitative research strategy that is similar to Neale and Smart's to do this.

Commitment and Responsibility

As Anderson (1997) acknowledges, men's relationships with women are one fundamental source of their desires for children, and these relationships are likely to have a significant impact on timing of entry into parenthood. Some authors have used the increasing rates of cohabitation and children born outside of wedlock alongside the decline in marriage and increase in divorce to suggest that men are now less inclined to commit to their paternal roles and relationships with partners. Additionally, authors such as Furstenburg (1988) suggest that fatherhood is assuming a more voluntary dimension as there is less pressure on men to be good providers, meaning men are now able to retreat from their responsibility. However, the interview analysis does not support this notion, as the overwhelming majority of men still keenly felt the responsibility of providing and were eager to be involved with all aspects of their children's lives, feeling that by delaying fatherhood they were now better able to do this. For example, many of the older fathers interviewed stated that they had waited to have children until they had a stable job, owned their own house and were in a secure relationship in order to provide the child with stability and be able to offer the commitment required.

> I never really wanted to start a family when I was too young. But at this stage I think at twenty seven you know a bit more about what is going on around you. You know a bit more about what you want out of life and what career prospects that you have your basic security as opposed to a person who is twenty one or twenty two or something like that. My wife has always wanted children from when we met, I was a bit reluctant at first because I wanted to get my career going. I wanted other things, like having a house and all the rest of that before you bring a child into the world. But everything just sort of fell into place, we got here I have got a good job. We are in the process of buying a house like I said, so everything looks as if it is going for us at the moment. (Frank, age 27)

Bergnéhr (2007) has suggested that men and women reflect carefully on their relationships before deciding to embark on parenthood. She suggests that as there become fewer obligations to remain in a romantic relationship but more requirements to fulfil, people experience stress and anxiety over the adequacy of their relationship, which is increased when thinking about having children. Subsequently, this may account for longer periods between marriage and parenthood than was common in previous generations. In addition, Bergnéhr contends that cohabitation does not signify a weaker inclination to commit; in reality, she argues, people use a period of cohabitation as a trial period to test how stable the relationship is before bringing in the additional complication of children.

It appears that children are seen as a much bigger responsibility for men than they were in previous generations. Bergnéhr states that children are seen as tying people down, making it harder to be flexible and mobile; highly valued characteristics of a society permeated by what Beck & Beck-Gernsheim (2002) refer to as "institutionalised individualism". In addition, as people are likely to have fewer children, they have the responsibility to invest more in them. Gittins (1993, pp. 110–111) writes:

> The fact that the majority of people in contemporary society have very few children or none at all, means that for those who do have one or two children more is expected of them. More, too, is 'invested' in them in terms of education, aspirations, emotional demands and fears.

The implication of this is that with this increased responsibility, men are waiting until they are emotionally mature enough to fully commit to it.

Several of the men implied that their partners had wanted children for a while but they had persuaded them to wait. For example, Simon had been with his partner for 10 years, and whilst she had always wanted children, he felt that it was only the "right time" now because of a combination of age, maturity and employment status. Other participants acknowledged that they had gone through periods of adulthood where they did not want children, or did not feel ready for them and had persuaded their partners to delay parenthood until their views about fatherhood had changed. One participant said that he was going along with what his wife wanted in having children, but did not really want a child as he was concerned it would "upset the apple cart" and interfere with their current lifestyle (Howard, age 36). However, this participant was an exception, as most of the men were pleased about the pregnancy, whether it had been planned or not. Subsequently, we can argue that some men may not feel ready for parenthood at the same time as their partners, and that some women may become mothers later than they would have ideally liked. Other research has found high levels of marital dissatisfaction when partners disagree on the timing of parenthood (Cowan & Cowan, 2009).

A Life of One's Own

One suggestion for men's postponement of fatherhood that has been briefly touched on is that there are ever increasing demands and expectations for being a good father, meaning much more of an input is required from men. Although the ideal of the man as a sole breadwinner has apparently become less prominent in recent years as increasing numbers of women are entering the workforce, and there are more dual earner families, in practice, men still appear to view the role of provider as fundamental to fathering. Alongside the breadwinner role, men are expected to spend time with their children, share all aspects of childcare and be emotionally open, warm and demonstrative. Many of the men interviewed reflected that this stream of demands left them with little time for themselves:

> When the father, in my case is a sole breadwinner but also coming home I have to be a father when I get home, whereas my wife is looking after the baby and probably when I get home she can switch off and become herself again, spend some time on her own. From that point of view probably my time is going to be more condensed into when can I have time, so to speak, quality time on my own. (Sebastian, age 26)

Bergnéhr asserts that people are strongly influenced by notions of self-fulfilment, but families and relationships restrain the freedom to do this. Liefbroer (2005) suggests that the decision to have children is usually the result of weighting social and emotional benefits against financial and opportunity costs. Liefbroer draws on Van de Kaa's (1993) "Second Demographic Transition Theory" (1993) which suggests that processes of modernisation, secularisation and individualisation in Western societies have reduced people's inclination to adhere to normative guidelines, whilst increasing the value of individual autonomy. As children are seen as impinging on autonomy, individuals will only choose to have children if the responsibilities can be accepted and if it will contribute to their "self". Liefbroer therefore argues that the postponement of fertility decisions is driven by the notion that having children will seriously diminish individual autonomy. Subsequently, it appears that men often view themselves as making better fathers in their 30s and 40s because they are then able to have an individualistic phase during their teens and 20s where they can achieve educational qualifications, build a career, establish a secure relationship and gain life experiences through things like travelling. In other words, they have time to do what they want before committing to putting someone else first.

Well when I was in my 20s it was the last thing that I wanted seeing other people, seeing my two sisters, brother, who've got children, and friends made me feel that it was something very restricting and something that inhibits sort of being able to fulfil myself, you know. I mean, in my 20s it was very much about, for me, it was very much about, er, travelling and enjoying meself and relationships were important but the relationships were more about exploring myself through a relationship, but, yeah, I suppose as I got round to about 30, I sort of felt, you know, that "I'm thirty", and okay, work is fine and I'm sort of succeeding with that and you know that, er, I'm about to buy my own property, financially things were okay, you know, but I just felt that I'd gone through a series of different sort of relationships and things and it was becoming a bit shallow, you know, and that something in me needed more than that. Then the final thing, it felt to me that it was quite an instinctual thing really, it just started surfacing, you know, that, sort of looking at people with children and really being attracted to children and to young children and being sort of emotionally drawn to them and thinking "Oh, this is a wonderful, wonderful thing". (Rick, age 35)

It appears that men still intend to be fathers at some stage in their lives, but do not envision a particular age at which they will do so. For many, natural life course transitions, of which a man's perceptions of his partner's biological clock are but one part, lead them to becoming delayed fathers.

I suppose it's being settled in our lives in that you find yourself um, when we first knew each other, before we first married, we went out a lot to pubs and clubs what have you and friends did as well, and as they all married off and indeed we got married as well you find, or we found that there's less people who we enjoy spending time with out on the social scene, and we were quite happy spending time at home, or round our friends houses drinking bottles of wine, just getting quietly drunk together rather than loudly drunk out, at which point it sort of crossed our minds that, my wife being thirty, she's thirty five at the moment, time's ticking away if we want to have a family, and we did, so it just seemed like a natural progression really. We reached the point where a baby would no longer, or we think would no longer be a, you know, a bond, it would be something that we'd really enjoy. (Pete, age 35)

The Unknown

One further reason that men may decide to delay fatherhood is that they have no idea what is expected of them, or what to expect from parenthood, and are concerned about facing the unfamiliar. Many men stated in the interviews that they had not received adequate information from the health service about their impending fatherhood, leaving them feeling detached, helpless and concerned about the unknown. This supports previous research which has suggested that the health service does not provide adequate information to impending fathers (Anderson, 1997). Twelve of the men interviewed had very little or no experience of children, leaving them completely in the dark about what dealing with a baby would involve, which was described as "daunting". However, although men feel anxiety about the unknown, many men relish the opportunity offered by this new challenge, which they anticipate will be fulfilling. This supports previous research by Lupton & Barclay (1997, p. 145):

Fatherhood, for most of the men in our study, did challenge their sense of being 'in control'. This loss of control was associated with distress and frustration, as well as anxieties about dealing with a tiny infant. At the same time, however, they found much pleasure in being part of 'the family unit' and taking on responsibility for a child.

In addition to concerns over not knowing what to expect from fatherhood, men also experience anxiety about how the child will affect the spousal relationship. As one of the participants in Bergnéhr's study states: "you know what you've got but not what you'll get" (2007, p. 8). Several participants in the interviews believed that having a child would alter their relationship with their partner and were not entirely sure how this change would manifest itself, although some suspected their partner would have less time for them, which may result in feelings of jealousy.

You keep hearing how things change after you have a family and I'm fairly sure it will but I don't know how yet. I think I will have to sort of share her so I suppose I, in some ways I've had it all to myself in the house, whereas, you know, it will be having to compete with the first-born. (Keith, age 31)

These concerns about the unknown are compounded by men not being able to talk to anyone about their feelings. Several of the men felt that they could not talk about impending fatherhood at work, as people without children would be bored by the topic. Interestingly, those men who worked with predominantly female colleagues were much more likely to discuss the pregnancy and fatherhood than those with male colleagues in more traditionally masculine occupations. The men interviewed were also particularly reluctant to ask advice from people with children, although they acknowledged that if advice was offered they would take it on board. Some of the men stated that they did not feel able to talk to friends, parents or even their partners about their worries and concerns over fatherhood. However, when men had access to other men in the same circumstances; through ante-natal classes, or friends at work, they found it useful to talk about fatherhood and know somebody else was experiencing the same things. It is possible that this reluctance to discuss feelings about fatherhood may prove an impediment to being an emotionally open and involved father.

Alongside these uncertainties over impending fatherhood and the future of their relationships, some researchers have suggested that men contend with the nebulous concept of the "new father", leaving men confused over what is expected of them (Dermott, 2003). This supports Aitken's (2000) contention that there are mixed messages on how to be a modern man and whilst some characteristics are publicly defined, men are often still unclear of what is now expected of them in private. Burgess (1997) suggests that because of this confusion over what fathering involves, men are often inhibited regarding their behaviour in public; feeling unable to openly raise their concerns about fatherhood and lacking the social outlets to discuss childcare that women have access to; therefore these anxieties are never satisfied, meaning men may continue to delay having children.

Similarly, Frosh (1997, p. 51) contends that there is a crisis of masculinity which positions men in a strained position regarding ideals of fathering:

> To father a child requires something other than the traditional boundary-setting and pro-hibitive stance, as no authority is vested in the father to sustain that stance; but to reach out in a loving way requires a shift of masculine consciousness, involving not just some more gentleness but a whole gamut of alterations in relations of dependency, intimacy, vulnerability and trust.

These arguments imply that this position of uncertainty is likely to have a significant impact upon men's decisions to become fathers; as they may delay having children whilst these uncertainties play on their minds. However, these explanations may be a little outdated, as for example Lupton & Barclay (1997) argue that the family gains more strength from the "new father" than from the "traditional strong father" archetype as men are now able to take an equal role in parenting and feel able to express their nurturant feelings. Similarly, many men in the interviews had a clear view of what fatherhood would involve and what was expected of them, and saw the changing image of fatherhood as positive as it offered them a different way to express masculinity, by being an involved, loving father.

> I think a lot of the bravado in men has gone. The big 'I am, I'm the hard disciplinarian, the breadwinner', or whatever. I think this modern man issue has come into it. I think men aren't so scared to show their feelings. (Malcolm age 32)

Many of the men also had clear ideas of how they would like to be seen as a father.

> Someone who's there, someone who's approachable, full involvement down to changing nappies, washing nappies, whatever. I think, to some degree, I would prefer to look at myself as a 'mother' figure. I know it sounds quite silly, but the role of the mother because they seem to be there all the time, involved all the time, and they're 'best friends' so to speak. I wouldn't want to be, my relationship with my father I wouldn't say was particularly very good. He was quite Victorian, and there's certainly no way I'd like to be like that. I'd like to be a bit more modern and approachable. (Malcolm age 32)

This supports the finding by Lupton & Barclay (1997) that the men interviewed overwhelmingly saw their own fathers as "emotionally distant" and contrasted this with how they wanted to be involved with their children. These changing conceptions of fatherhood provide advantages for men in that being a caring, emotionally open father is no longer at odds with being a masculine man, enabling men to become more involved in all aspects of their children's lives. As Lupton and Barclay note, the closeness between father and child is seen as beneficial for both parties, by providing emotional fulfilment for both.

The Child's Best Interests

Whilst fertility experts have been concerned about the trend of delayed parenthood because of its implications for population demographics, research has demonstrated that men who delay parenthood often make better fathers. For example, Heath (1994) conducted a study to compare the father-child relationship of on-time fathers (under 35) with late-time fathers (35 and older). Findings indicate that late-time fathers were more likely to spend time in leisure activities with their children, have higher expectations of their children's behaviour and be more nurturant towards their children. This may be indicative of greater maturity in late-time fathers.

> I just hope that we will both be healthy, because that is the danger isn't it for late parents. I mean people who perhaps have kids in their forties that they are just not going to see out you know very much of their child's life. I suppose that Janet and I are thirty eight now and I mean I suppose that that is a bit of a reality too. But I don't know why but I always thought of people who had really old parents as being quite lucky children when I was small, because it just seemed that parents seemed to be so much sorted with the way that they dealt with their children. Because they were more mature, than they were when they were really young. It just seems to be easy to be a parent to handle things like disciplinarians safety and various kind of making a decision seems to be, I don't know, seems to be when you are more experienced or probably easier to make. You might agonize over it more but probably those decisions are probably easier to make. (Terry, age 38)

Heath puts forward advantages of late-time fatherhood; these children enter families when the breadwinner has achieved some success in the workplace and consequently has a higher salary and more freedom to spend time with the child, with the men also getting emotional fulfilment from time with the child rather than at work. Pleck (1997) notes that whilst several studies have found older fathers are more involved with their children, substantial proportions of working fathers report stress in combining work and family roles. Yet, Pleck argues that paternal engagement has increased over the last three decades and this engagement is associated with desirable outcomes in children (cognitive competence, empathy, less gender-role stereotyping), also promoting psychosocial development in fathers themselves. Because these men wait to have children, it may be more likely that the child was wanted and that men have more interest in the father role. However, because these men had waited years to have a child, anxieties about child-rearing abilities and losing the child could be triggered.

The Changing Role of Fathers

Brannen & Nilsen (2006) compared fathering within families of four generations in order to examine how it has changed. They found that the current generation of fathers achieved fatherhood over a longer period and via a pattern of life course transitions *before* embarking on fatherhood, in contrast to the world war two generation, whose transitions into work, marriage and fatherhood happened within only a few years of each other. Brannen and Nilsen note that with a trend towards increased working hours, some fathers in the current generation were more work-focussed than their own fathers had been, giving them less time for their families. They conclude that although there is both transmission and change in fathering over time, the work-focussed father permeates the ideology of all generations. However, it is no longer acceptable for men to be exempt from active involvement with their children because of their breadwinner status. Thus it could be argued that society's expectations of men as fathers are higher than ever before.

Henwood & Procter (2003) note that whilst interviewees in their study welcomed the opportunities offered to them by the new model of fatherhood, there were also some areas of tension; providing cash and care, valuing selflessness and autonomy and negotiating fairness, equity and decision making. The men in their study showed a clear preference for involved fatherhood, in contrast with the previous disciplinarian figure, which was seen to have inhibited their fathers in developing relationships. However, these raised expectations meant that prior to the birth, some men were anxious about making the change to being a selfless, sensitive child-centred parent and questioned their ability to do so.

Whilst men are expected to embody aspects of the "new father", they are also expected to fulfil traditional "masculine" roles such as providing and breadwinning. These conflicting expectations can place men in a position of uncertainty, which renders them unwilling to embark on parenthood. For example, Gatrell (2005) argues that culture of long working hours is not conducive to being an involved father, yet the social identity of fathers remains inextricably linked to their occupational status due to constraining social expectations. Interview research with men about their experiences as fathers, and which has identified tensions introduced by different fatherhood discourses into the lives of men who have become fathers, has prompted some similar observations and reflections.

> Nonetheless, there was still evidence that at least some of the men were struggling with the privileged discourse of emotional 'involvement' with their children. The men's tendency to draw on notions of 'protector' and 'provider', the person who ideally is 'strong' and 'controlled' when describing how best to deal with fatherhood, suggests a discourse of fatherhood that continues to be phrased through gendered assumptions. (Lupton & Barclay, 1997, pp. 145–146)

Lupton and Barclay argue that whilst men are now more able to express their desire for intimacy with their children, they do this within a socio-cultural setting in which men are still expected to work in order to support their families, meaning that men's interactions with their children are constrained by the demands of paid employment.

Conclusions

In interviews they conducted with young men about how they imagined their adult lives, Edley & Wetherell (1999) found that almost all their participants anticipated getting married and having children; indicating that men's intention of becoming fathers has not altered, but the change has been in the age they enter into fatherhood. Where research has considered expectations for women to "have it all", it appears the same phenomenon may be increasingly applicable to men; who are expected to excel in the workplace, be loving, sharing partners and involved and emotionally open fathers. In addition, where men are uncertain about what fathering a child actually involves, or concerned about their capacity to meet expectations of fathers, this can compound their anxieties, meaning that they are likely to delay parenthood to when they feel they have the time and resources to devote to being a committed and responsible parent. From this perspective, delayed fatherhood does not have to be seen as a negative phenomenon, as these men are likely to have more time and resources for the child, providing them with better opportunities.

> Yeah, I think, it's always been there, I've always wanted to have children, and, erm, it's not a career term ambition but it's not the word I'd use, 'ambition', it's something that I've always thought that, you know, it's part and parcel of a marriage and part and parcel of what my life, you know, I want my life to be, I want to be a father, and, erm, it really, it just obviously seemed right. (Trevor, age 32)

Reflecting upon the demographic argument that has recently been made in media discussions (Beckett, 2006) in favour of men matching their own biological clocks with that of their partner, our suggestion would be that this is an unrealistic stance, and does not fit with findings about the social and subjective logics at work in men's lives. Such a position would require many men to become fathers before they felt ready, and could lead to resentment towards the child for causing them to miss out on time and experiences they could have had before parenthood. In addition, earlier fatherhood may mean bringing a child into a less stable environment, as men would have less time to establish a secure relationship with their partners, and less time to ensure they had a reliable job. With increasing numbers of men and women spending longer amounts of time in education, and therefore longer before starting paid work and establishing a career, it appears inevitable, for higher socioeconomic groups at least, that the age of first parenthood will be delayed.

Whilst this chapter has sought to demonstrate that delayed fatherhood can have positive outcomes for both father and child, it is important not to pathologise young parents. Teenage or young parents are frequently portrayed by the media as irresponsible and inept parents, having children as a result of an accident. However, in research focussing upon teenage mothers, the point has been made about that it is important not to neglect the specific circumstances affecting such young women's lives, their reproductive decisions, and their transition into motherhood (see e.g. Phoenix, 1991). Likewise, the same point can be made about teenage fathers' adult transitions, reproductive trajectories, and role in parenting children.

Boys from disadvantaged backgrounds (low socioeconomic status, behavioural and educational difficulties, divorced parents) are those most likely to become young fathers (Sigle-Rushton, 2005), which raises concerns about the kind of start in life that they can offer their children. The lack of educational qualifications amongst these fathers may make it more difficult to secure well-paid, stable jobs, leaving them vulnerable to marginalisation. However, rather than seeing teenage fatherhood as an irresponsible accident, some research has indicated that a proportion of teenage parents choose to have their children young as a way of changing their lives for the better (Cater & Coleman, 2006). From in-depth interviews with 51 young parents (aged 14–21) who had all planned to have children, Cater and Coleman found that these parents saw having a child as a route out of family hardships and unhappiness, a chance for independence and an opportunity to gain a new identity. For the young fathers, bringing up a baby was seen as providing a purpose and sense of capability and satisfaction, which they did not get from paid work. Therefore, children could offer a way of achieving status and purpose for this marginalised group, who may be able to create a loving family of their own to compensate for negative childhood experiences. The youngest father interviewed by Henwood & Procter (2003) felt that impending fatherhood had helped him to mature and become a better person.

This chapter has sought to depart from the methodology of previous studies by interviewing fathers independently. Research such as by Berrington (2004) usefully provides statistical information based on a large number of respondents. By contrast, interview data is highly responsive to contextual influences, raising questions about the effects of interviewing men and their partners at the same time. The interviews conducted by Henwood & Procter (2003) offered men the opportunity to discuss their views, feelings and fears about fatherhood within a space where partnership and relationships were included as a substantive focus to be addressed, but where enactment of the ongoing relationship with a partner did not set the framework for discussion. As a feature of in-depth qualitative research more generally, the data produced by the interviews, along with the need to pay rigorous attention to the challenges of interpreting such data, offered insights into explanations behind statistical trends.

So what about the future of motherhood? It should be considered that it is not just men, but also women who may decide to delay having children. A study by Tyden et al. (2006) of 300 female students in Sweden found that on average, women wanted to be aged 29 at the birth of their first child and 35 at the last. There was some indication that fertility issues were not paramount for many of these women, as only 18% ranked having a child before they got too old as very important. There were certain factors in the study that women saw as important in their decision to have a child: being sufficiently mature, having completed studies and having a stable partner to share parenthood with. It is possible that the contemporary and growing emphasis on "sharing parenthood" may be because once women have established a career, they have more to lose from having children and may be unwilling to take on a "second shift" of extra housework and childrearing responsibilities (Hochschild, 1989). With fathers who increasingly expect to share parenting and take an active role in the care of their children, some women may have more time and opportunities for self-development and investment in their careers.

Acknowledgement This study was funded initially by the Economic and Social Research Council (Grant No: R0222 5016). It is now part of the national ESRC collaborative network "Timescapes" (Grant No: RES-347-25-0003).

References

Adkins, L. (2002). Reflexivity and the politics of qualitative research. In T. May (Ed.), *Qualitative Research in Action* (332–348). London: Sage.
Aitken, S. (2000). Fathering and faltering: "Sorry, but you don't have the necessary accoutrements". *Environment and Planning*, 32, 581–598.

Anderson, D. (1997). Men, reproduction and fatherhood. International Union for the Scientific Study of Population, Policy and Research Paper No 12.

Asthana, A., & Hill, A. (2009). Late Motherhood: Time for a vital wake-up call. The Observer. Sunday 9th August 2009.

Beck, U., & Beck-Gernsheim, E. (2002). *Individualization: Institutionalised Individualism and Its Social and Political Consequences*. London: Sage.

Beckett, A. (2006). Who's broody now? Guardian Unlimited. Available at http://www.guardian.co.uk/science/story/0,,1766358,00.html (accessed 17/03/07).

Beets, G. (1983). Vruchtbaarheidsverwachtingen van mannen en vrouwen (Birth expectations of males and females). In *Maandstatistiek van de bevolking (CBS)* (Statistics Netherlands – Monthly bulletin of population statistics), 31(2), 26–36.

Bergnéhr, D. (2007). Love and family: Discussions between Swedish men and women concerning the transition to parenthood. *Forum Qualitative Social Research*, 8(1) Art 23, January (online journal – www.qualitative-research.net/fqs)

Berrington, A. (2004). Perpetual postponers? Women's, men's and couples' fertility intentions and subsequent fertility behaviour. *Population Trends*, 117, Autumn, 9–19.

Brannen, J., & Nilsen, A. (2006). From fatherhood to fathering: transmission and change among British fathers in four-generation families, *Sociology*, 40(2), 335–352.

Bunting, L., & McAuley, C. (2004). Research review: teenage pregnancy and parenthood: the role of fathers, child and family. *Social Work*, 9, 295–303.

Burgess, A. (1997). *Fatherhood Reclaimed: The Making of the Modern Father*. London: Vermillion.

Cater, S., & Coleman, L. (2006). *Planned Teenage Pregnancy – Perspectives of Young Parents from Disadvantaged Backgrounds*. York: Joseph Rowntree Foundation.

Charmaz, K. (2006). *Constructing Grounded Theory: A Practical Guide Through Qualitative Analysis*. London: Sage.

Coffey, A., & Atkinson, A. (1999). *Making Sense of Qualitative Data*. London: Sage.

Cowan, P., & Cowan, C. (2009). *News you can use: are babies bad for marriage?* A Research Update from the Council on Contemporary Families. Chicago, IL: University of Illinois, January 9, 2009

Daly, K. (1996). Spending time with the kids: meanings of family time for fathers. *Family Relations*, 45, 466–476.

Dennis, N., & Erdos, G. (2000). *Families Without Fatherhood*. Third edition. Trowbridge: Cromwell Press.

Dermot, E. (2003). The 'intimate father': defining paternal involvement. *Sociological Research Online*, 8(4).

Edley, N., & Wetherell, M. (1999). Imagined futures: young men's talk about fatherhood and domestic life. *British Journal of Social Psychology*, 38, 181–194.

Fisher, C. (2004). *Fatherhood and Mental Health: A Qualitative Study of Fathers with Mental Health Difficulties Who Live with Their Children*. Unpublished DClinPsy Thesis. Cardiff: University of Wales.

Frosh, S. (1997). Fathers' ambivalence (too). In W. Holloway, & B. Featherstone (Eds.), *Mothering and Ambivalence*. London: Routledge.

Furstenburg, F.F. (1988). Good dads-bad dads: two faces of fatherhood. In E.J. Cherlin (Ed.), *The Changing American Family and Public Policy* (193–218). Washington, DC: The Urban Institute Press.

Gatrell, C. (2005). *Hard Labour: The Sociology of Parenthood*. New York, NY: Open University Press.

Gittins, D. (1993). *The Family in Question: Changing Households and Familiar Ideologies*. Second edition. Basingstoke: Macmillan.

Heath, T. (1994). The impact of delayed fatherhood on the father-child relationship. *Journal of Genetic Psychology*, 155(4).

Henwood, K.L. (2004). Reinventing validity: reflection on principles and practices from beyond the quality-quantity divide. In Z. Todd, B. Nerlich, & S. McKeown (Eds.), *Mixing Methods in Psychology: The Integration of Qualitative and Quantitative Methods in Theory and Practice*. Hove and New York, NY: Psychology Press.

Henwood, K.L. (2008). Qualitative research, reflexivity and living with risk: valuing and practicing epistemic reflexivity and centring marginality. *Qualitative Research in Psychology*, 5(1), 45–55.

Henwood, L., & Pidgeon, N. (2003). Grounded theory. In P. Camic, L. Yardley, & L. Rhodes (Eds.), *Qualitative Research in Psychology: Expanding Perspectives and Methods*. Washington, DC: American Psychological Association.

Henwood, K.L., & Procter, J. (2003). The 'good father': reading men's accounts of paternal involvement during the transition to first time fatherhood. *British Journal of Social Psychology*, 42, 337–355.

Hochschild, A.R. (1989). *The Second Shift. Working Parents and the Revolution at Home*. New York, NY: Viking.

Hollway, W., & Jefferson, T. (2000). *Doing Qualitative Research Differently: Free Association, Narrative and the Interview Method*. London: Sage.

Liefbroer, A. (2005). The impact of perceived costs and rewards of childbearing on entry into parenthood: evidence from a panel study. *European Journal of Population*, 21, 367–391.

Lupton, D., & Barclay, L. (1997). *Constructing Fatherhood: Discourses and Experiences*. London: Sage.

Mason, J. (2002). *Qualitative Researching*. Second edition. London: Sage.

May, T. (Ed.) (2002). *Qualitative Research in Action*. London: Sage.

Neale, B., & Smart, C. (2002). Caring, earning and changing: parenthood and employment after divorce. In A. Carling, S. Duncan, & R. Edwards (Eds.), *Analysing Families: Morality and Rationality in Policy and Practice* (183–198). London: Routledge.

ONS – Office for National Statistics (2001). Social focus on men. London: The Stationery Office. Available at http://www.statistics.gov.uk/downloads/theme_social/Social_Focus_on_Men/SfoM(Final).pdf (accessed 17/03/07).

ONS – Office for National Statistics (2005). Birth statistics: review of the Registrar General on births and patterns of family building in England and Wales, 2004. Series FM1 No. 33. London: ONS.

Pears, K., Pierce, S., Kim, H., Capaldi, D., & Owen, L. (2005). The timing of entry into fatherhood in young, at-risk men. *Journal of Marriage and Family*, 67, 429–447.

Phoenix, A. (1991). *Young Mothers*. Oxford: Polity Press.

Pidgeon, N., & Henwood, P. (2004). Grounded theory. In M. Hardy, & A. Bryman (Eds.), *Handbook of Qualitative Data Analysis* (625–648). London: Sage.

Pleck, J. (1997). Paternal involvement: levels, sources and consequences. In M. Lamb (Ed.), *The Role of the Father in Child Development*. Third edition. New York, NY: Wiley and Sons.

Quinton, D., Pollock, S., & Golding, J. (2002). The transition to fatherhood in young men: Influences in commitment. ESRC Report. Available at www.regard.ac.uk (accessed 17/03/07).

Reeves, J. (2006). Recklessness, rescue and responsibility: young men tell their stories of the transition to fatherhood. *Practice*, 18(2), 79–90.

Sigle-Rushton, W. (2005). Young fatherhood and subsequent disadvantage in the UK. *Journal of Marriage and the Family*, 67, 735–753.

Tanfer, K., & Mott, F. (1999). *The meaning of fatherhood for men*. Paper prepared for NICHD Workshop "Improving data on male fertility and family formation" at the Urban Institute, Washington, DC, January 16–17, 1997. Available at http://fatherhood.hhs.gov/CFSForum/apenc.htm (accessed 17/03/07).

This is London (4 September 2006), Older dad's six times more likely to have autistic children. Evening Standard. Available at http://www.thisislondon.co.uk/newsarticle-23365716-details/ Older+dads+six+times+more+likely+to+have+autistic+children/article.do (accessed 17/03/07).

Tyden, T., Svanberg, A.S., Karlstrom, P.O., Lihoff, L., & Lampic, C. (2006). Female university students' attitudes to future motherhood and their understanding about fertility. *European Journal of Contraception and Reproductive Health Care*, 11(3), 181–189.

Van de Kaa, D.J. (1993). The second demographic transition revisited: theories and expectations. In G.C.N. Beets et al. (Eds.), *Population and Family in the Low Countries 1993: Late Fertility and Other Current Issues* (81–126). Lisse: Swets and Zeitlinger.

Chapter 12
Women's Lifestyle Preferences in the 21st Century: Implications for Family Policy

Catherine Hakim

Introduction

Declining fertility rates in virtually all modern societies are forcing social scientists and policy analysts to look again at the reorganisation of social life and family life that followed women's readmission to the labour market in the second half of the twentieth century. Until recently, the focus has been primarily on women's employment, paid work in the market economy, and the impact of equal opportunities policies in giving women genuine access to jobs and careers. There is now a change of perspective, with greater attention being given to all forms of unpaid household and family work as well, and to the wider impact of equal opportunities policies on family life and fertility rates. Demographers' explanations for declining fertility generally point the finger at female employment as a principal explanation, but without any overarching understanding of the broader changes in women's position in society.

Preference theory provides a new perspective on all these developments, in particular the polarisation of female employment and fertility patterns. It enables us to make sense of recent social trends, and provides a solid, evidence-based framework for the development and review of social policy in all its forms, including family policy and population policy.

Today, one-third of the countries in the world have fertility rates (TFRs) at or below the 2.1 replacement level (Tsui, 2001, p. 184). By the mid-1990s, over 80% of Western countries had period fertility rates below 1.8 (Frejka & Ross, 2001, p. 217). This unprecedented and widespread decline in fertility across the globe is forcing politicians as well as social scientists to consider the economic, social and political consequences of fertility decline and to reconsider the need for pronatalist policies. By 2003, the United Nations and the OECD were reporting a huge surge of interest in family policy among governments, especially in countries with tight labour markets. Most OECD governments have radically changed their views concerning

C. Hakim (✉)
Senior Research Fellow, Sociology Department, London School of Economics, London, UK
e-mail: c.hakim@lse.ac.uk

G. Beets et al. (eds.), *The Future of Motherhood in Western Societies*,
DOI 10.1007/978-90-481-8969-4_12, © Springer Science+Business Media B.V. 2011

fertility levels in the last 30 years. Whereas fertility was generally regarded as satisfactory or even too high in the past, today, most OECD countries regard their current fertility rate as too low for comfort, and increasing numbers see active policy interventions to be necessary (UN, 2004; d'Addio & d'Ercole, 2005, pp. 45–46).

Recent reports from the European Commission regularly worry about declining fertility and an ageing society, and their economic consequences for the labour market and welfare policies (European Commission, 2005a, b). At the start of the twenty-first century, the Commission organised a report on the policy options to deal with these new problems (Grant et al., 2004). In the past, childbearing has always been regarded as something that happened "naturally", hence something that public policy did not need to encourage. It has taken a long time for politicians and policy-makers to realise that the old assumptions no longer operate in the twenty-first century.

The sharp decline in fertility that occurs everywhere after the contraceptive revolution of the 1960s gave women easy access to reliable modern forms of birth control has also confounded demographers. The key distinction drawn by demographers has generally been between those using, or not using, any contraception. Sometimes a further distinction is drawn between modern, reliable, forms of contraception (the pill, IUD, and sterilization) and older, less reliable forms (condoms, withdrawal, etc.), but decisions are presented as being made jointly by couples – as illustrated by Preston (1986). However, as Keyfitz (1987) recognised early on, the crucial distinction is between male and female control of contraception. All the older forms of contraception were controlled by the male. What makes modern contraception unique is that it gives a woman independent control of her fertility[1] – if necessary without the knowledge or cooperation of her partner. In both developed and developing countries, some wives use the pill to avoid pregnancy without their spouses' knowledge. Similarly, some young women choose independently to pursue an accidental pregnancy and have a child without the father's agreement, sometimes relying on their own resources.

This puts the spotlight on women, and women's life goals, instead of the conventional perspective in economics and demography of treating couples as a single, integrated unit with a single set of priorities (utilities), especially if they are formally married. It appears, in retrospect, that fertility levels were determined primarily by men in the past, by accident or by design, and thus by the partner who did not carry the main responsibility for carrying the child, birth, and childrearing. We now need to know a lot more about women's values, life goals, and relative priorities between employment and family work.

---

[1] Studies of contraceptive practice using the old methods show that they left women feeling helpless, not in control, and fatalistic (Fischer, 2000). It is modern contraception that gives women personal and independent control of their fertility and thus produces a change of perspective, even a psychological change, creating a sense of autonomy and personal freedom (Hakim, 2000, p. 45). It is this change that starts to make lifestyle choices meaningful for women. Modern contraception eliminates the "contingency" orientation over women's life course and empowers women (Presser, 2001, p. 178).

Women's life goals and priorities have changed significantly since the 1960s. The contraceptive revolution and the equal opportunities revolution fundamentally altered the relative rewards of paid work for women, making it far more attractive than it has ever been (Hakim, 2000). Equal pay for doing the same job, the opening up of professions hitherto reserved for men (such as medicine), and the end of direct and overt discrimination in recruitment and promotion, in the educational system as well as in the workforce – all these changes make financial independence, non-marriage and childlessness genuine options for women as well as men. In some European countries, half or more of all women in the senior levels of management and the professions remain childless (Hakim, 2003c, 2004a, pp. 112, 181). The choice between a major investment in a career, or in family life and childrearing, is now a real one. Across Europe, women's new freedom to control their fertility and to plan their (work) lives has resulted in a significant increase in women's overall life satisfaction (Pezzini, 2005). One could even argue that public policy has now swung to a strong bias in favour of female full-time lifelong employment over the role of mother and homemaker. The terms and conditions of paid work have improved dramatically in modern societies since the 1960s. In contrast, the terms and conditions for full-time homemakers and parents have declined.[2] As Manne (2005) points out, the case for motherhood now has to be argued in rich modern societies. The case for full-time motherhood is almost never aired in schools or in the media, so that young women can be taken by surprise at their positive reactions to caring for their first born child.

A common trend across Western European and Northern American countries is the polarisation of women's employment, and the polarisation of women's lifestyles more generally. There is a new social group of careerist women, many of whom become high achievers, and almost half of whom remain childless. However they remain a small minority. The majority of women have jobs rather than careers, and have discontinuous patterns of employment rather than continuous employment like a man (Hakim, 2004, pp. 121–143). Some women, admittedly a shrinking minority, choose to remain full-time homemakers. At present, this diversity of lifestyles is not adequately recognised or explained by social science theory, and it is not acknowledged by diversified policies.

Preference Theory

Preference theory provides a new theoretical basis for analyses of women's choices between paid work and family work in modern societies, and for the development of social policy and family policy as they affect women in the twenty-first century.

---

[2] Countries that switch to individualised taxation implicitly withdraw fiscal support for marriage and the full-time homemaker spouse – as illustrated by Sweden and Britain. In addition, the role of housewife or homemaker has lost status. In the past, it had the same status as a secretary, one of the most common female occupations, falling roughly in the middle of the occupational prestige scale (Hakim, 2004, Table 2.7). Today, unpaid household work seems to have less status than a paid job.

Table 12.1 The four central tenets of preference theory

---

1. Five separate historical changes in society and in the labour market which started in the late twentieth century are producing a qualitatively different and new scenario of options and opportunities for women. The five changes do not necessarily occur in all modern societies and do not always occur together. Their effects are cumulative. The five causes of a new scenario are:
   * the contraceptive revolution which from about 1965 onwards gave sexually active women reliable control over their own fertility for the first time in history;
   * the equal opportunities revolution which ensured that for the first time in history women had equal access to all positions, occupations and careers in the labour market. In some countries legislation prohibiting sex discrimination went further to give women equal access to housing, financial services, public services, and public posts;
   * the expansion of white-collar occupations which are far more attractive to women than most blue-collar occupations;
   * the creation of jobs for secondary earners, people who do not want to give priority to paid work at the expense of other life interests; and
   * the increasing importance of attitudes, values and personal preferences in the lifestyle choices of affluent modern societies
2. Women are heterogeneous in their preferences and priorities on the conflict between family and employment. In the new scenario they are therefore heterogeneous also in their employment patterns and work histories. These preferences are set out as ideal types in Table 12.3. The size of the three groups varies in rich modern societies because public policies usually favour one or another group
3. The heterogeneity of women's preferences and priorities creates conflicting interests between groups of women: sometimes between home-centred women and work-centred women, sometimes between the middle group of adaptive women and women who have one firm priority (whether for family work or employment). The conflicting interests of women have given a great advantage to men, whose interests are comparatively homogeneous; this is one cause of patriarchy and its disproportionate success
4. Women's heterogeneity is the main cause of women's variable responses to social engineering policies in the new scenario of modern societies. This variability of response has been less evident in the past but it has still impeded attempts to predict women's fertility and employment patterns. Policy research and future predictions of women's choices will be more successful in future if they adopt the Preference Theory perspective and first establish the distribution of preferences between family work and employment in each society

---

Source: Hakim (2000).

It is especially helpful for identifying the policy levers that will be effective with particular groups of women.

Preference theory is a historically informed, empirically based, multidisciplinary and predictive theory about women's choices between market work and family work in rich modern societies (Hakim, 2000, 2003a, c). It argues that a series of social and economic changes (Table 12.1) produce polarisation between three groups of women making distinctive life choices (Table 12.2). *Work-centred or careerist women* give priority to their jobs, often remain childless even if married, and endorse the competitive, achievement-oriented values of the marketplace. *Home-centred or family-centred women* prefer not to work after marriage and childbearing, often have many children, and espouse caring and sharing family values. *Adaptive women* seek a balance between employment and family work over the lifecycle as a whole; they

Table 12.2 Classification of women's work-lifestyle preferences in the twenty-first century

Family-centred *20% of women* *(varies 10–30%)*	Adaptive *60% of women* *(varies 40–80%)*	Work-centred *20% of women* *(varies 10–30%)*
Family life and children are the main priorities throughout life	This group is most diverse and includes women who want to combine work and family, plus drifters and unplanned careers	Childless women are concentrated here. Main priority in life is employment or equivalent activities in the public arena: politics, sport, art, etc.
Prefer *not* to work	Want to work, but *not* totally committed to work career	Committed to work or equivalent activities
Qualifications obtained as cultural capital	Qualifications obtained with the intention of working	Large investment in qualifications/training for employment/other activities
Number of children is affected by government social policy, family wealth, etc. Not responsive to employment policy	This group is very responsive to government social policy, employment policy, equal opportunities policy/propaganda, economic cycle/recession/growth, etc. Including income tax and social welfare benefits, educational policies, school timetables, child care services, public attitude towards working women, legislation promoting female employment, trade union attitudes to working women, availability of part-time work and similar work flexibility, economic growth and prosperity, and institutional factors generally	Responsive to economic opportunity, political opportunity, artistic opportunity, etc. Not responsive to social/family policy
Family values: caring, sharing, non-competitive communal, focus on cohesion	*Compromise between two conflicting sets of values*	*Market place values*: competitive rivalry, achievement orientation, individualism, excellence

Source: Hakim (2000).

tend to be torn between the two competing value systems of the marketplace and family life. Female heterogeneity emerges clearly only from the 1970s onwards in modern societies, after the contraceptive and equal opportunities revolutions are fully implemented, and it is reflected in polarised lifestyle choices.

It is possible that female heterogeneity always existed. What is certain is that it is only revealed to its full extent after five key social and economic changes, in

Table 12.3 National distributions of lifestyle preferences among women and men

	Family centred	Adaptive	Work centred
Britain			
All women aged 16+	17	69	14
Women in full-time work	14	62	24
Women in part-time work	8	84	8
All men aged 16+	?	< 48	52
Men in full-time work	?	< 50	50
Men in part-time work	?	< 66	34
Spain			
All women aged 18+	17	70	13
Women in full-time work	4	63	33
Women in part-time work	7	79	14
All men aged 18+	?	< 60	40
Men in full-time work	?	< 56	44
Belgium-Flanders			
All women	10	75	15
Women with partners	12	75	13
All men	2	23	75
Men with partners	1	22	77
Germany			
Women	14	65	21
Men	33	–	67
Czech Republic			
All women aged 20–40	17	70	13
Women in employment	14	69	17
Wives aged 20–40	14	75	11
Sweden			
Women in 1955 birth cohort: actual lifestyle choices by age 43 (1998)	4	64	32
Japan			
Ideal lifecourse of unmarried women 1987	37	55	8
Idem 2002	21	69	10

Data for Belgium-Flanders extracted from Corijn and Hakim (forthcoming) based on a 2002/3 survey.

Data for Germany extracted from Bertram et al. (2005).

Data for Czech Republic from Table 1 in Rabusic & Manea (2008) based on a November 2005 survey.

Data for Sweden extracted from Huang et al. (2007) reporting analysis of a longitudinal dataset.

Data for Japan from National Institute of Population and Social Security regular surveys of Views of the Unmarried about Marriage and Family in Japan.

Sources: Data for Britain and Spain, 1999, extracted from Tables 3.14 and 3.15 in Hakim (2003a, pp. 85, 87).

particular the contraceptive revolution and the equal opportunities revolution of the 1960s and 1970s (Table 12.1). By the end of the twentieth century, women had genuine choices to make, as to how they live their lives. They could actively choose to prioritise career or family, or else to seek some compromise between the two. Choices reflect a normal distribution of responses to the conflict between full-time careers and a serious involvement in family life.

Preference theory has already been operationalised and tested in national surveys in two contrasting European countries – Britain and Spain (Hakim, 2003a). In both countries, three lifestyle preference groups were identified, as expected, with very similar national distributions, close to those posited by Hakim and shown in Table 12.2. Lifestyle preference groups were also identified among men, on a more rough and ready basis. The key finding was that lifestyle preferences predict women's employment and fertility even more strongly than the "social structural" variables usually underlined as most important, notably educational qualifications (Hakim, 2003c). The three lifestyle preference groups have also been identified, using a variety of methods, through surveys in other countries, with broadly similar distributions for women and men (Table 12.3).

Preference theory deals only with social processes in modern societies, after the contraceptive revolution, and is forward-looking rather than retrospective in orientation. It is predictive, combines historical and psychosocial explanations, and incorporates the most recent relevant micro-level qualitative research on how women choose between employment and family work. It provides a framework for understanding how social policies, family policy, and employment policies work, in terms of their success and failure within particular groups of women (Hakim, 2000, pp. 223–253).

Since the contraceptive revolution marks a qualitative change in women's perspective on childbearing, research on fertility trends before 1960 may be essentially of historical interest. For the same reason, we can expect an immediate decline in fertility wherever modern contraception is introduced, even in developing countries, where nearly all (93%) of contraception involves modern methods (Tsui, 2001, p. 191).[3] After the contraceptive revolution, it is women's values and lifestyle preferences that become the driving factor, with the social and economic context facilitating or impeding the realisation of women's preferences. On the evidence for at least one country (Spain), women's lifestyle preferences are not closely linked to, or shaped by, political and religious values (Hakim, 2003a, p. 206). So it is perhaps not surprising that the three lifestyle preference groups are found in the previously socialist and secular countries of Eastern Europe as well as in Western Europe and Japan (Table 12.3). Similarly, the three lifestyle preference groups cut across

---

[3]Tsui (2001) quotes a United Nations study summarising contraceptive patterns in 57 developing countries: 58% of married women of reproductive age used some form of contraception, and this was almost invariably modern methods, mainly sterilization, the oral pill and IUDs (United Nations, 1996, Table 15). Some fast-moving Asian countries, such as Singapore, have already switched family policy to a pronatalist position.

education levels, social class and income levels, so none of these variables can be used as proxy indicators for lifestyle preferences (Hakim, 2003a, pp. 93–105).

In sum, we should now focus on women's values, life goals and priorities, as well as the social and economic context for achieving work-life balance. We need data on women's *personal preferences* as regards employment and fertility, as well as data on their partner's preferences. This is not the same as collecting data on societal norms regarding fertility, sex-roles, and women's employment. These societal norms differ between countries, but display relatively little variation within countries (Philipov, 2005), whereas personal preferences vary a great deal. For example, most people regard the two-child family as the ideal family size, even when they themselves prefer to have no children at all. Most people will agree that smoking is harmful, yet many still choose to smoke themselves. People can be aware of societal norms, and confirm them, but still reject them; it is only personal preferences that predict respondents' behaviour (Hakim, 2003a, pp. 139–140, 157–159; 2003b, 2004). Unfortunately, most social surveys collect data on societal norms (which are not causal) rather than on personal preferences (which can be causal), so they do not test preference theory, as they claim.[4]

The most recent illustration of this fundamental problem is in an otherwise admirable comparative study of eleven European countries, including Britain, Germany, Sweden and Spain. Vitali et al. (2007) analysed the 2004 European Social Survey, which collects opinion poll-style data on societal norms (what people in general *should* do) but no data on personal lifestyle preferences (what I want for myself). They used survey questions that Hakim has classified as measures of patriarchal values, with demonstrably weak links with behaviour (Hakim, 2003a, pp. 68–69, 139–140, and 157–159) to construct a classification of careerist, home-centred, and adaptive women. With these proxy indicators, they found that all three groups could be identified in every European country; however there was little or no link to behaviour in most countries (Vitali et al., 2007) as predicted by Hakim. Like others, they purport to test preference theory, but in fact study patriarchal values and societal norms instead.[5]

All available national surveys find a profound difference between men's and women's priorities between paid work and family work. Over half of men, and up to three-quarters, are work-centred – compared to around 20–25% of women. Only a tiny minority of men are family-centred. Numbers in this group are generally so small that exact measurement is difficult, but at present home-centred men remain well below 5–10% nationally. Adaptive men are a more important group than previously assumed, in the region of 20–40%. These conclusions are based on recent survey data for Britain, Spain, Belgium-Flanders and Germany, four contrasting societies in Europe (Table 12.3).

---

[4]This is the most common problem with critics' attempts to falsify preference theory: their tests have been obliged to utilise data on societal norms (rather than personal preferences) and thus find weak linkages with behaviour (Hakim, 2007a).

[5]The study also confirmed that Britain differs from other European countries, as Hakim has argued.

The evidence is that men and women differ substantially in lifestyle preferences. At the same time, the difference is one of degree, not a qualitative difference, with a large overlap in the distributions. This research finding is welcomed by some (for proving common sense knowledge) but rejected by others (for supporting outdated stereotypes).

Feminist Debates

One impediment to objective assessment of sex differences in lifestyle preferences is the feminist thesis that there are simply no "natural" sex differences at all, that *all* sex differences in values and behaviour are socially constructed and thus "artificial". At the extreme, this has led social scientists to argue that research on sex differences must not be published at all, because such information supports "essentialist" views of men and women as fundamentally different. This extreme feminist position has had an impact on policy-makers. For example, it is reflected in European Union (EU) policy positions that expect, even demand, symmetrical roles in the workforce and the family for all men and women in the EU, irrespective of personal preferences.

For example, in March 1995, the *American Psychologist* carried a debate between Eagly and others on the feminist and political correctness constraints on research that seeks to establish which sex differences in personality, ability and social behaviour are vanishing, and which remain important after the equal opportunities revolution. Similarly, the March 1996 issue of the *British Journal of Sociology* carried a debate on Hakim's paper "Five feminist myths about female employment" (Hakim, 1995), with eleven sociologists and economists attacking the substance of the article, and even the idea that feminist ideology was producing new myths. These are not ephemeral debates that have already run their course. Crompton has repeatedly attacked preference theory, accusing it of being an essentialist heresy, unacceptable within social science, despite its solid basis in research evidence (Crompton, 2007; Crompton & Lyonette, 2005; Hakim, 2007a, b). These debates and critiques are taken further in a compendium which discusses feminist theory and preference theory, and examines the research evidence on sex differences in physiology and behaviour (Browne, 2007).

The feminist thesis of essentialism is that research evidence showing sex differences in any aspect of attitudes and behaviour is either irrelevant or tendentious. Such differences only exist due to sex discrimination and men's exploitation of women; they are thus pernicious, unjust as well as unnatural, and should be eradicated by every means available as quickly as possible. All sex differences are assumed to be to women's disadvantage, and are rephrased as gender inequalities rather than as simple differences (Crompton, 2007). Through this logic, accepting that there are any enduring sex differences (however small) becomes tantamount to endorsing injustice. As Van Hooff and Swaab show in their Chapters 3 and 4 in this book, the scientific evidence for certain sex differences is accumulating, but debate continues over the practical social implications of such differences.

Policy Implications of Female Diversity

The unprecedented fertility decline of the late twentieth century has led to a new perspective among social scientists and policy-makers, with renewed interest in the household economy, unpaid and reproductive labour. The change is reinforced by a widespread view that equal opportunities policies have been effective, and no longer need to remain centre stage, at least in some countries.[6]

The change of perspective is also found within economics. Throughout the twentieth century, economics focused almost exclusively on market work, and even ignored women's employment until the equal opportunities revolution made sex and race discrimination standard topics in labour economics. But there is now a new determination to measure household work and other unpaid work within national statistics and national accounts, despite the technical difficulties. European statistical offices are committed to publishing satellite accounts on the household economy, prompting innovative research based on the new time budget survey data that has to be collected (Hakim, 2004, pp. 27, 56–57). Reproductive and other household work becomes more visible, and gains importance from official valuations stating that it adds anywhere from 50 to 100% to GDP.[7]

The change in perspective is illustrated in a comprehensive economic literature review on women's work in OECD countries (Boeri et al., 2005). Instead of the customary focus on market work alone, this review gives equal attention to women's reproductive work and to the (negative) impact of rising female employment on fertility, on children's development and welfare, and on household income distribution. It points out the need for structural changes in the labour market to resolve the conflict between full-time employment and childrearing work, notably opening up part-time work options on a large scale. Similarly, a recent economic research synthesis on the family notes that the emphasis on child quality rather than on quantity shifts attention to the mother's time investment in childrearing (Ermisch, 2003). Today, economists no longer ignore reproductive work, and other unpaid work, and are willing to discuss its contribution to the economy. Economists are also focusing on how women divide their time between, and choose between, market work and unpaid work, employment and fertility. This represents a fundamental change of focus in research on women's work (Hakim, 2004, 2010).

Policy-makers are also looking at the costs of pronatalist family policy in a new light. In the first decade of the twenty-first century, the European Commission began

---

[6]For example in Britain, it is recognised that 30 years after the creation of the Equal Opportunities Commission and introduction of sex equality legislation, the social, economic and legal situation of women had been transformed dramatically, with sex discrimination no longer the main problem in explaining the pay gap, for example (Watson, 2005; Women and Work Commission, 2006). The emphasis switched instead to the question of work-life balance, which affects everyone, and has serious consequences, as reflected in declining fertility rates across Europe.

[7]Such valuations had been produced previously by academics (Thomas, 1992, pp. 21–26). The publication of official statistics on the topic represented a major investment in research and reflected a major change of political perspective.

to be openly concerned about declining fertility and the economic consequences of an ageing population, an ageing workforce, and little or no population growth. Europe no longer has a "demographic motor", has lost its "demographic engine", it worried. Comparisons are being drawn with the USA, "where fertility is now 40% higher than Europe". For a time, it was thought that increased immigration might fill the shortfall in the workforce, but recent studies dispute this solution (Coleman & Rowthorn, 2004). So far, the response from the Commission is to reiterate gender equality policies and demand rising female employment, family-friendly employment arrangements, and more public childcare (European Commission 2002, 2003, 2005a, b), solutions that actually aggravate the problem of declining fertility (Dey, 2006). In Britain, the Labour government generally follows the lead of the European Commission, and policy-advisors are equally politically correct in their insistence that labour market gender equality policies must always take priority over pronatalist policies (Dixon & Margo, 2006, p. 85).

One sign of changing perspectives is the European Commission's decision to commission a Rand study of the causes and economic consequences of declining fertility and population ageing, and the policy options for solving it (Grant et al., 2004). Adequate fertility rates are being recognised as a crucial contribution to economic growth and avoiding a decline in human capital (Grant et al., 2004, p. 135). In line with all other such reviews (Gauthier, 1996a, b, 2007; Gauthier & Hatzius, 1997) the report admits the difficulty of demonstrating conclusively that particular policies have visible effects on fertility rates, and concludes that it is impossible to show the impact of any individual policy, because the wider pronatalist culture can be crucial to the effectiveness of schemes (Grant et al., 2004, pp. 96, 131). However the study concludes that policy aimed at increasing or sustaining fertility rates does have an impact, sometimes a strong impact. France's long-term pronatalist family policies have maintained relatively high fertility rates. In Spain, fertility rates collapsed under democracy, after Franco's pronatalist policies were withdrawn. Fertility rates collapsed in East Germany after reunification, and in Poland after the transition to capitalism, after economic uncertainty made forward planning more risky. All these events suggest that the preceding pronatalist policies were effective, and that economic uncertainty is a powerful contraceptive. The Rand study also recognises that policies to raise female employment can exacerbate the problem of low fertility and population ageing in the longer term (Grant et al., 2004, p. 140). Perhaps most important, no single policy can be recommended as universally effective. And policies can only be effective if substantial funding is invested in family policy. Weak policy effects are typically due to the low (and declining) economic value of family allowances and tax benefits, for example. Population policy can be expensive, but then so are other social policies that are now taken for granted – such as income support for the unemployed, the disabled, and the retired.

The Rand report for the European Commission is unusual in recognising that there are many ways of achieving the same goal, and no single solution to the problem of fertility decline. Preference theory explains why it is that many different policies can all have an impact, and why it is so difficult to identify the impact of any single policy. Each policy favours one or another subgroup of women, and its effect depends in part on the relative importance of the three preference groups, and how well policies are targeted to them. Most are poorly targeted, because they focus on the typical, or average woman (the adaptive woman in the preference theory classification), who is not universal. Thus, the wide availability of part-time jobs (including jobs with very short hours) in the Netherlands and Britain can be just as effective as strong fiscal support for families in the USA and France.

One important research finding that has yet to be fully understood or appreciated is that (long) parental leaves are found by many studies to be irrelevant or counter-productive as regards raising fertility (Gauthier & Hatzius, 1997; OECD, 2006, p. 65), a finding that attracts debate. In contrast, studies are broadly unanimous in showing that income transfers to families to reduce the costs of children raise fertility, to varying degrees (Diprete et al., 2003; Gauthier, 2007). Overall, cash benefits, and the flexibility they offer, are more attractive to people, and have greater impact than benefits in kind and schemes controlled by someone else. Yet most governments, and most recent evaluation studies, focus on the latter, especially parental leave, under the general label of promoting work-life balance (Houston, 2005; Gauthier, 2007). Yet parental leave schemes can be relatively unimportant for achieving work-life balance among careerists. In addition, some occupations and jobs are so demanding, or "hegemonic" that they can never be made family-friendly. They may be a minority, but they tend also to be the most highly paid (Hakim, 2006).

A new analysis of data for 1980–2002 for 18 OECD countries has shown that policies that increase *compatibility* between family life and jobs (such as parental leave and childcare) are less effective than policies providing workforce *flexibility* (such as part-time jobs and telecommuting). Workforce flexibility has twice as much impact on fertility rates as compatibility policies (Yamaguchi, 2007). This helps explain many of the contradictory findings from other studies (Gauthier, 2007). Another factor is that policies on housing, education and health may support or impede family policies. For example, the difficult school timetable in Germany tends to limit family size and promote childlessness, in contrast to German fiscal policy.

The two policies that appear to have the greatest potential impact in encouraging women to achieve their ideal family size are, first, raising family allowances (direct benefits for children) to help compensate for the costs of children and, second, the homecare allowance, which gives full-time mothers financial compensation for the job they do. The homecare allowance remains the least well-known, although it has been operating successfully since 1985 in Finland (Ilmakunnas, 1997), and was copied in Norway from 1998 onwards, although it proved politically infeasible in Sweden (Vikat, 2004; Hoem, 2005). The homecare allowance involves paying one parent (typically the mother) an allowance for their work as full-time carer and is offered to families who do not use state-subsidised childcare (thus ensuring parity between users and non-users). The money can be regarded as a wage for childcare at home, as a partial replacement for earnings foregone, or it can be used as a subsidy for purchased childcare services which enable the parent to return to work, full-time or part-time. It has proved a popular alternative to state nurseries because it allows parents to choose their own timetables and childcare – including the option of paying close neighbours or relatives for their help, for example. The homecare allowance has proven popular in Finland and Norway, in part because of this flexibility, although the original rationale was to offer parity between families using, and not using, state-funded childcare. It has been proposed for Britain also (Hakim et al., 2008). The homecare allowance has been shown to raise fertility, mainly by supporting couples to go beyond the two-child norm to have a third child. The policy is most attractive to home-centred women (Hakim, 2000, pp. 232–233; Schone, 2004; Ellingsæter, 2007; Aassve & Lappegård, 2009; Lappegård, 2010).

The latest French policies are moving in the same direction, paying mothers with a second or third child a substantial salary for her work in the home. In autumn 2005, the French government announced a new scheme of financial incentives to encourage higher-paid middle class women to have a third child. At a conference on family life, the Prime Minister announced that the government proposed to pay up to 1,000 Euros per month, double the current maximum and close to the 1,200 Euros minimum wage, to women who have a third child, in an attempt to encourage highly paid and professional women to have larger families (Randall, 2005). Like the homecare allowance, the scheme pays a parent (in practice, the mother) who stays at home to look after their children – raising the total allowances up to around 1,000 Euros a month on top of family allowances (child benefits) (Randall, 2005; Dixon & Margo, 2006, p. 37). This new scheme builds on the success of the APE (Allocation Parentale d'Education) which, from 1994 onwards, paid mothers caring full-time for two children a monthly benefit of around 500 Euros during the 3 years following the second birth. The APE was so popular and successful that it resulted in a visible decline of around 10% points in employment rates for mothers aged 20–38 years, and was thus criticised by feminist scholars for supporting sex-role differentiation and "gender inequality" (Fagnani, 1998; Hakim, 2000, pp. 233–245; Lanquetin et al., 2000; Dixon & Margo, 2006, p. 38). The APE, like the homecare allowance, actually pays full-time mothers a small salary for their work at home. It is thus more effective than the more common approach of offering tax rebates to families with children, which does not actually reward the caregiver directly. For example in Singapore, families who have a second child within marriage before the age of 28, or a third or fourth child at any age, receive a Singapore $20,000 tax rebate (Dixon & Margo, 2006, p. 38).

Finland and France now have the highest fertility rates in the EU, higher than in Sweden (Hoem, 2005). They also have relatively high levels of women with three or more children. The homecare allowance increases the probability of a third birth in Finland (Vikat, 2004) and in Norway (Lappegård, 2010). Despite this, the homecare allowance is rarely discussed in social policy and population policy reports, and is often criticised (Fagnani, 1998; Lanquetin et al., 2000; Dixon & Margo, 2006, p. 38). Feminists regard the homecare allowance as controversial, because it rewards and validates full-time motherhood and family work. For example Heitlinger (1991) and Hoem (2005) reject all subsidies for full-time mothers as sexist, and only endorse family policies that keep mothers in the labour market throughout their lives.[8] Since these schemes are available to whichever parent stays at home, the schemes are not sexist. They are especially attractive to family-centred men as well as women, and 10–16% of users are fathers. However the main problem with feminist objections to such schemes is that they fail to recognise and accept the heterogeneity of women's (and men's) lifestyle preferences, and thus insist on one-size-fits-all policies. Preference theory points out that all policies are differentially attractive to family-centred, work-centred and adaptive men and women. So it makes sense to have schemes that benefit family-centred parents as well as schemes favouring adaptive people and the (frequently childless) careerist minority. As Gauthier et al. (2004) have shown, people who choose to become parents today in modern countries are an increasingly self-selected group with a particular interest in children. Time budget studies show that parents' investment of time in childrearing activities is increasing long-term. However non-employed mothers are a particularly self-selected minority, and their time investment in their children's development has risen more sharply over the past three decades than that of fathers and employed mothers (Gauthier et al., 2004; see also Vikat, 2004, p. 205). It appears that women who have a third birth are predominantly family-centred, so that the homecare allowance supports this minority group in Scandinavia (Vikat, 2004, p. 203). Female heterogeneity is producing increasing polarisation of women's choices and lifestyles. The current policy emphasis on working women thus needs to be counterbalanced by family policies that support home-centred women as well. The interests of women and children are not always compatible. Across Europe, feminist women are least likely to value children (Jones & Brayfield, 1997, p. 1260).

Conclusions

There is now greater willingness to recognise that equal opportunities policies have the side effect of raising disincentives to bear children, and that women's choices are now polarising, with some prioritising family life and children, while others prioritise careers (Burggraf, 1997; Hakim, 2003c; Wolf, 2006). There is also more realism about so-called "family-friendly" policies being in reality work-friendly policies that help to raise female employment rates rather than supporting families. The research evidence is that certain family-friendly employment arrangements, such as parental leave, have no impact on fertility rates, while others, notably part-time jobs and other forms of flexibility, are important facilitators and correlates of higher fertility levels. Cash benefits are the most effective, and a child-rearing salary paid directly to the mother seems to be the most effective of all. It might be argued that welfare payments to solo mothers have in effect been doing exactly that for years, thus raising fertility rates among non-partnered women.

---

[8] Feminists reject any division of labour in the family as sexist and disadvantageous to women. However economists have pointed out that even a minor (female) advantage in childrearing, or a minor (male) advantage in earnings, would lead to a rational division of labour in the family (Becker, 1991; Ermisch, 2003).

Preference theory is consistent with theory and evidence on economic incentives for childbearing and employment. It remains the only theory that can explain the polarisation process in women's activities that is increasingly visible across all modern societies, and that will eventually extend to men as well. Preference theory provides an evidence-based theoretical framework to inform the design and targeting of social policies. All policy objectives can be achieved once we recognise, and accept, the heterogeneous character of women's and men's lifestyle preferences. Instead of one-size-fits-all policies that suit no-one, we can develop differentiated policies which support the reproductive work of family-centred women and men, the productive work of careerists, and the needs of adaptives who want to combine the two activities throughout life. Pronatalist policies will be most successful if they are targeted at family-centred women and men. In some European countries, gender equality in the workforce is arguably almost achieved among careerists, many of whom remain childless.[9] New equal opportunities policies will be of most benefit to this group. Adaptives will benefit from both sets of policies because they have a foot in both camps. However policies that are targeted on the adaptive group generally exclude the family-centred and careerist groups. This may explain the success of French social and family policies. Alternating left-wing and right-wing governments have variously supported the family, or careerist women, producing a fairly balanced policy mix, overall. As a result, and despite having few part-time jobs, France has relatively high female employment and relatively high fertility. This outcome is due to polarised lifestyles (Hoem, 2005, Fig. 4), not due to a correlation, as implied by multivariate analysis.

Existing theories to explain fertility decline are too focused on periods predating the contraceptive and equal opportunities revolutions to be useful for policy development in the new scenario of the twenty-first century. Preference theory provides a new, solid evidence-based framework for the analysis and development of diversified family policy and population policies in modern societies. It can help to identify specific policy levers for raising fertility, but it demonstrates that policy must *differentiate* between groups of women, and be even-handed in supporting all groups and value systems. One size fits all policies are no longer appropriate in the twenty-first century.[10] Careerist and family-centred women respond to *different* economic incentives. Their interests conflict at times, which is why there can be no single influential women's lobby in politics, despite the fact that women make up half (often more than half) the population.

Finally, population policy cannot be subordinated to gender equality policy. Once this is recognised, there are few barriers to effective pronatalist policies, apart from cost. As predicted by preference theory, there will be conflicts of interest between

---

[9]The pay gap between men and women has effectively disappeared, replaced by what is called the "family gap": an average earnings differential between childless women and women with children (Waldfogel, 1993).

[10]One exception to this might be Murray's proposal for a standard Guaranteed Minimum Income for all combined with the elimination of all welfare state benefits and attached administrative costs (Murray, 2006).

careerist women and family-centred women. By and large, "gender equality" policy as currently formulated in Europe focuses primarily on the interests of careerist women and, to a lesser extent, adaptive women. In the USA, there is a parallel maternalist feminist lobby which represents the interests of family-centred women. There is no equivalent in Europe, and the interests of home-centred women are poorly represented in the political arena except, possibly, in Germany, where the idea of different but equal contributions by husband/father and wife/mother became an important interpretation of the principle of sex equality (Schiewe, 2000, p. 94). This may be one reason why fertility decline has already progressed so far in Europe. Full-time mothers are the weakest political lobby group of all. We need to support this group and give women real choices on the balance between paid jobs and family life.

References

Aassve, A., & Lappegård, T. (2009). Childcare cash benefits and fertility timing in Norway. *European Journal of Population*, 25, 67–88.

Becker, G.S. (1991). *A Treatise on the Family*. Cambridge, MA: Harvard University Press.

Bertram, H., Rosler, W., & Ehlert, N. (2005). *Nachhaltige Familienpolitik*. Berlin: Bundesministerium für Familie, Senioren, Frauen und Jugend.

Boeri, T., Del Boca, D., & Pissarides, C. (Eds.) (2005). *Women at Work: An Economic Perspective*. A report for the Fondazione Rodolfo Debenedetti. Oxford: Oxford University Press.

Browne, J. (Ed.) (2007). *The Future of Gender*. Cambridge: Cambridge University Press.

Burggraf, S. (1997). *The Feminine Economy and Economic Man*. Reading, MA: Addison-Wesley.

Coleman, D., & Rowthorn, R. (2004). The economic effects of immigration into the United Kingdom. *Population and Development Review*, 30, 579–624.

Corijn, M., & Hakim, C. (forthcoming). Lifestyle preferences in Belgium-Flanders.

Crompton, R. (2007). Gender inequality and the gendered division of labour. In J. Browne (Ed.), *The Future of Gender*. Cambridge: Cambridge University Press.

Crompton, R., & Lyonette, C. (2005). The new gender essentialism – domestic and family 'choices' and their relation to attitudes. *British Journal of Sociology*, 56, 602–620.

d'Addio, A., & d'Ercole, M. (2005). *Trends and determinants of fertility rates: the role of policies*. OECD Social Employment and Migration Working Papers No. 27. Paris: OECD Publishing.

Dey, I. (2006). Wearing out the work ethic: population ageing, fertility and work-life balance. *Journal of Social Policy*, 35, 671–688.

Diprete, T.A., Morgan, S.P., Engelhardt, H., & Pacalova, H. (2003). Do cross-national differences in the costs of children generate cross-national differences in fertility rates? *Population Research and Policy Review*, 22, 439–477.

Dixon, M., & Margo, J. (2006). *Population Politics*. London: Institute for Public Policy Research.

Ellingsæter, A.L. (2007). Old and new politics of time to care: three Norwegian reforms. *Journal of European Social Policy*, 17, 49–60.

Ermisch, J.F. (2003). *An Economic Analysis of the Family*. Princeton and Oxford: Princeton University Press.

European Commission. (2002). *Employment in Europe*. Luxembourg: OOPEC.

European Commission and European Foundation. (2003). *Perceptions of living conditions in an enlarged Europe*. EF/03/114/EN, Dublin: European Foundation for the Improvement of Living and Working Conditions.

European Commission, Directorate-General for Employment, Social Affairs and Equal Opportunities. (2005a). *Social Agenda*, No. 11.

European Commission, Directorate-General for Employment, Social Affairs and Equal Opportunities. (2005b). *Confronting Demographic Change: A New Solidarity Between the Generations – Green Paper*. Luxembourg: OOPEC.

Fagnani, J. (1998). Recent changes in family policy in France: political trade-offs and economic constraints. In E. Drew, R. Emerek, & E. Mahon (Eds.), *Women, Work and the Family in Europe* (58–65). London: Routledge.

Fischer, K. (2000). Uncertain aims and tacit negotiation: birth control practices in Britain, 1925–1950. *Population and Development Review*, 26, 295–317.

Frejka, T., & Ross, J. (2001). Paths to subreplacement fertility: the empirical evidence. *Population and Development Review*, 27(Supplement), 213–254.

Gauthier, A.H. (1996a). The measured and unmeasured effects of welfare benefits on families: implications for Europe's demographic trends. In D. Coleman (Ed.), *Europe's Population in the 1990s* (295–331). Oxford: Oxford University Press.

Gauthier, A.H. (1996b). *The State and the Family*. Oxford: Clarendon Press.

Gauthier, A.H. (2007). The impact of family policies on fertility in industrialised countries: a review of the literature. *Population Research and Policy Review*, 26, 323–346.

Gauthier, A.H., & Hatzius, J. (1997). Family benefits and fertility: an econometric analysis. *Population Studies*, 51, 295–306.

Gauthier, A.H., Smeeding, T.M., & Furstenberg, F.F. (2004). Are parents investing less time in children? Trends in selected industrialised countries. *Population and Development Review*, 30, 647–671.

Grant, J., Hoorens, S., Sivadasan, S., van het Loo, M., DeVanzo, J., Hale, L., Gibson, S., & Butz, W. (2004). *Low Fertility and Population Ageing: Causes, Consequences and Policy Options*. Report to the European Commission. Cambridge: RAND.

Hakim, C. (1995). Five feminist myths about women's employment. *British Journal of Sociology*, 46, 429–455.

Hakim, C. (2000). *Work-Lifestyle Choices in the 21st Century: Preference Theory*. Oxford: Oxford University Press.

Hakim, C. (2003a). *Models of the Family in Modern Societies: Ideals and Realities*. Aldershot: Ashgate.

Hakim, C. (2003b). A new approach to explaining fertility patterns: preference theory. *Population and Development Review*, 29, 349–374.

Hakim, C. (2003c). *Childlessness in Europe*. Report to the Economic and Social Research Council. London: London School of Economics.

Hakim, C. (2004). *Key Issues in Women's Work: Female Diversity and the Polarisation of Women's Employment*. London: Glasshouse Press.

Hakim, C. (2006). Women, careers, and work-life preferences. *British Journal of Guidance and Counselling*, 34, 281–294.

Hakim, C. (2007a). Dancing with the devil? Essentialism and other feminist heresies. *British Journal of Sociology*, 58(1), 123–132.

Hakim, C. (2007b). The politics of female diversity in the 21st century. In J. Browne (Ed.), *The Future of Gender*. Cambridge: Cambridge University Press.

Hakim, C. (2010). How can social policy and fiscal policy recognise unpaid family work? *Renewal*, 18(2), 23–33.

Hakim, C., Bradley, K., Price, E., & Mitchell, L. (2008). *Little Britons: Financing Childcare Choice*. London: Policy Exchange.

Heitlinger, A. (1991). Pronatalism and women's equality policies. *European Journal of Population*, 7, 343–375.

Hoem, J.M. (2005). Why does Sweden have such high fertility? *Demographic Research*, 13, 559–572. (www.demographic-research.org)

Houston, D. (Ed.) (2005). *Work-Life Balance in the Twenty-First Century*. London: Palgrave Macmillan.

Huang, Q., El-Khouri, B.M., Johansson, G., Lindroth, S., & Sverke, M. (2007). Women's career patterns: a study of Swedish women born in the 1950s. *Journal of Occupational and Organizational Psychology*, 80(3), 387–412.

Ilmakunnas, S. (1997). Public policy and childcare choice. In I. Persson & C. Jonung (Eds.), *The Economics of the Family and Family Policies* (178–193). London: Routledge.

Jones, R.K., & Brayfield, A. (1997). Life's greatest joy? European attitudes toward the centrality of children. *Social Forces*, 75(4), 1239–1270.

Keyfitz, N. (1987). The family that does not reproduce itself. *Population and Development Review*, 12(Supplement), 139–154.

Lanquetin, M.-T., Laufer, J., & Letablier, M.-T. (2000). From equality to reconciliation in France? In L. Hantrais (Ed.), *Gendered Policies in Europe: Reconciling Employment and Family Life* (68–88). Houndmills: Macmillan and New York, NY: St Martin's Press.

Lappegård, T. (2010). Family Policies and Fertility in Norway. *European Journal of Population*, 26, 99–116.

Manne, A. (2005). *Motherhood: How Should We Care for Our Children?* Crows Nest NSW: Allen & Unwin.

Murray, C. (2006). *In Our Hands: A Plan to Replace the Welfare State*. Washington, DC: American Enterprise Institute Press.

OECD. (2006). Women at work. In: *Employment Outlook*. Paris: OECD, 61–125.

Pezzini, S. (2005). The effect of women's rights on women's welfare: evidence from a natural experiment. *Economic Journal*, 115, C208–C227.

Philipov, D. (2005). *Comparative Report on Gender Roles and Relations and Summary Policy Implications Regarding Gender Roles*. DIALOG/IPPAS Report Nos 16/17. Vienna, Austria: Vienna Institute of Demography of the Austrian Academy of Sciences.

Presser, H.B. (2001). Comment: a gender perspective for understanding low fertility in post-transitional societies. *Population and Development Review*, 27(Supplement), 177–183.

Preston, S.H. (1986). Changing values and falling birth rates. *Population and Development Review*, 12(Supplement), 196–200.

Rabusic, L., & Manea, B.-E. (2008). Hakim's preference theory in the Czech context. *Czech Demography*, 48(2), 46–55.

Randall, C. (2005). Middle class mothers will be paid to start baby boom. *Daily Telegraph*, 20 September 2005.

Schiewe, K. (2000). Equal opportunities policies and the management of care in Germany. In L. Hantrais (Ed.), *Gendered Policies in Europe: Reconciling Employment and Family Life* (89–107). Houndmills: Macmillan and New York, NY: St Martin's Press.

Schone, P. (2004). Labour supply effects of a cash-for-care subsidy. *Journal of Population Economics*, 17, 703–727.

Thomas, J.J. (1992). *Informal Economic Activity*. London: Harvester Wheatsheaf.

Tsui, A.O. (2001). Population policies, family planning programs and fertility: the record. *Population and Development Review*, 27(Supplement), 184–204.

United Nations. (1996). *Levels and Trends of Contraceptive Use as Assessed in 1994*. ST/ESA/SER.A/146. New York, NY: United Nations.

United Nations. (2004). *World population policies*. New York, NY: United Nations (available at www.un.org/esa/population/publications/wpp2003/)

Vikat, A. (2004). Women's labour force attachment and childbearing in Finland. *Demographic Research*, 3(8), 175–212. Special Collection. (www.demographic-research.org)

Vitali, A., Billari, F.C., Prskawetz, A., & Testa, M.R. (2007). Preference theory and low fertility: a comparative perspective. *European Demographic Research Paper 2007/2*. Vienna, Austria: Vienna Institute of Demography of the Austrian Academy of Sciences.

Waldfogel, J. (1993). *Women Working for Less: A Longitudinal Analysis of the Family Gap*. STICERD Working Paper No. WSP/93. London: London School of Economics.

Watson, J. (2005). Sex equality fit for the 21st century. Speech on the 30th anniversary of the Equal Opportunities Commission.

Wolf, A. (2006). Working girls. *Prospect*, April, 28–33.

Women and Work Commission. (2006). *Shaping a Fairer Future*. London: Department for Trade and Industry.

Yamaguchi, K. (2007). The relationship between female labour force participation and total fertility rate among OECD countries: two roles of work-family balance. Paper presented to CGP-SSRC seminar on Fertility Decline and Work-Family Balance: Japan, the USA and other OECD countries, held in Tokyo, May 2007.

Chapter 13
The Future of Motherhood: Conclusions and Discussion

Gijs Beets, Joop Schippers, and Egbert R. te Velde

Conclusions

Te Velde starts from the fact that the age at *first* birth has been rising over the past decades in most Western countries: both women and men are increasingly older when they have their first child. The mean age at first birth is, in some countries, approaching 30 years for women with substantial variation around the mean. Their male partners, the fathers, are normally 2–3 years older at first birth. Although the age at first birth has decreased over the past century to reach a bottom low in the 1960s, it has never been so high as it currently is in recorded history. That makes the issue unique.

With the introduction of effective contraceptives the evolutionary link between sexuality and procreation was broken. Having children is still highly valued but has become a personal choice. The same holds for its time path towards getting them. In many eyes, life is controllable: unwanted conceptions can be prevented by contraceptives, unwanted pregnancies can be interrupted by abortion, and reproductive problems can be solved by doctors using their state of the art in reproductive techniques. However, the "technical solution" does not always work, and certainly not without substantial financial and especially emotional costs, following from stress, disappointment and medical problems. In the end one should not forget that compared to the offspring of other mammals humans have to make exceptionally large investments in gestation, delivery, breastfeeding and rearing their children until adulthood (see the Chapter 2 by Te Velde). From an evolutionary perspective reproduction is essential for "not becoming a dead end", but in the mammal world it is not self-evident that men and women form couples the way humans do. Mating strategies vary widely. Males and females are characterised by different reproductive strategies as females will normally be fertilized but they may worry about by whom, while males may worry whether they will ever fertilize a female at all (Chapter 3 by

G. Beets (✉)
Senior Demographic Researcher, Netherlands Interdisciplinary Demographic Institute (NIDI), The Hague, The Netherlands
e-mail: beets@nidi.nl

G. Beets et al. (eds.), *The Future of Motherhood in Western Societies*,
DOI 10.1007/978-90-481-8969-4_13, © Springer Science+Business Media B.V. 2011

Van Hooff). Humans stand out in their mating strategy of men supporting women to more successfully raise their children also because these are so helpless for a relatively long period. Men and women also differ in their feelings, as well as in their day-to-day behaviour and responses. To a large extent that is related to the fact that the male and the female brain is not similar. Consequently these different brains will not lend themselves for a completely equal division of tasks between men and women, nor in the family, nor on the labour market (Chapter 4 by Swaab). The difference in brain structures result from the interaction of sex hormones and developing brain cells and is thought to be the basis of gender identity and gender roles, as well as in our sexual orientation. Since the contraceptive revolution women can fully control their reproduction and can really choose to have a child or not, but gender differences in behaviour have remained. Couples and individuals also have the basic right to decide freely and responsibly on the number and spacing of their children (Chapter 5 by Van de Kaa), but making reproductive decisions is one of the most difficult issues to tackle because of their lifelong consequences. It depends on other preferences and commitments, and the availability of a partner while the reproductive clock ticks further every day. The contraceptive pill was initially seen as the perfect tool towards closing the gap between the wish for children and the ultimate family size, but it brought, unforeseen and paradoxically, demolition of control over sexual behaviour and marriage as well as postponement of childbearing (Chapter 5 by Van de Kaa).

In our knowledge based society women are better educated than ever before, and participate on the labour market in much larger numbers. Late parenthood can be considered a rational outcome that is not easy to turn (Chapter 7 by Schippers). Labour market orientation partly reflects changing educational levels, wishes for gender equality and for economic independence. Given the various socio-economic and socio-cultural developments that Western welfare states have gone through over the past decades, there does not seem to be a ready-made and ideal solution for a "better world" – a world in which all citizens are happy and can operate according to their own preferences all the time –, and certainly not one solution that fits all. None of the existing welfare state regimes seems to provide for "the optimal world", although the social-democratic regime (Scandinavia) is thought to come closest, as institutional structures and public family policies widely support people to find their way in making family and economic careers compatible. In this respect Scandinavia is much and much closer to this "better world" than for example the conservative or the Mediterranean familist regimes where individuals seem to be left "on their own" in finding solutions for the problem of reconciling work and family life (Chapter 8 by Van Doorne-Huiskes and Doorten). In modern societies gender equality is a most relevant issue but children are very important: "if investments in their quantity and quality stay out, Europe can say goodbye to its dream of becoming the world's most competitive knowledge economy", Esping-Andersen argues in his chapter. He therefore pleas for a more egalitarian division of paid and unpaid work, and for universal and affordable quality childcare, which even yields a respectable return on the initial investment as he shows with the Danish model. Also Beck-Gernsheim pleas for solving the incompatibility issues between labour market and family careers from a policy perspective and not from trying to find solutions via for example new reproductive technology. However, Te Velde refers in his chapter to "fertility insurance" as a likely future, where women will be able to freeze their own eggs at a young age.

Evolution provided that motherhood requires stronger commitments for women than fatherhood for men. For men combining a family and a labour market career is almost self-evident, and many employers expect their male workers to be fulltime available. Men differ in their anticipation on parenthood from women. They have their own concerns about what parenthood will bring. Men may contribute to (extra) postponement but will eventually become a father and consider being a provider and breadwinner as essential to good fatherhood (Chapter 11 by Henwood et al.). Most women also opt for parenthood and nowadays prefer to combine the best of both worlds: a good family life and a career in the labour market. However, many women have hesitations on how to manage this combination, as they want to do both "jobs" properly, but want to prevent to become overburdened too. Promoting women's employment should thus not involve that women have to choose between the two but find an easy way of compatibility (Chapter 12 by Hakim).

If we translate the outcomes of the various chapters into some more general conclusions the first one may be that the decision on whether to have children or not and, if yes, when to have the first, has become a very personal one in Western societies. Women and men stand rather different in this matter, and it may take much time and energy to make up one's mind.

The second conclusion is that two major perspectives are working more or less against each other: a health perspective and a socio-economic perspective.

- From the *health* perspective "late fertility" (defined here as having a first child when the mother is 30 years or over) is beyond the biological optimum for women. Risks on health deficiencies for both the mother and the first child are lowest when women are in between the age range from about 18 to 30 years. Having a first baby before the age of 18 or after age 30 is therefore less recommendable, also in the era of Assisted Reproductive Technology (ART). Health issues related to late fertility are, for women (and their partners), increases in the so-called waiting-time-to-conception, increased risks of remaining involuntarily childlessness, increased problems with conception and, during gestation, miscarriage, a higher chance of ending up with a Caesarean delivery, and a higher risk of developing breast cancer before age 75; and for babies, an increased risk of a preterm delivery with adverse mental and/or health consequences, and an increased risk of perinatal and infant mortality.
- In contrast, from a *socio-economic* perspective, late fertility is quite understandable as it offers many advantages, both at the personal and couple level (feeling more mature/ready for parenthood and having a more solid financial household and welfare situation), as well as on the macro level (more tax incomes from young, employed, still childless adults). In our knowledge-based society it is quite normal nowadays that individuals are well-educated and have a job before embarking on having children. Having and raising children during educational enrolment is rather exceptional. Fertility postponement has become the more or

less obvious solution for individuals that first have to settle, emotionally and financially. Only after individuals have finished education, found a position on the labour market and a nice house, and have had a "bit of fun" and explored "the world" they may enter into a stable relation with a partner and take up the responsibility for children. Having children is an expensive exercise, an irreversible adventure, and hardly generates income. In earlier days children were an old-age insurance; nowadays children are mainly "taken" for emotional, social and psychological reasons. So, in stead of an "investment good" children have evolved more and more into what economists would call a "consumer good". Investments are high, but the parents expect to receive much positive energy and new challenges from having children.

In terms of our central question on the compatibility of women's emancipation and motherhood the contributions of the different authors result in the conclusion that it is not necessarily impossible to combine the two, but in today's Western society it requires a lot of effort to have the best of both worlds: having a family, taking good care of your children and your partner and having a proper professional career too. The various chapters also show that the central question put up is a multi-layered one. It relates to questions of preferences and restrictions, to questions of voluntary versus traditional behaviour, to the question of what is typically female and typically male behaviour and to whether sociologists or biologists would answer this question in the same way.

Discussion

Emancipation and Gender Equality

The prevailing concept of gender equality in the 1960s and 1970s assumed that at birth men and women were the same with regard to work, behaviour, preferences, social and economic abilities and that differentiation occurring thereafter mainly resulted from upbringing in a male-dominated society (Chapter 2 Te Velde). Male/female differences were considered to be "social constructs" propagated by men "as an excuse to suppress women and maintain male dominance" because "women are not born as women, they are made into women". These quotes and views from the philosopher Simone de Beauvoir – and many others[1] expressed similar views – have inspired generations of feminists, psychologists, sociologists and policy-makers. They assumed that if circumstances were to change by implementing appropriate policy measures, unjust and undesirable male/female differences would disappear within short notice. However, the results from biological and genetic research from the 1970s onwards indicate that some of the major differences

---

[1] See for example *Male and Female* written in 1949 by Margaret Mead or *Sexual Politics* (1970) by Kate Millett.

between men and women emanate from variations in hormone levels in early pregnancy (Chapter 4 by Swaab) and are determined by differences in our genetic profile as established over millions of years of evolution (Chapter 3 by Van Hooff). In spite of many similarities, men and women differ in some essential aspects. Now that we have taken the irreversible decision to separate sexuality from reproduction (Chapter 2 by Te Velde), we must not delude ourselves that the innate differences between men and women no longer exist or will disappear within a generation, is the lesson to be learnt. Men and women are not only different in appearances and reproduction, also in feelings, thoughts and behaviour. As a result much has changed in the nature versus nurture debate. True gender equality does not imply that men and women should be the same with regard to their abilities and attitudes towards work and children – the implicit assumption of early emancipation policies promoted in several countries. Through the "sameness" concept of gender equality, the male became increasingly the standard and role model for the female: only if she was able to adapt to his lifestyle and ambitions, she will be able to succeed in this male-dominated world. It does not come as a surprise, that under such circumstances women do not find it easy to combine the development of a professional career and the start of a career as a mother. As a consequence they may delay childbearing or have no children at all. Research shows that many European women prefer to have their children earlier than they in fact have. In addition, increasing numbers of men also feel forced to adapt to the straitjacket of traditional male behaviour, even if they would like to give more room to their "soft side" and would like to be involved more with and spend more time on caring for and raising children. On the other hand, a growing share of ever higher educated and emancipated women wants to design their own life course. They want to experience freedom and the wide variety of opportunities that is open to them to spend their time, energy and money. Sometimes explicitly, but more often by implication they decide "not to have children yet". Convinced as they are that they live in a world "where everything is possible all of the time" they postpone motherhood to a later stage in life – and sometimes end up in a trap when having a child is no longer as easy as it would have been 5 or 10 years earlier.

More often than men, women experience the absence of a child as a painful deficit causing sorrow and grief. Such feelings do not easily fit in emancipation programmes, in which women are primarily regarded as an important source of labour. In our opinion, true equality must entail the notion that both sexes are equivalent in the sense of having the same value, which is different from being the same. True gender equality accepts that both sexes are different in some essential aspects. Unique female features and abilities such as the deep rooted wish to have a child to care for, to be able to become pregnant, deliver a child, breastfeed, and look after babies and small children, should be taken into account and appreciated. Both men and women should have equal opportunities for self-development and self-fulfilment. However, because of their innate differences these equal opportunities can not always be the same; for example for many women motherhood is part of their self-fulfilment and usually that is more important for them than fatherhood is for men. True emancipation implies an interpretation of equality that not only accepts, but also appreciates the differences between men and women. True emancipation also includes the appreciation of differences *among* women and among men. Some women – as demonstrated by Hakim in her chapter in this book – set higher priorities to motherhood, while others define themselves primarily as a labour market professional. Similarly, some men still resemble the traditional "hunter", looking for success in the outside world of jobs and money, while others (often defined as more "female" men) settle for a less challenging role in the outside world and have high preferences for family life. Moreover, true emancipation also recognises that people can change over time and develop new preferences. The problem for women, of course, is that the biological clock keeps ticking. The process of harmoniously decision making with their partners may therefore follow different time paths and not perfectly match in scope. Men also have to make up their mind and prepare for parenthood. They are as responsible for postponement behaviour as women are. Finally, true emancipation would also imply that the biological and genetic male-female differences should not have spill over effects into domains where these differences are not or no longer relevant. Whereas in the past some occupations were not suitable for women, because they lacked the physical power for the job, the introduction of engines and computers in many jobs has made the biological difference irrelevant. So, the relevance of biological differences is partly, but certainly not completely, a matter of the organisation of society and the development of values, norms and ideas. Some people would take the argument even one step further. Pointing to the welfare state as the most successful experiment so far to take the edge of the "natural condition of mankind" they would argue that the welfare state has a task to reduce gender differences following from gender related biological and genetic differences. In the same way they would argue that the welfare state has as one of its tasks to pin down men on their role and responsibility as a father.

The Consequences for Motherhood

Does such a view tacitly imply that we make a plea for a type of housewife motherhood as it was in the past? Not at all, as we think that the achievements of the contraceptive revolution and female emancipation such as equal opportunities of education, having a job, financial independence and sexual freedom are never to be reversed. But it should be made possible to easily combine these achievements with having a family.

What are the consequences of a concept of gender equality whereby the achievements of female emancipation and the endorsement of motherhood are being combined? In a society that embraces such a vision, women are offered ample opportunity to develop themselves, have a job and enjoy life, just like men, but at the same time have the possibility to get their children within their "biological window of opportunity" whenever they wish to have these, and raise the children in full harmony with and support from their partners and society as a whole. Society should welcome the arrival of children, warmly embrace them and their parents, and partners should be able to deal with the "combination scenario" in the way they want it: from both sharing in managing the family and household tasks, and in their labour market commitments towards a continuation of what their ancestors did in the one-income family era (with one partner specialised in earning the income, while the other, most often the woman, in being responsible for the tasks at home).

Towards a New Policy Approach of Motherhood

What path do we have to go towards developing a new society that accepts that true gender equality appreciates both sexes to be different in some essential aspects? On average, women are still more family oriented than men, and both should become more aware of that. In such a new world we assume that the age at first birth will not be beyond the biological optimum. In order to arrive there we plea for (1) much more *information* and (2) much more *facilities*.

- *Information*, already in the school curriculum, on how to deal with combining several life course commitments from young adulthood onwards:

  - discuss in schools how boys and girls behave, how men and women behave, what are their drives and feelings. Discuss the gender-specific similarities, but also the dissimilarities, for example the difference in age pressure of getting the first child during one's early 30s. If it is normal practice to provide in schools information on healthy life, sexually transmitted diseases and contraceptives, why are school children not informed then on managing a personal intimate relationship and family life, in combination with raising an income? Should our future adult generations not also aim at optimising rational decision making processes, at optimising mental health, and for example at preventing too many lives to be disrupted by broken families? Why not inform high school children also on risks of remaining childless with increasing age, and on dealing with "proceptives": everything you should know if a wished for pregnancy stays away,
  - discuss the fact that most early mothers[2] had preferred to have their first child somewhat later, and that many late mothers had preferred the first child to have arrived somewhat earlier in their life. Or more in general, discuss how to make rational choices and how to deal with uncertainties. Everyone, boys and girls, men and women, should be informed about good and bad family life, on what contributions s/he should make, on what s/he may expect from having a family and keeping it ongoing, even on the pros and cons of going for separation or divorce. One should not only reflect on the own perspective but also on that of the partner and the child,
  - everyone should also know that it is not true that you are perfectly fertile as long as you do not get a signal from your body that something is wrong with

---

[2] Early motherhood may of course also result after an unwanted (teenage) pregnancy, for example due to non-use or failing contraceptives.

your reproductive system. Finding out about failures in one's reproductive system normally comes as a shock, maybe just because people assume that they would have had a signal earlier on. Also those youngsters who already know very early that they like to remain childless should be informed, since we know that the wish to remain childless may change over time, like the wish to become a parent also changes over time.

- *Facilities* to really and easily make choices for a happy and healthy life. Should not we get rid of gender stereotypes on labour market, income and child care issues, and provide fair and flexible facilities and opportunities to everyone, men and women, to fulfil own life time preferences? What other people (parents, siblings, peers, church, etc.) say, is becoming of less importance, we are more or less individualised, find our own way, make our own rational choices. Men and women do so in different ways, have different queries and concerns. In a time that all possible information is available, for example via the Internet, it is of importance to guide people easily towards that information and towards those facilities that really make a difference for them. We therefore suggest a sort of "cafeteria"-system:

  - like one can arrange one's own preferred meal in a cafeteria by picking up several food ingredients and leaving out others, we can imagine a public window where one may arrange one's own lifetime set of facilities providing an easy way towards the preferred combination of labour and family career,[3]
  - a window of flexible opportunities for gender equality, where family oriented men and women can for example easily raise an extra income during the period they lower working hours (the amount of money to be saved in advance or to be paid back later on in life), where "adaptive people" (cf. Hakim) can claim all kind of tailor made combination arrangements and facilities, and where "work centred people" can arrange child care facilities and outsource other (household) issues according to their wishes. We should realise that labour market oriented people might otherwise not consider to have children. Such a public window also provides opportunities and support for those who remain childless, voluntary or not,
  - arrangements include of course the option of fully paid and adequate maternity leave (with retention of job and salary), paternity and parental leave, various affordable ways of outsourcing child care facilities and household chores, fine tuning the couple's labour market commitments towards their personal preferences, emergency plans if all of a sudden things run differently (like long-term leave for sick children). In short, a coherent package of optional supportive arrangements covering all facets of life that people are confronted with and want to ease when they intend to start a family,

---

[3] A concrete proposal for such a public policy window has been developed in the Netherlands as part of the so-called "Verkenning Levensloop" (SZW, 2002) that was presented to Parliament in 2002. Due to a coalition change after the 2002 elections this initiative did not get any serious follow up.

- arrangements should be focussed on advancing health and wellbeing, on preventing stress and poverty. A coherent package likely has an effect on the (earlier) timing of the first child and maybe subsequently on the ultimate family size, although this is debated by those who see a direct relation between (increasing) welfare and (decreasing) family size,
- but, most importantly, couple's and individual's preferences should lead the availability of arrangements and facilities. The main goal is to support people, via a gender balanced, flexible and child-parent friendly society, to easily fulfil people's wishes (with demographically spoken a more or less constant population size and age structure, i.e. a stationary population).

If people are better informed and if a cafeteria window of flexible opportunities is available then citizens can much easier comply with their preferences. Such a more ideal and flexible gender balanced child-friendly society requires a new way of thinking, a thinking away from the short term considerations that currently almost always prevail – next year's budgeting and the coming up political elections – towards a system that favours people's long term life course preferences. It starts from the idea that if a person is born a certain socio-economic trajectory is set for about 80 years of this person's life including a corresponding budget. As life is costly and financial support will not be provided free early in adult life the system works via tax (back) payments later in life. Collective provisions should be available for those who for one or another reason (early death, physical or mental incapacity, one parent family) are unable to easily provide later back payments.

We speculate (but are of course not completely sure) that in such a world the age at first birth will settle at an ideal level, ideal as a compromise from both the health and the socio-economic perspective. This might be somewhat earlier than it has become now in the forerunning countries. Settling at an ideal level may also arrive via a larger share of the population having the first child at a smaller age difference from the mean, for example lower teenage motherhood rates, larger shares of first children born to mothers between 25 and 30 years, and smaller shares to mothers of 30 or over than currently is the case.

From a health perspective, such a society would be more ideal with respect to the age at first birth. Is that also the case for the socio-economic perspective? The better a society succeeds in smoothly incorporating its reproductive function in all other activities going on in society, including production and consumption, the lower the friction costs involved and the higher overall welfare will be. This holds when one looks at welfare from a financial perspective with the focus on the Gross Domestic Product (GDP). It holds the more if one looks from a broader welfare perspective as proposed by Hennipman (1962), who also includes non-financial items among the determinants of welfare. From this broader welfare perspective people realise higher welfare levels the more they are able to fulfil their preferences. Of course, if people – women and men – can have their children at the desired moment in their life cycle and face little or no obstacles in the reconciliation of work and family life this will surely contribute to higher levels of welfare. It will probably also contribute to higher levels of labour market participation *over the life course*. The latter addition is important as the result of the measures proposed earlier in this chapter could be that lower participation rates would occur for the current cohorts of young parents (especially when measured in hours). However, if people become really convinced that a career as a parent can be successfully combined with a career in the labour market more mothers and fathers will invest in this combination, with a higher supply of hours and of human capital over the life course. If parents are not "worn out" during the so-called "rush hours of life" they will be able to prolong their labour market activities beyond current retirement ages. And if fathers contribute more to care and parenting, mothers may invest more in human capital and that offers them better labour market opportunities. Finally, better opportunities for people from *all* social and educational classes to realise their desired number of children at the preferred time contributes to overall welfare (see the Box for an example of the Nordic countries).

A Common Nordic Fertility Regime?

In line with other Western countries, also in Scandinavia first parenthood is postponed. But what distinguishes the Nordic countries is the strong recuperation of fertility at older ages, and the weak role of educational attainment in completed fertility. "These patterns can, to some extent, be attributed to the impact of Nordic social policies that facilitate fertility recuperation and make social differences in behaviour small (...) Similar welfare policies have contributed to more similar childbearing patterns (...) The structures of the Nordic welfare states, and their orientations towards equality, support of employment, provision of care services, and maintenance of high living standards, are associated with the smoothing out of various temporary fertility fluctuations" (Andersson et al., 2009).

Illusion or Goal within Reach?

Would this new society be an illusion or a goal within reach? Can we and must we – from an ethical perspective – be willing to guide or even steer reproductive behaviour? If it is a goal: what are the effective arrangements that we can provide, and how do we get there? Will indeed everyone be happy or will the reform raise new unthought-of impediments? Will women and men be able to better find and understand each other or will their conflicts even be heavier? Will focussing more on micro preferences clash with macro interests? Will reforms in various countries ultimately converge to one standard format for all nations, or consist of different regional models and solutions, or will models emerge per subpopulation?

Although such questions remain unanswered it is clear that doing nothing and just continuing our current path leads to a demographic, socio-economic and healthy future which seems far from ideal. We believe a fundamental societal change towards complying with (real) personal preferences will lead to a more (the most?) optimal situation with respect to family life, health and wellbeing issues for every citizen, including the timing of the first child. We learn from Esping-Andersen's chapter that the ultimate lifetime wage gains are much larger than the investments governments have to provide for making available child care in a full-time employment society: the net result to the exchequer yields a respectable return on the initial investment. It supports our plea for stopping with short-sighted measures and facilities, and for developing instead plans that assist people during major shares of their life course.

The Future Timing of the First Child

At the end of this book we can only speculate about what is really going to happen with the future timing of the first child. Given the fact that:

- the majority of women and men remain interested in having children,
- women and men will most likely be better educated in the future than today (and the higher the educational level, the higher the age at first birth),
- many make a longer and increasingly less successful search for the perfect partner to share parenthood with (i.e. leaving more people without steady partner at the moment that they actually wish to have children),
- many have divorced or separated parents, which has a lowering effect on their own ability to settle a solid partnership and become a parent "in time",
- many have also other life-time priorities which they would like to see materialised and which may conflict with early parental responsibilities,
- making a decision about having children already now or not yet remains among the most difficult and time consuming ones in the adult life time, and is easily further postponed,
- many on earth are concerned about ever growing populations and that families should preferably be small; even if starting late it is still possible to have a small family,

we suppose that there are not many reasons to believe that the age at first birth will soon lower by itself. More likely, if nothing happens from the outside, the age at first birth will continue to rise further up until a certain ceiling. A significant share of the future western first babies will be born to mothers in their 30s. From a health perspective that is beyond ideal but only if health costs will rise alarmingly the age at first birth may lower. More awareness of unhealthy fertility boundaries may have some toning down effect. But we believe that a coherent package of fundamental supportive arrangements, making society more child and gender friendly, would have much more impact, not only on the age at first birth but on wellbeing in general. In that new society the feeling of being part of a family, looking after children and household work, are important assets of life both for women and men. Men are "e*woman*cipated", and family policy measures are formulated in the context of life courses. If a societal reform into that direction stays away, we suppose that also motherhood will increasingly stay away, or will last-minute be assisted technologically. The disadvantage of assisted reproductive technology is however that the chance of success is only moderate and further we do not (yet) know whether it is completely safe, i.e. what are evolutionary seen the effects for coming generations. Moreover, people may wrongly get the idea that reproductive technology is the future solution for anyone if in trouble. They may be inclined to even postpone further supported by the idea of this safety net, but ultimately end up with a rude awakening.

To a large extent society as we know it now, was designed over the past century by males, at least the basic socio-economic arrangements. Many women obviously do not feel very much at home there. Yet, watchers of the future from different disciplines are inclined to say that Western societies are becoming more and more feminine. If this development goes on for another quarter of a century, how much would tomorrow's society deviate from the existing, male design? Would it also make a perfect socio-economic, health and demographic performance? Would it endorse that men are more work oriented and women more family oriented, that men are more short term oriented on making profits and women more long term value oriented? Would women perceive and treat the time spend at home on raising the next generation of workers as economic activity? We believe that in a more feminine world all humans have similar opportunities, and gender equality will be based on accepting the biological variation. That women take less risks, are less power oriented, more often on the safe side, more careful, more empathic, more oriented towards good and long-lasting relationships – not only privately but also in their professional life – is translated into practical family policies where both women and men fit in well. Very likely policy measures, to be obtained from the above mentioned cafeteria window, differ per gender. Men and women are not supposed to have exactly the same roles or tasks. Pregnancies and child care are not perceived as a problem but as a common responsibility for employers, employees and society. Long-term thinking appreciates the arrival of the future employee; short-term thinking only appreciates this year's profits. In an anticipating society both motherhood and fatherhood will have another meaning, another life fulfillment, and become ideally timed.

References

Andersson, G., Rønsen, M., Knudsen, L.B., Lappegård, T., Neyer, G., Skrede, K., Teschner, K., & Vikat, A. (2009). Cohort fertility patterns in the Nordic countries. *Demographic Research*, 20(14), 313–352.

Hennipman, P. (1962). Doeleinden en criteria der economische politiek. In J.E. Andriessen & M.A.G. van Meerhaeghe (Eds.), *Theorie van de economische politiek*. Leiden: Stenfert Kroese,

1–106. Also published as Hennipman, P. (1977). *Welvaartstheorie en economische politiek*. In J. van den Doel & A. Heertje (Eds.), Alphen aan den Rijn/Brussel: Samsom, 17–113 (both in Dutch).

SZW (Ministry of Social Affairs and Employment – the Netherlands) (2002). *Verkenning levensloop, beleidsopties voor leren, werken, zorgen en wonen*. The Hague: Ministry of SZW.

Author Index

G. Beets et al. (eds.), *The Future of Motherhood in Western Societies*,
DOI 10.1007/978-90-481-8969-4, © Springer Science+Business Media B.V. 2011

Subject Index

CPSIA information can be obtained at www.ICGtesting.com
233786LV00010B/35/P

9 789048 189687